THE BEST OF

The **Oldie**
1992–2012

OLDIE PUBLICATIONS

'Does my bonus look big in this?'

Published by Oldie Publications Ltd
65 Newman Street, London W1T 3EG
www.theoldie.co.uk

ISBN 978-1-901170-19-1

A catalogue record for this book is available from the British Library

Printed and bound in the UK by Butler Tanner & Dennis Ltd

Acknowledgements
The Oldie would like to thank all the writers, illustrators and cartoonists whose work is reproduced in these pages

Production and design by Sonali Chapman, Joe Buckley and Silvia Baz

THE BEST OF
The **Oldie**
1992–2012

THE FIRST TWENTY YEARS
With an introduction by Jeremy Lewis

Alec Guinness December 2003

CONTENTS

INTRODUCTION

JEREMY LEWIS

Like many of the best ideas, *The Oldie* was conceived in a pub. One day in the summer of 1991 Richard Ingrams and Alexander Chancellor met for a drink. Ingrams had retired as the editor of *Private Eye* in 1986, after twenty-three years at the helm, Chancellor was a former editor of the *Spectator*, now editing the *Independent*'s colour magazine, and they both agreed that, as Ingrams put it, 'with the disappearance of the *Listener*, the sad decline of *Punch* and the *New Statesman,* and the takeover of the *Spectator* by the *Daily Telegraph*', it was the right moment to start a new magazine that would be independent of the big newspaper conglomerates. As men in their fifties, they deplored the cult of youth and the way in which,

egged on by misguided marketing men, 'even "serious" newspapers nowadays pander to what they think, in our view mistakenly, will appeal to young readers.' The magazine they had in mind would 'deliberately focus on the old, but it would not be '"targeted" at old readers, nor aim to exclude any particular age group.' Fired up with enthusiasm, they discussed their ideas with Stephen Glover, one of the three founders of the *Independent*, who had recently left the paper to embark on the freelance life.

Starting a magazine is a dauntingly expensive business, and although family and friends (including Beryl Cook, Patrick Marnham and Emma Soames) invested sums ranging from £5,000 to £20,000, far more substantial backing was called for. It was decided to approach

The Oldie's editor with contributors and friends at a lunch at Wheeler's in 1992

Back row, left to right: John Mortimer, Larry Adler, Roy Greenslade, Carmen Callil, Miles Kington, Naim Attallah, Bill Deedes. Front row, left to right: Jennifer Paterson, Candida Lycett Green, Richard Ingrams, Beryl Bainbridge and Harry Enfield

the Palestinian-born Naim Attallah as a possible backer. Famed for his iridescent socks and suit linings and the bevy of upper-class beauties who staffed his offices, Attallah was one of the most colourful and flamboyant figures in the publishing world. He already owned two magazines – the *Literary Review*, edited by Auberon Waugh, and *Wire*, a jazz magazine – as well as the book publishers Quartet; he had recently been appointed the managing director of Asprey's, the Bond Street jewellers, and had compiled a book of interviews with famous names. He was generous to a fault, and was willing to back literary enterprises that harder-headed businessmen would have dismissed as insignificant or unprofitable. Ingrams, Chancellor and Glover went round to Attallah's offices in Poland Street, and over lunch Ingrams had what he 'thought was a brainwave. I suggested to him that he could do a series of in-depth interviews for the new magazine. I could see his eyes light up, and by the end of the lunch he was close to getting his cheque book out.'

Naim Attallah agreed to back the new magazine to the tune of £225,000. A board of directors was appointed, with Attallah as chairman: the other members were Ingrams, Chancellor, Glover, Auberon Waugh, Patrick Marnham and John McEwen, all of whom had invested money in the new enterprise. In due course board meetings would be held in an office over Asprey's, and later in the Lansdowne Club, and the directors would be paid £500 each for attending. In the meantime Richard Ingrams rented a room in Naim Attallah's offices in Goodge Street, and enlisted his son-in-law, David Ford, to set up the nuts and bolts of a publishing business. David Ford went on to become *The Oldie*'s General Manager and, although he had

no experience of the magazine world, he set about finding a printer, distributor and advertising manager, hiring a sub-editor and a lay-out man, printing stationery, and rustling up computers, desks, filing cabinets, paper-clips and the other essential props of office life.

Almost all of those involved were journalists, and their plans soon attracted attention in the Press. One side effect of this was the confirmation of the new magazine's contentious title, which had been suggested by Richard Ingrams (Alexander Chancellor had come up with the traffic sign logo of a bent and ageing couple hobbling across a road, which embellished the magazine's cover for many years). Although Ingrams later admitted to doubts about whether the name would appeal to advertisers, a 'somewhat premature' article in the *Sunday Telegraph* not only referred to *The Oldie* by name, but provided an 'unstoppable' momentum: offers of cash and contributions flooded in, and from then on '*The Oldie* was a goer'. Excitement mounted when Ingrams was interviewed on television by Terry Wogan, and appeared on Jonathan Ross's show with Auberon Waugh: there was talk of selling 200,000 copies per issue, and a spirit of optimism prevailed.

Not all the Press comments were complimentary. 'It sounds like the sort of project dreamed up by drunks and forgotten the next morning,' declared Peter McKay in the *Evening Standard*: he gave it six weeks at most, and suggested that Naim Attallah would have had 'more chance of seeing a return if he financed a troupe of geriatric piano accordionists working

Naim Attallah by Willie Rushton – detail from the cover of Attallah's book, *Singular Encounters* (Quartet, 1992) – a collection of his interviews

Larry Adler (1914–2001), *The Oldie*'s former video critic, at The Oldie of the Year Awards, 1993

Beryl Bainbridge, *Oldie* theatre critic until her death, and Barry Cryer, a regular lunch attendee, at The Oldie of the Year Awards, 2000

the Northern Line on Sunday evenings.' 'There's no fool like an Oldie fool,' Toby Young pronounced in the *Financial Times*, though he gave the new magazine 'a slim but fighting chance of success'. But Bill Deedes, a veteran journalist and former *Daily Telegraph* editor, understood what Ingrams and company were getting at: 'Each generation is left out of step with the previous generation,' he announced. 'With this generation the gap is the widest because of the speed of change due to science and technology. We also have fashion cults moving at bewildering speed with the sense of cultural isolation for the old.' And despite the carping from Fleet Street, so great was public interest and faith in *The Oldie* that 4,000 subscribers paid up for a year's worth of copies without having glimpsed a single copy.

'I don't want anything to do with young fogeys,' Ingrams told Zoë Heller from the *Independent on Sunday*, who wanted to know what sort of people would read and write for *The Oldie*, and how similar it might be to the *Spectator*; on the other hand he would like to make use of good writers who had been 'thrown on the scrapheap'. (Ingrams made good his promise: a long and distinguished list of writers who had fallen on hard times found a new home in *The Oldie*.) Heller then asked him what he meant by an 'oldie'. 'It's, er, it's... well, I suppose it's partly a description of me,' he told her – whereas 'a fogey is a Tory and a bore, I think.' Ingrams himself wore specs, was going deaf and had greying hair, and readily admitted that 'I don't like pop music. I don't like modern films. I hate nearly everything that's on television.

So I am *an* oldie.' (Elsewhere he defined an oldie as 'someone who can't set the video'.) After he had described feminism as a 'malign force' to which the Labour Party, the BBC and the Church of England were all in thrall, Heller hurried to break the news to the feminist publisher Carmen Callil, who hoped to be the new magazine's architectural correspondent. Callil 'stamped her foot and said she wasn't going to put up with it. "I only went along because Liz Calder [from the publishers Bloomsbury] dragged me there. I told her they'd be chauvinistic and anti-homosexual. Well, Ingrams is just going to have to watch his step."'

Carmen Callil was not the only one eager to contribute. At a *Private Eye* lunch Beryl Bainbridge asked if she could be the drama critic, a post she held with distinction until her death in 2010, while Larry Adler 'desperately wanted to write about restaurants – he liked to eat out free', but settled instead for reviewing videos of old films. Auberon Waugh offered to write a 'Rage' column, given over to:

1. Inveighing against the ignorance, idleness, stupidity, dishonesty and sexual incompetence of the young.
2. Insulting the young in any and every manifestation.
3. Insulting the old who seem to be deferring or otherwise sucking up to the young.
4. Promoting the idea of 'age fascism' whereby the young are automatically seen as inferior.
5. Denouncing new things, new ideas, modernism in any form, especially anything proposed in the name of youth or by anyone under the age of forty.

Nor were ideas in short supply. 'There are a lot of people we assume to be dead who are no such thing,' Ingrams told the *Sunday Times*, so paving the way for *The Oldie*'s long-running 'Still With Us' column. He cited a 103-year-old Romanian pianist who had recently resurfaced and given a concert, and went on to attack the *Independent* for devoting two pages to pop music ('rubbish'), and to the marketing men's notion that the young have money to spend ('All the ones I know are broke').

Ingrams was rapidly emerging as the dominant figure in the enterprise: as Naim Attallah put it, he 'assumed total control and moulded the contents to suit

his own perception of what it should be as a new organ. As an organ-player himself, he was deft at the fine tuning it needed to produce the melodies that charmed his ears. The atmosphere of *bonhomie* at the outset helped him achieve his ambition without the least resistance from the board. The euphoria following the launch indirectly gave him the mandate to link the magazine with himself so that it became an indivisible entity.' One area which Ingrams would keep strictly to himself was the choice of cartoons: some of them outraged his readers – in which case they were promptly reprinted in the next issue, alongside the angry letters of protest – but before long it was agreed that *The Oldie* published better and funnier cartoons than any of its rivals.

The first issue of *The Oldie* was published on 21st February 1992 from offices rented from a firm of architects in Charlotte Street; 52 pages long, it appeared – like *Private Eye* – on a fortnightly basis. 'As far as I was concerned *The Oldie* began life as a joke,' Ingrams told readers in his editorial. 'But as soon as I announced it, I found that everyone was taking it seriously. People rang up wanting to invest. Before I knew what was happening, I was leading a crusade.' He thanked Naim Attallah for backing the magazine, and Andreas Whittam-Smith, the editor of the *Independent*, for his timely sacking of Germaine Greer, who was now free to write the first of her 'News from Stump Cross' columns for *The Oldie* (with accompanying wood engravings by John O'Connor). Other ingredients of that first issue included Candida Lycett Green's inaugural 'Unwrecked England' (on Kelmscott Manor), Auberon Waugh's 'Rage', 'Pin-Ups' provided by Jilly Cooper, John Michell's 'An Orthodox Voice', a 'Still With Us' on Godfrey Evans, a Naim Attallah interview with Bill Deedes, a 'Modern Life' on Heavy Metal, Peter Wilsher on 'Money', and a piece I wrote on Magdalen Goffin's neglected masterpiece, *Maria Pasqua*; long-serving columnists already *en poste* included Beryl Bainbridge on theatre, Richard Osborne on music and Valerie Grove on wireless. Eagle-eyed readers were amused to find a scathing review of a Madonna biography by *The Oldie*'s future 'God' columnist, Alice Thomas Ellis, despite an earlier claim that no mention would be made in its pages of 'Madonna, Gazza or rap – whatever that may be.'

105,000 copies were sold amidst a furore of publicity, and the future looked bright indeed – still more so when Ingrams

received a letter from Julie Burchill, a columnist once famed for her forceful views, in which she congratulated him on 'producing the most pathetic magazine ever published'. 'The viability of *The Oldie* remained in doubt until, on the day of publication, we received a faxed message from Ms Julie Burchill,' Ingrams declared in his second editorial. 'So concerned was Ms Burchill that her message of ill will should reach the *Oldie* office that she faxed it no less than three times – printed in capital letters. It persuaded me that we might have a future. It was such a magnificent tribute from exactly the right sort of icon of the modern Britain that I took some convincing that it wasn't in fact a hoax.' But Burchill was not alone in her views. 'To me, *The Oldie* is the ultimate conceit and folly of Richard Ingrams,' Nigel Dempster wrote in the *Daily Mail*. 'His day, as proved by this silly venture, is over.' It was rumoured that Dominic Lawson had banned any references to *The Oldie* in the *Spectator*, while Jocelyn Target in the *Guardian* announced that its editor was a sex maniac and an anti-semite.

Nor was *The Oldie*'s name universally admired. 'What a ghastly name for a magazine. Sounds like old fogeys, white hair, obvious dentures and red fingernails,' wrote Joan Swinge from Bournemouth, before suggesting *Dignity, Seniority, Doyen* and *Maturity* as preferable alternatives. 'The name makes me cringe and I would be embarrassed to buy it,' declared E Hulse from Essex. 'On the other hand, I would definitely go for *Ripe...*' Writing in the *Daily Telegraph*, Jane Thynne reported that some people were convinced that the whole venture was a hoax, for which the name was partly responsible. 'There have been complaints, but they know it's hopeless to try to persuade me. I don't think Bron liked the name either,' she quoted Ingrams as saying. 'I call it hip replacement – putting hip into old,' declared the deputy editor, Emma Soames, when asked by the *New York Times* to define *The Oldie*. Nigel Dempster had told his readers how Ingrams now spent his days in the Groucho Club in Soho, 'surrounded by young acolytes', so Kate Muir of the *Times* went along to case the joint, noting how 'among the sharp suits he sticks out like an escaped don in his corduroys and cashmere sweater which is riddled with either moth or bullet holes.'

The editorial in the third issue referred to the 'undisguised viciousness' of some of the Press coverage: Nigel Dempster

Miles Kington (1941–2008), *Oldie* columnist from 1992 until his death

Richard Ingrams, as drawn by David Hensley on the cover of issue 53, February 1994

Oldie TV, which ran for two series on BBC Two in 1997, was hosted by Richard Ingrams, Mavis Nicholson and Edward Enfield (*above*). Guests included Ludovic Kennedy, Jennifer Paterson and Martha Gellhorn

with eccentric slices of memoir, travel and adventure. To list all those who wrote for the magazine as regular columnists or occasional contributors would be tedious and invidious, but over the next few years Miles Kington and Edward Enfield became household names to *Oldie* readers; Jennifer Paterson (one of television's *Two Fat Ladies*) provided a food column, and was eventually succeeded by Elisabeth Luard, while Mavis Nicholson's predecessor, Ursula Wyndham, was the magazine's first agony aunt. Ned Sherrin covered memorial services – a task now undertaken by James Hughes-Onslow of the *Evening Standard*. Jane Bown, the *Observer*'s legendary photographer, provided portraits of those interviewed by Naim Attallah; Barbara Cartland was eventually sacked for over-promoting herbal remedies ('Every time she mentioned these wretched things we used to get hundreds of people ringing up wanting to buy them').

Oldie Literary Lunches were introduced in 1996: held at Simpson's-in-the-Strand, they featured three authors, each of whom was given ten minutes after lunch in which to describe their new books: and whereas at the more pompous Foyles Literary Lunches grandees and authors drained their champagne in a separate room from the 'punters', *Oldie* readers were encouraged to mix with the celebrities, and were only banned if they proved boring or obstreperous. The first Oldie of the Year awards had been handed out in 1993 – the cricketer David Gower took the crown – with Bill Deedes, Mavis Nicholson, Barry Took and Victoria Mather on the judging panel, and Hugh Trevor-Roper, Yehudi Menuhin and Spike Milligan among the guests.

Like many of the best editors, Richard Ingrams had no time for readership surveys, opinion polls and the like, and invariably hurled the pollsters' findings into the nearest waste-paper basket. But although he showed no interest in reading tabulated lists of readers' preferences, he was all in favour of their expressing their views in the letters pages; and, unlike most magazine editors, he was happy to publish pieces sent in by *Oldie* readers and members of the public. 'I am beginning to realise at last my dream of a magazine, a very large part of which is written by its readers,' he announced after two years at the helm: 'There is too much of a myth about journalism nowadays... My

continued to snipe from the wings, devoting two pages in the *Daily Mail* to *The Oldie*'s 'lacklustre layout' and 'unsound reporting'. And the stupendous sales proved to be a flash in the pan. Those who had wrongly assumed that *The Oldie* would be an alternative *Private Eye* quickly jumped ship, and novelty value swiftly fades: sales of the second issue dropped to 40,000, descending to 25,000 by the twelfth issue and 15,000 by the end of the first year.

Though the sales figures were falling, the editorial confidence of the magazine grew, and the carping from the Press died away as the magazine gradually found its voice and its *raison d'être*. A letter from the atheist Oxford don Richard Dawkins attacking John Michell provided evidence that *The Oldie* was doing its job of irritating and entertaining at the same time, and other contributions to early issues included Dr Tom Stuttaford on the health-giving properties of red wine, and a short story from William Trevor: *The Oldie* rarely publishes short stories but Trevor and Jane Gardam proved fine exceptions to the rule, just as the publisher and poet James Michie was allowed to break the 'no poetry' embargo.

Like all good magazines, *The Oldie* combined the familiar with the unexpected, memoirs, dependable experts writing on gardening, wine, films and television, belief is that anyone with a typewriter is a journalist.' Later that year he was kept at home by a gammy leg: re-reading some early issues, he 'was absolutely appalled by the general air of amateurishness – compared to the polished and streamlined product you see before you today.' The first issues lacked vitality because the magazine had no readers – and 'it is the readers who breathe life into a paper with their letters, their ideas and contributions.' 'In the end *The Oldie* seemed to write itself, with very little commissioning on my part,' Ingrams wrote in a retrospective editorial: some years later, when I joined the staff of *The Oldie* on a part-time basis, I was given the grand but misleading title of 'Commissioning Editor' – and soon realised that although book reviews were commissioned, as were the regular columns, the free-standing articles were written on spec, and the role of 'commissioning editor' was a contradiction in terms.

Such views were at odds with those of Emma Soames, who left in September 1992 to become the editor of the *Evening Standard* (her departure coincided with that of the 'Supreme Consultant', Alexander Chancellor, who was briefly lured across the Atlantic to work with Tina Brown on the *New Yorker*). Soames targeted topical subjects and then tried to match them up with suitable journalists, many of whom had covered the ground umpteen times before. 'After a short time I realised that this was going about it the wrong way. The best thing was to get the writers first and let them write about anything they liked,' Ingrams recalled, adding 'that way, at least you avoided having to pay "kill fees".' 'I Once Met', suggested by *The Oldie*'s literary editor, James Michie, was far more in tune with Ingrams's notions of how a magazine should be assembled, and remains his favourite feature in *The Oldie*: almost all the best 'I Once Mets' have been provided by members of the public, so proving that 'the amateur is often best qualified to tell a good story,' while the 'Memory Lane' slot is exclusively filled by *Oldie* readers.

Ingrams's receptivity to readers' offerings and suggestions is combined with a fierce adherence to Lord Beaverbrook's adage that 'readers have got to be annoyed'. Annoyance reached incandescent levels in the letters pages when a regular column was offered to the

Oxford-educated Wilfred De'Ath, who had abandoned his family and a successful career at the *Sunday Times* and the BBC for a life of petty crime: readers were particularly incensed by his accounts of stealing out of country hotels without paying the bill, and wrote angry letters threatening to cancel their subscriptions if the editor continued to offer space to this fiend in human form. 'Why give the silly sods space?' Hugh Cudlipp once wrote apropos Ingrams's enthusiasm for publishing letters from 'moaners', but Ingrams would have none of it. 'A "silly sod" cancelling his subscription will, in my experience, annoy at least six people so much that they will reach for their cheque books and take out a sub,' he told the former editor of the *Daily Mirror*, himself an occasional contributor.

But *The Oldie*'s editorial self-confidence was not reflected in sales or profitability. According to Naim Attallah, the original capital had 'evaporated' by the spring of 1993, and his magazine 'was going to need much greater resources and more sustained backing if it was going to stay afloat'. A further contribution of £20,000 from Lord Lambton had proved a welcome drop in the ocean; Auberon Waugh admitted that '*The Oldie* is in trouble', and that it 'never had enough wind behind it.' There was talk of a merger with *Punch*, which was enjoying a short-lived resurrection, and rumours of *The Oldie*'s financial difficulties prompted old foes to sharpen their quills: Peter McKay referred to Ingrams's 'loony magazine' in the *Sunday Times*; Nigel Dempster in the *Daily Mail* suggested that Attallah should be awarded a knighthood for keeping afloat a magazine which was 'edited by ageing hypocrite Richard

Columnist Wilfred De'Ath at The Oldie of the Year Awards, 2012

Spike Milligan (left) and Peter O'Toole at The Oldie of the Year Awards, 2000

Ingrams and employs other deadbeats'. 'As was my wont, I continued in the role of knight in shining armour and rode to the rescue,' Naim Attallah admitted after revealing that he had borrowed a further £300,000 from his bank to keep *The Oldie* afloat. 'I must have been mad. There was no way I could sit back and see it fail, despite my better judgment; I just could not bear to see our past efforts wasted. As an optimist by nature and a fighter by instinct, I frequently ignored the voice of reason.' Nor was Attallah's involvement with the magazine restricted to dipping into his coffers and providing a dash of colour at Literary Lunches. His interviews were widely admired: before talking to his subjects he was briefed in detail by Jennie Erdal, an editor at Quartet, who then edited and wrote up the taped interviews at her home in St Andrew's. 'You didn't tell me it was a woman!' Attallah expostulated after interviewing the octogenarian Frances Partridge: but such lapses were few and far between.

With the magazine's monetary problems in temporary abeyance, life resumed its familiar pattern. Lunches were held in the basement of the Charlotte Street offices, to which contributors and well-wishers were invited; on my first visit to *The Oldie* I made a mercy dash to an ironmonger in Goodge Street after the office corkscrew had gone missing. In the spring of 1994 the editor took two months' leave of absence to finish his biography of Malcolm Muggeridge: Donald Trelford, a former editor of the *Observer*, held the fort in his absence, and broke new ground with a regular sporting column, now provided by Frank Keating. The 'World's Worst Dumps' feature made its first appearance; aerial photographs of crop circles – a particular enthusiasm of John Michell's – became an annual occurrence; Bloomsbury published the first *Oldie Annual*; John Gibben joined the staff as a 'token beard', and the editor revealed that, according to the marketing department, 251 *Oldie* subscribers had double-barrelled names. But losses in the year up to March 1994 amounted to £274,000, and the magazine was losing £10,000 per issue. The *Times* reported that *The Oldie* was 'limping to an early grave', the *Evening Standard* mourned its 'sad if inevitable demise', and Toby Young likened it to Eddie the Eagle, then celebrated as the most incompetent practitioner ever to take part in competitive skiing.

Although 'in my heart of hearts I knew this was a decision I would live to regret,' Naim Attallah once again dug into his pocket: Auberon Waugh spoke of the 'generous and loyal support' of a man 'who deserves a statue in the hall of modern British heroes,' and Mary Kenny referred to Mr Attallah as a 'great hero'. Richard Ingrams admitted that he had made two fundamental mistakes: he had underestimated the amount of money needed ('why anyone had thought it possible to launch a new magazine with a mere £250,000 is hard to explain'); and he had mistakenly opted for fortnightly publication, with the result that *The Oldie* had a larger staff than it could afford (looking back, David Ford suggests that Ingrams in particular had been too influenced by the success of *Private Eye*: as a topical magazine, it needed to keep up-to-the-minute, whereas most of the material which appeared in *The Oldie* in 1994 reads as well in 2012 as it did at the time). By the summer of 1994 *The Oldie* was losing £20,000 a month: there were no plans to keep it going, and Attallah and the Board decided that there was no alternative to closing it down. Publication ceased in August, and was widely reported in the Press. But the super-energetic business manager, James Pembroke, who was then in his late twenties, remained convinced that *The Oldie* could survive, and break even, if it was published on a monthly basis: he won round Richard Ingrams, and Naim Attallah agreed to go ahead provided he was not called upon to invest another penny in it. Ingrams later credited Pembroke with 'saving *The Oldie*': not only did he have to restructure and reorganise

An *Oldie* staff trip to Chatsworth, 2000. From left: Tony Cole (aka Beardie), Helen Richardson, Siva the accountant, Jeremy Lewis, Richard Ingrams, the late Duke of Devonshire, Ben Tisdall, Tony West (aka Swiss Tony), Nick Parker and Jenny Naipaul

its publication, but – given the adverse publicity caused by its closure – convince subscribers, advertisers and retailers to keep faith in the magazine. In September 1994 *The Oldie* was reborn, with a smaller staff and new offices in Poland Street, where other of Naim Attallah's Namara publications were housed. Switching to monthly publication was a pivotal moment in *The Oldie*'s history. It had survived by the skin of its teeth: writing in the *Sunday Times*, Joanna Pitman marvelled at how it kept going on 'a budget that would barely have fed a family of sparrows'.

Richard Ingrams admitted to 'a somewhat curmudgeonly attitude towards the advertising department of this magazine', but in the mid-Nineties the revenue from display and classified advertising soared from £3,000 to £20,000 per issue. Advertisements appeared in colour as well as in black and white; advertisers included holiday operators, the makers of stair-lifts, zimmer frames and incontinence pads, ladies of ill repute operating in the Paddington area, makers of alternative footwear, mail-order clothing firms (one of whose advertisements featured *The Oldie*'s Commissioning Editor wearing a scarlet nightshirt – *see page 17*) and a Yorkshire butcher who specialised in 'real oldie-style bacon'. All this was thanks to the new advertising manager, Tony West ('Swiss Tony') – a former policeman with a *Viva Zapata* moustache and a straining waistband, who had put himself up for the job – and his dapper deputy, Dave Sturge. When not on the phone to potential advertisers, Messrs West and Sturge spent a good deal of time chanting in mock-African voices, simultaneously beating their desk-tops like tribal drums, their heads thrust back like wolves serenading the moon. I started work at *The Oldie* in January 1997, coming in one day a week, and as soon as I poked my head round the door a chant of 'Je-zza, Je-zza' went up, accompanied by much banging of desks. Every now and then a serious-looking man with a beard came into the office to discuss some matter of business: no sooner had he left than a chant of 'Bear-die, Bear-die' went up, and a bearded face shot round the door to see if he was needed.

Apart from the tribal drumming, the Poland Street office was remarkable for its apparent chaos, the epicentre of which was Richard Ingrams's desk. I had seen some heavily laden desks in my time – André Deutsch's and Alan Ross's were particularly fine examples – but

this was in a league of its own. The disorder was deceptive, however: the papers at the bottom of the mound may have been years old, and composted down to a kind of mulch, but Ingrams knew exactly how and where to find the items he needed, and the system only broke down if, to his intense annoyance, some busybody or reforming spirit tried to tidy him up. We shared a desk – or rather two old-fashioned kneehole desks pushed together end to end – and to get to my seat I had to pick my way past cardboard boxes brimming over with yellowing sheets of paper, while at the same time trying not to trip over an obsolescent vacuum-cleaner, the nozzle of which trailed away under my desk. Before I could get down to any work I had to clear a space for myself, pushing back the mountains of bumph which rolled towards me from the editor's end of our communal desks. My weekly clearances were ephemeral triumphs: by the following Tuesday my end of the desk had been entirely covered over, as if by an ever-encroaching Amazonian jungle. I was not alone in being stunned by the noise and the muddle. Jenny Naipaul, who joined us from the *Spectator*, was so stupefied by the chaos that she went into a near-catatonic trance before deciding that she must do something about it; Caroline Law could bear the chanting no longer and fled to *The Week*, which she now edits; finding himself surrounded by 'broken furniture and sagging storage boxes covered in black soot' when he arrived for his interview in Poland Street, Nick Parker assumed he had wandered into a derelict office, but went on to spend ten happy years at *The Oldie*.

Despite the background noises and the teetering mounds of paper, sales were gradually increasing, hovering round the 20,000 mark, and the wealth of advertisements made it possible to expand the magazine to 68 pages (and on to 84 pages in 2000; nowadays most issues are 92 pages). The Literary Lunches in Simpson's-in-the-Strand proved a huge success. For a time they were sponsored by Stannah Stairlifts; by a cruel irony it was not possible to fit one of their stairlifts into the restaurant, and halt or wheelchair-bound speakers and lunchers had to make their way up to the first floor by traditional

Former *Oldie* columnist Germaine Greer, as drawn by Willie Rushton on the cover of issue 27, February 1993

Sir Paul Getty (1932–2003): an admirer and former proprietor of *The Oldie*

Bob Marshall-Andrews (left) and *Oldie* publisher James Pembroke at The Oldie of the Year Awards, 2012

means. Highlights of Literary Lunches included a waiter tipping a bowl of soup down Peter O'Toole's neck, and Larry Adler turning green during the first course: he was manhandled out of the dining-room, presumed dead, but reappeared at the pudding stage, pale but in good spirits, and entertained *Oldie* readers to a performance on the mouth organ. A welcome presence at many Literary Lunches, then and now, was the comedian and script-writer Barry Cryer, who could always be relied upon to step into the breach should one of the speakers fail to turn up, and set the tables aroar with a non-stop stream of jokes.

Naim Attallah was a genial host on such occasions, and had diversified into phallic chocolates and erotic key-rings, but by 2000 he had decided that he could no longer afford to support *The Oldie* and the *Literary Review*, and both magazines were put up for sale. Several potential buyers were approached, including John Brown, a former book publisher who had made a name for himself as a 'contract' magazine publisher – publishing, among other things, the Waitrose magazine – and as the publisher of the Newcastle-based comic magazine, *Viz*. Brown offered to get in touch with Paul Getty, an admirer of *The Oldie* who had sponsored some Oldie of the Year lunches. Although he was, by then, in poor health, and had not long to live, Getty warmed to the idea: John Brown negotiated the purchase of *The Oldie* from Naim Attallah in August 2001 – the *Literary Review* had gone its separate way – and in due course found himself publishing it through his firm, John Brown Ltd, together with *Viz*, the *Fortean Times* and *Gardens Illustrated*: he had told Getty that if he would invest £250,000 in *The Oldie*, Brown could get it to break even.

After the sale to Getty, a new cast of directors was appointed, and *The Oldie* moved from Poland Street to its present offices in Newman Street, five minutes' walk from *Private Eye* and the Star Café in Great Chapel Street (where editorial lunches are held). Rosie Boycott was made the travel editor, and a director of the magazine; Richard Ingrams revealed that an article by the Marquess of Aberdeen describing his exploits in brothels [*see page 97*] had 'led to an unprecedented and welcome burst of publicity for *The Oldie*', and thanked readers for taking part in a Readership Survey ('Already the results are being fed into the computer, which will shortly issue me with my instructions to make *The Oldie* a bigger, brighter and better read. Cynics have

warned me to be wary of the opinions of readers who have nothing better to do with their time than fill in forms...') With *The Oldie*'s tenth anniversary looming in February 2002, 'Some of the country's top designers have been working for months to create this breakthrough in magazine presentation... some of you may not notice any difference, so sensitively and discreetly have the changes been made.'

'One of the inevitable hazards of employing elderly contributors is that they are likely to die,' Ingrams wrote early in the new millennium, citing Peter Black and Patricia Highsmith as recent examples. Auberon Waugh had died in 2001, in his early sixties: the years to come would see the deaths of Miles Kington, Ned Sherrin (memorial services), Alice Thomas Ellis, Larry Adler, Jennifer Paterson, E S Turner (who became a contributor in his nineties) and Geoffrey Moorhouse (whose 'Pennine Life' column was welcomed as evidence that *Oldie* writers and readers are not, as is sometimes claimed, restricted to the Home Counties). The death of Paul Getty had its own implications for the future of *The Oldie*. He had been a benign and well-disposed proprietor, but his son Mark did not share his enthusiasm for the magazine; the link with John Brown Ltd had been severed after its founder sold his business, but Brown himself remained as the non-executive Chairman. His role had been to hold the fort, and before long *The Oldie* would be on the market once more.

I n May 2007 Ingrams's editorial announced that 'a group of highly proactive venture capitalists' had bought *The Oldie* from Mark Getty. Getty had been about to conclude the sale to another publisher, but agreed to hold off when Richard Ingrams asked him to give James Pembroke, *The Oldie*'s former business manager, more time in which to raise the money ('He's got twenty-four hours,' Getty replied). Two friends of Pembroke's came up trumps, with the result that the magazine now had three proprietors: David Kowitz, a hedge-fund manager described in the cast list as 'Our Quiet American', who agreed to invest on the strength of having the cover of the first issue of *The Oldie* pinned up in the lavatory of his New York apartment, and now hosts *The Oldie*'s Christmas party in his sumptuous flat in St James's Place, one floor down from Rupert Murdoch; Richard Beatty, the then owner of Britain's largest ad sales agency, who had done work for *The Oldie* and now owns the Polpo restaurants in London; and James Pembroke, who succeeded John Brown as Publisher. A dynamic figure with flashing blue eyes and a flamboyant telephonic presence, Pembroke had left *The Oldie* to set up his own contract publishing in Bath: but he retained a passion for the magazine and longed to return to it, and no sooner had the sale been concluded than he hurried off to Newman Street to see what could be done.

James Pembroke's impact on *The Oldie* has been incalculable, and entirely beneficial. Sales have rocketed from 26,000 to over 40,000; the great majority of copies of magazines like *The Oldie* are sold to subscribers rather than through the retail trade, and huge efforts have been made to build up the subscription list. More pages have been added – most issues now are 92 pages – and the magazine is published thirteen times a year (i.e. on a four-weekly rather than a calendar month basis). The *Oldie Review of Books*, a quarterly supplement, has been followed by money supplements and gift guides; Oldie books have been published, among them Oldie Annuals, a selection of Candida Lycett Green's 'Unwrecked England' pieces, cartoon books, James Michie's *Last Poems* and a cookery book by Elisabeth Luard. Oldie Piano Weekends have been succeeded by Oldie Writing Courses and Cartoon Courses; Oldie Food and Wine seminars have been held in Italy and Spain; Oldie speakers have spread the word on cruises arranged by Swan Hellenic, who sponsored the Oldie Literary Lunches after Stannah Stairlifts, and by Noble Caledonia, who then took over from Swan Hellenic; and in September 2011 the first Soho Literary Festival, sponsored and organised by *The Oldie*, took place over three days at the Soho Theatre in Dean Street, and proved a great success. Despite the gloomy state of the economy, much of this was made possible by a doubling of advertising revenue, masterminded by Chris Mace and his successor, Lisa Martin, and her colleagues Azmi Elkholy and Jack Watts. Nor was the editorial side immune to change: new items included 'Top Chumps' and 'Tips for Meanies', incorporated in the 'Old Un's Diary' alongside old favourites like 'Great Bores of Today' and 'Not Many Dead'. And whereas all too many newspapers, magazines and book publishers refuse to read pieces submitted by readers or the general public, and return them (if at all)

with a printed rejection slip, *The Oldie* still takes trouble on that score, even if we can't provide the detailed critiques that authors invariably long for.

This year marks the twentieth anniversary of *The Oldie*. It employs far fewer people than it did when I joined it fifteen years ago: the one-room Newman Street office is a good deal tidier than its predecessor in Poland Street, but the editor's desk is, as ever, a quagmire of paper, not a sheet of which can be moved or replaced by hands other than his own. Richard Ingrams remains at the centre of *The Oldie*'s solar system, with Sonali Chapman, Deborah Asher, Joe Buckley, Charlotte Fairbairn and myself rotating round him in stately formation, and James Pembroke whizzing across the firmament like a meteor in perpetual motion; Sarah Shannon, late of *Private Eye*, masterminds the long-running 'Old Un's Diary'. Working at *The Oldie* is hugely enjoyable and entertaining, but – as with any publishing venture – the magazine will be judged by the writers who appear in its pages, and the work they produce. The rest of this book will give you some idea of who they are, and what some of them came up with.

★　　★　　★

DECIDING WHAT to include in an anthology of this kind is, inevitably, an invidious business, made more so by limitations of space and cost. Almost everything that has appeared in *The Oldie* over the past twenty years has been entertaining and well written: to some extent any selection is bound to seem arbitrary, flattering to those who have been included but hurtful to those – the great majority – who have not. We have excluded pieces that have dated in terms of their subject matter, including reviews and pieces that were tied to particular exhibitions or events; and we have restricted those who have been included to one entry apiece. A magazine like *The Oldie* depends, above all else, on those who write for it: we've been extremely lucky in our contributors, regular or sporadic, and we're eternally grateful to all those who have appeared in our pages.

I'm very grateful to the following for talking to me about days gone by at *The Oldie*: Richard Ingrams, James Pembroke, John Brown, Alexander Chancellor, David Ford, Stephen Glover and Nick Parker. Naim Attallah's memoir, *Fulfilment and Betrayal: 1975–1995* (Quartet, 2007) was an invaluable source of information.

Raymond Banning – the piano tutor at *The Oldie*'s piano weekends – watching *Oldie* columnist Giles Wood play at a piano weekend in 2003

Jeremy Lewis, the Commissioning Editor himself, modelling a striking red nightshirt on *The Oldie*'s roof terrace

The CARTOONISTS and ILLUSTRATORS of The Oldie

RICHARD INGRAMS

Since our launch in 1992 *The Oldie* has featured the work of about one hundred and twenty-five different cartoonists – an extraordinary range of different ages and styles. Some of them were known to me from my years at *Private Eye* – veterans like Martin Honeysett, Mike Williams, Ed McLachlan, Tony Husband and Larry – but many more were new and some were very young.

One or two came from abroad, like our most prolific contributor, the American cartoonist Nick Downes, whose macabre and often gruesome humour makes an especial appeal to me.

In the course of the twenty years, we have not surprisingly lost a fair share. I think particularly of Larry, Ged Melling, Hugh Burnett (famous for his monk cartoons), Les Barton – but others have come forward to take their

place. The number of submissions is as great as ever.

As far as illustrators are concerned, we have tended to rely on a small band of regulars. They include, most notably, Peter Bailey (many of whose illustrations are featured in the book) and Bob Geary, who is also an outstanding caricaturist. Bob has been responsible for a number of covers, as well as supplying a regular portrait for the Book Review pages, a task previously performed by Trog (Wally Fawkes) and before him by Michael Cummings, formerly the *Daily Express* political cartoonist in the Beaverbrook days.

Other regular cover artists have been Ham Khan, Axel Scheffler (of Gruffalo fame) – who also provided the cover to this book – Martin Honeysett, Alan de la Nougerede, Arthur Robins, Bill Belcher, David Stoten and Bob Wilson.

Quentin Blake (like Posy Simmonds) has done occasional covers (see page 117). I was also grateful to him when the magazine was still in its infancy for recommending two of his former pupils from the RCA, Steven Appleby and John Watson (who provided the cover of issue one but died tragically young at the age of forty in 2000).

Clockwise from bicycle illustration above right:
Bill Belcher's two freewheelers; autumn leaves by Ed McLachlan; pigs – detail from Steven Appleby's expenses scandal cover, July 2003; Oldie chain – detail from Ed McLachlan's Christmas cover, 2005; Harold Wilson and Daphne du Maurier by Michael Cummings; Bob Wilson's man in hat

The Joys of ALCOHOL

DR THOMAS STUTTAFORD *argues that drinking can prolong your life*

DR THOMAS STUTTAFORD

The Oldie's resident doctor since 1992, Dr Stuttaford has also been a *Times* columnist and Conservative MP for Norwich South.

Despite the efforts of the politically correct puritans from the United States, and their craven followers in Britain, ninety per cent of British people still enjoy a drink. Any guilt about the effect of an occasional drink, or even three or four daily drinks, which has been inculcated by the propaganda of the health promoters, can be tempered by the thought that even the most puritanical doctors in America now admit that there is overwhelming evidence that moderate drinkers live longer than abstainers.

The most recent research, from New Zealand, Holland and Britain, published last autumn, so convincingly showed that a moderate daily alcohol intake reduced the death rate from heart disease that the revenue from sales of red wine to Americans increased by forty per cent. It seems that their obsessive fear of coronary thrombosis outweighs their preoccupation with 'alcohol abuse'.

Many writers, and a few doctors, have broadcast the results of research projects which, since the 1970s, have shown that alcohol in modest quantities is beneficial; but these results, because they tended to confound the preconceptions of the puritans, have been largely ignored until now, when the evidence is so great that it has to be accepted. Science has only confirmed the common observation that moderate drinkers do well, that abstainers are often as unhealthy as they look, and that drunks die young.

of older patients, which concluded that two or three glasses of wine a day was one of the seven clues to a longer life.

Over the last few years there have been attempts by pressure groups such as Alcohol Concern to persuade doctors, and the lay public, that society is permeated with hidden elderly 'problem drinkers', the physical and mental victims of a society tolerant of alcohol, who are now suffering the torments of the damned because of their capricious habits.

This is largely nonsense, for careful research has shown that most elderly heavy drinkers usually drank heavily

Science has only confirmed the common observation that moderate drinkers do well, that abstainers are often as unhealthy as they look and that drunks die young

Few writers have done more to promote common-sense drinking than Jane MacQuitty, the wine correspondent of the *Times*. In particular she has done an invaluable service in counteracting the fear that even a few drinks taken while pregnant will damage the unborn child. There is no evidence that any child has been damaged by modest social drinking.

Miss MacQuitty might as easily have written of the advantages of wine drinking for older age groups by reference to her father, William. Dr William MacQuitty, a former banker, film producer, author and photographer, who later became the founding managing director of Ulster TV, still, at 87, swims daily despite artificial hips, and continues to travel the world. Last year he wrote his autobiography, *A Life to Remember*. One of William MacQuitty's recipes for a long and enjoyable life is spartan food and hard work during the day, followed by a half-bottle of wine with a good dinner in the evening.

As long ago as 1980, public health doctors working in California completed a nine-year study on the health

long before they reached old age, and that, as one might expect, most people drink less as they grow older because experience has taught them that they tolerate alcohol less well. Far from being damaged, those who drink moderately in old age suffer no more depression than non-drinkers, are no more likely to attend out-patient clinics or be admitted to hospital and even, rather surprisingly, don't suffer from any more falls than the abstainers.

Total abstainers tend to be less alert, less sociable, and presumably more boring, than those who drink.

An example from the writing of one prominent gerontologist seems to sum up the trendy, bigoted and humourless approach of the new puritans. 'Wellness refers to emphasising a lifestyle which encompasses a healthy existence in all areas of one's life. We need to educate the ageing population as to the benefits of a health-enhancing behaviour as an alternative to dependence on alcohol.' He continued by advocating 'nutritional awareness', 'physical fitness' and 'environmental sensitivity', but most of us would be better educated, and more healthy, if we confined our nutritional awareness to sharing a bottle of claret with Dr MacQuitty.

We could drink to the knowledge that the two or three drinks we would enjoy would reduce the chance of a coronary thrombosis by at least forty per cent (*BMJ*, 1991), by more if we were women, and that when we reached really old age we, as drinkers, would be more interesting than the conformist abstainers; we would be more active, more sociable, less incontinent, would sleep better and swallow fewer pills. We would be less depressed, and no more likely to be attending the local hospital.

Although the Government's recommendation is that men should not exceed twenty-one units a week and women should not exceed fourteen, the evidence for this is slight. Much larger surveys have shown that the chance of damage for people of normal build is unlikely at double these figures. This has been confirmed by recent research in New Zealand. An earlier survey of around 80,000 American nurses showed that those who drank two to five units a day had a better expectation of life than the total abstainer.

A memorial service was held for George Barker on 26th February 1992, two days after what would have been his 79th birthday, not a bad age at all. For three generations the Barker family worked out their rages and aggression in very different ways: grandfather Barker, a Lincolnshire farmer, would, when overcome with anger, wrestle with the bullocks in the cattle yard; George's father, who was a butler, shouted around the house before settling down with port and a cigar; George the poet outraged his father, and society, in a host of ways, and was not averse to relieving his inner tensions with a few drinks. He died at nearly 79 years of age, young compared to Winston Churchill who drank more in a day than the Royal College of Physicians would recommend for a week, and lived to ninety. Both men, together with many others less famous, would seem to disprove the accepted rule that drinking to excess is inevitably dangerous.

Most of us, wisely, should confine our drinking to no more than a half-bottle of claret or so with dinner. Who knows, it might even be beneficial.

My First Job

by KEITH WATERHOUSE, *novelist and playwright (1929–2009)*

I LEFT MY LOCAL College of Commerce at the age of fifteen with shorthand and typewriting 'skills', as they would nowadays be called, hoping to become a newspaper reporter. Since this was out of the question until I was a little older, I became an undertaker's clerk instead.

My careers teacher thought it an eccentric choice but I knew what I was doing. I should have access to a typewriter, which would enable me to pursue my journalistic ambitions in my lunch hour. The only other job on offer was at Lloyd's Bank and I could not see myself composing submissions for *John O' London's Weekly* and *Britannia & Eve* on an adding machine.

It was a small, family-run business – one of those old-fashioned offices where the partners are known as Mr Percy, Mr William and so on – called J T Buckton & Sons, motto: We Never Sleep. Why, unless they had a contract with a latterday Burke and Hare, a firm of 'funeral furnishers' (as they preferred to call themselves) should feel the need to stay up all night was never explained to me. What it boiled down to was that the last clerk to leave each evening was supposed to switch the telephone through to Mr Percy's house. The task was as often as not forgotten, and there were no midnight burials.

The office, run on pleasantly paternal lines, was absurdly overstaffed and my duties were light. One of them was to look after the postage book – very handy for a budding journalist sending out a constant flow of self-addressed envelopes to editors. Buckton's had a rule that all correspondence within the Leeds postal district was to be delivered by hand, to save on stamps. This provided me with a pleasant daily amble around the city centre, with plenty of time for a coffee at the Gambit Café, where the tables were marked out as chessboards and elderly clerks wearing celluloid collars and paper cuffs played their tournaments.

Another enjoyable task was to attend funerals, where I was required to stand in the church or crematorium porch with a notebook and take down the

My teacher thought becoming an undertaker's clerk an eccentric choice

names of all the mourners and whoever or whatever they might be representing. This was for the benefit of the next of kin, but I always slipped a carbon copy to the *Leeds Guardian*, the local weekly, who paid ten shillings a column.

Otherwise, apart from a certain amount of larking about with shrouds in the basement stockroom, and the necessity to look suitably solemn whenever a bereaved party came in to discuss funeral arrangements with Mr Percy, our office routine was pretty much like that of any other small business. There would be the occasional crisis when we had two funerals on the go at once and there were not enough limousines to go round, and I would be sent galloping along to the cab rank to requisition three or four taxis; but that served only to remind us that in the midst of life we were on the edge of black comedy.

One day I was over at the mortuary on some errand or other when I encountered one of Mr Percy's rivals cautioning his pall-bearers as they carried the coffin (or casket, as it is known in the trade) out to the hearse: 'Now don't forget that's the late Mr Parkin you've got in there – we don't want a repetition of last week's fiasco.'

It was all to come in useful.

News from Stump Cross

GERMAINE GREER *wrote about rural life at Stump Cross, her home near Saffron Walden: in this column she declares war on the rabbits...*

GERMAINE GREER

Feminist writer, critic and essayist Germaine Greer – author of *The Female Eunuch* (1970) – was an *Oldie* columnist until December 1993.

Rain. More rain. Waterbutts full for the first time in a year. A soft grey mist hanging in the hedgerows. The snowdrops did their best in dry, warm ground, and quickly went their way. Now the scillas and the narcissi and the wood anemones are keeping their jubilee, their petals sleeked by the damp air, glowing against the new green that is rushing up over the land. Under the beech trees a clump of sweet violets has appeared; by the pond in the wood is another. A dome of frog spawn nudges the surface of the water and the white marsh marigold is in flower. Up on the chalk hill Farmer Hamilton's beet is beginning to show.

The grass grows like mad, and the geese graze like mad upon it, for the time of their brood is almost at hand. They are already so plump that the folds of fat beneath their bellies drag up on the new grass, leaving trails like the slime of a giant snail. The gander, for want of anyone else to show off against, bullies the widowed grey goose. A Canada gander came courting her but she, not wanting to know that unlike the white geese she can fly, stayed on the ground. Since the fox took her grey mate she has been an outsider. The gander 'treads' her though and there are more of her narrow pointed eggs than there are of the big chalk-white ones of the white geese, so she will have her day, I hope. Mother-son incest is not frowned upon in the goose community; she and her son-consort may head up a grey flock yet.

If I cannot control the rats there will be as few goslings as there are chicks. First the rats stole the eggs from under the setting bantams. Then we moved the setting bantams out of the house, which was by now thoroughly undermined, into coops. The rats dug under the coops, so we kept moving the coops. The chicks hatched, the rats dug faster and dragged the tiny birds through the holes they made. We now have one chick left, immured with its mother in an outhouse. It is enough to make a woman invest in a pack of Jack Russells, and be buggered to the anti-blood sports movement.

I can't myself see the difference between digging out a badger and digging out a rat family. Rats are intelligent; they love their children and they are passionately attached to life. A rat will drag its trap around for days, because no one can get near enough to free it or kill it. Some time ago I wrote about the way country people deal with trapped rats, which is by dropping the rat, trap and all, into the waterbutt. I got passionate letters from hairdressers and fashion designers. How could you? they wailed. How cruel. I pondered the advisability of sending these correspondents a live rat of their own to deal with, but while I was pondering, Charlie and the game-keeper, fed up with all the nonsense about rats' rights, poisoned nearly all the rats. Then I asked the RSPCA officer the best way to deal with trapped rats. 'Drown them,' she said.

The cats bring in live rabbit kittens, screaming piteously, and punch them around

A rat with a day-old chick is not a pretty sight, no prettier a sight indeed than someone vivisecting a day-old chick. It is all bloody cruel out there. Creatures suffer and die horribly all the time. The cats bring in live rabbit kittens, screaming piteously, and punch them around to get the juices flowing, before biting their faces off. At what stage cognition ceases I have no idea. Some cats start at the rear. Both of mine begin at the front, and seldom bother with the rear, which is usually left under the dining table. Guests have risen from dinner parties and tramped the contents of a warm and steaming rabbit caecum all over the house. Inexperienced guests sometimes intervene to stop the slaughter; one brought a rabbit to me as I lay in bed and placed it reverently on the coverlet. It lay and trembled. One of its feet kicked spasmodically. It was paralysed down one side. 'Shall we get the vet?' she asked. We didn't. I have given up intervening since I rescued a dormouse five times. When the red cat, who specialises in the rarer species and small songbirds, brought the dormouse in for the sixth time, I decided the dormouse gene pool would be better off without it.

As I see it, the ecological balance is already so buggered up that you cannot simply live and let live. We have a thousand or so rabbits and about the same number of rats on my three acres because there is nowhere else for them to go. The population that should be spread over the hundred-acre field lives with me because I neither plough nor poison my ground with fungicides, herbicides, insecticides and fertilisers. Because of the environmental stress none of the critters who lives under my hedgerows and my poultry houses is quite sane or quite well. The rabbit population is full of myxomatosis. Because none of the predators will take a sick rabbit, the myxy ones are compelled to live out a normal life-span, and to reproduce. When the ferreters come these days they get no hassle from me. Strange to relate, they get no hassle from the anti-blood sports people either. Funny that, when you think about it. Foxes live by hunting and could expect to die the same way, but rabbits? What harm did rabbits ever do?

Well, I'll tell you. Rabbits are bloody bastards. Absolute bloody bastards. They don't kill other animals. They kill plants. Foxes, unlike dogs and mink, kill for food for themselves and their young. Rabbits don't kill trees for food. I don't know why they kill trees. They will do just enough damage to a young tree to ensure that it dies, and then they will move on to the next one. They will nose their way through spiral guards and gnaw out a neat half-inch strip all the way round the tree; that's all it takes to kill even a mighty tree. They will climb on each other's shoulders to attack the tree above the guard – I reckon, because

otherwise I don't know how the hell they do it. Build a cage for a young tree and they will burrow under it. If they can't get at any other part of the tree, they will dig under it and eat the roots. They will kill larch, oak, sycamore, hornbeam, whitebeam, beech, birch, horse chestnut, willow, alder, poplar, aspen, apple, medlar, cherry, maple, cedar, cypress, hazel, pine, spruce, juniper, whitethorn, blackthorn, but not brambles or bracken or elder. I have just planted twenty planes and they have yet to kill one, but they will. I have planted more than 700 trees since I have lived in this house and they have destroyed 400 of them, some when they were already twenty centimetres in girth. They have eaten whole yews and lived to tell the tale. They even managed to strip a monkey puzzle of its scales.

I do not protest when rabbits eat bulbs or gnaw their way into the cage to eat my salad. But I cannot bear it when for the sake of slightly different taste, some sort of oral novelty, they kill one of my trees. Do something for our struggling tree population. Kill a rabbit today.

MEMORY LANE

What were you doing 40, 50, 60, 70 or 80 years ago?

70 years ago, when I was eight, my father noticed that I could not bend over and I was subsequently diagnosed with TB of the spine. I was transported across London in a Green Line bus converted to take stretchers to Stockwood Park, a stately home in Luton complete with massive oil paintings on the wall.

I was placed in a plaster bed, a half cast of my body from knees to the top of my head, supported on a wooden frame. The only thing between the plaster and me was a thin piece of muslin. I spent three and a half years so confined, occasionally being lifted out for a blanket bath or X-ray, or for another cast to be made.

Life went on as normal for the four years I was there. We had schooling and we did craftwork and singing. When I came home I was ahead of the children at my secondary school.

There are so many memories: shaking a piece of soap in the bowl of water brought at 6.30 to convince nurse that you had washed – which you had not; the question 'Have you been today?' and the dose of senna if you had not; beds placed daily outside in the sun, and me wearing the skimpiest g-string; hearing boys who were temporarily out of plaster sliding around the floor on a blanket when the nurses had gone to supper; fortnightly visiting on Sundays from two till five.

Eventually it was decided that I was cured and could get up. But first I was laid for an hour a day on a board, the angle of which was increased until I could be upright without being dizzy. Then I was an 'up boy' and was finally allowed home.

That was how it was then.

Charles Cooper

23

The Doctor and the Rats

*The editor's Hungarian doctor **TIBOR CSATO** had a particularly intimate relationship with the rats which frequented his London office*

As usual, very late one night, I came home and sat down in my big bedroom/consulting-room by the small table opposite the Venetian blinds. These covered the wall of windows facing the courtyard in long, uninterrupted rows. I had hardly settled down to read when I was alerted by a sound of rattling in the blinds. I looked up and was fascinated to see small, black, Himalayan rats obviously running races to and fro on the parallel tracks of the shutters. When I looked at them, they stopped for a moment and, having made sure that I had no ill-will towards them, continued with their race-games.

Rats in general, and Himalayan rats in particular, have a high degree of ESP and are known to understand human language, if not by word, certainly by meaning. So, when I got sleepy and did not wish to be disturbed, I just looked up and said very quietly, 'Now boys, that'll do. Go away now, off to sleep.'

When I began to talk they instantly stopped and listened. Presently, one by one, they dropped to the ground and vanished. I didn't know where to, for I couldn't see a hole. But that didn't worry me, so long as they let me sleep.

Early one morning, my cleaning woman beckoned me to quietly follow her to the waiting-room. The room was floored with wooden boards running in parallel strips down the entire length of the room. It was nothing like parquet and in places there were gaps between the planks. There was one such gap in the middle of the room and there, on either side, was a neat little heap of some kind of masonry, looking like the road signs that signify 'work in progress'. Around the heaps, a group of my rats were performing a kind of circular dance like children doing ring-a-ring-a-roses.

This touching little scene explained to me the puzzle of a workman who rang my bell every day during the lunch-hour. He smiled at me broadly with nails sticking out of his mouth and went straight into the waiting-room. I was so relieved that he wasn't a patient that I hadn't asked my secretary if she knew what he was about. Now it was clear. The man had been filling the gaps between the boards with masonry, which the rats had been scraping out again during the night. All parties were happy with the game.

> **'Now boys, that'll do,' I said. The rats instantly stopped and listened. Presently they vanished**

The rats had incidentally never touched any of my food. But when I returned after a long weekend, I found the manuscript of my theories of social integration, along with that of the history of my aeronautical school, torn into fine strips by my little Himalayan rats and stuffed into empty jam jars, presumably nests for the coming generation. I took this as a hint *symbolique de quelque chose* and never attempted to rewrite either work.

However, our idyllic co-existence came to an abrupt end. I had been careless enough to talk about the rats to my patients, some of whom thought I was 'seeing things'. Others, who believed my experiences, felt that the consulting premises of a doctor should not be the place for loathed carriers of disease.

One night I sensed that they had been reporting me and my rats to the local extermination officer. I was so sure that my hunch was right that I stopped my Himalayans in the middle of their sport: 'Look here, boys,' (for some reason I used to call them 'boys'), 'you must know by now that I have nothing against you. But there are, alas, black-hearted humans who hate you and are preparing for your perdition. For your own safety's sake you must leave here right away. Do not wait for morning. What's more, I shall tell you where to go.' And, doing with my hands and fingers a kind of dumb crambo (like bees indicating to each other in which direction and how far they are going to find flowers), I explained that they should go across the courtyard and through the little house at the other side. This would take them into the next street where they would find an Indian shop with all kinds of food not yet touched by humans. They would be able to live there in plenty and in comfort and the owners would never know. No one would trouble them. 'Now boys, good luck and goodbye.'

The following morning I was visited by the Rodent Officer of the Borough of Marylebone. He found recent rat droppings and a tiny hole in the floor. He distributed morsels of poisoned food in various places, saying that he would come back next day to collect the corpses. Duly he returned but, lo and behold, none of the morsels had been touched and there were no corpses or rat droppings anywhere. Puzzled, he shook his head in disbelief. But I had learned my lesson and I never told anyone of my warning to the rats.

Not even when, six months later, Lord Trenchard, the venerated founder of the RAF, rose to his feet in the House of Lords to tell the story of the rats in one of the barns on his estate in Scotland. These rats did no harm to anybody and Lord Trenchard, like me, used to chat with them. His barn, like my room, was denounced and the extermination officers called. Trenchard convoked the rats in his barn and addressed the assembled congregation, assuring them of his friendship, warning them and telling them where they would find a nearby barn in such a state of neglect that they could live there in plenty, and remain safe and unbothered.

As in my case, the Rodent Officers found traces of rats but their traps remained empty. The rats were long gone, destination unknown.

I read the full report of Trenchard's speech in the *Times*, but I cannot recall what the occasion or his excuse had been for telling that unusual and lengthy tale. He was, however, a public figure far too respected to be interrupted or doubted by his fellow Lords, and I felt vindicated by his story.

'Ah, look! He's texting in his sleep again'

THE DEATH FILE

The Death File, a column in which well-known friends of The Oldie revealed their hopes for their final moments, was compiled by Richard Middleton. In 1992 journalist and broadcaster **LUDOVIC KENNEDY** *(1919–2009) shared his thoughts*

MY IDEAL WAY TO GO...
I would hope to slip away with the minimum amount of suffering, perhaps from a massive heart attack. I hate violent death so I would never shoot myself or jump out of a window. If I went down with a terminal illness I would have to endure the pain. That is until the law on voluntary euthanasia is changed.

MY LIFE EXPECTANCY...
I am seventy-two now and I would have thought that within the next ten years would be about right – perhaps eighty-five, providing I was still compos and active.

MY LAST WORDS...
'Fuck you, Jack.' Sorry, that's the first thing that came into my head.

MY METHOD OF DISPOSAL...
Four years ago I arranged my own burial at sea through a Devon shipping company of which I am a director. I love the sea. I have no fear of it. I served on destroyers with the Royal Navy Volunteer Reserve throughout the war. The sea is a watery womb from which we all emerged many years ago.

MY FUNERAL ARRANGEMENTS...
I'd leave the order of service to my next of kin but I should like it to be brief and attended only by close family. Besides, the funeral boat can only fit about ten mourners.

MY SPECIAL EFFECTS...
No fancy shrouds, there wouldn't be much point. The coffin – weighted and drilled with about forty holes – and everything in it would biodegrade within five years. I would like a piper to play a pibroch or lament as the coffin slips into the sea.

MEMORIAL SERVICE...
That's really up to the living I leave behind, isn't it? Besides, a memorial service would very much depend on popular demand.

THE OTHER SIDE?...
There is no other side. I am an atheist in the same way that people are asexual or apolitical. I have no interest in gods, they bore me.

MY THOUGHTS ON LIFE AND DEATH...
I don't know why we are here or where we are going or what the point is except what you make of life yourself. I've had a wonderful life and I wouldn't have missed it for anything, but overall there doesn't seem to be much point in it at all. As far as death is concerned, the poet Belloc summed it up best when he said in one poem, 'On with one's coat and out into the night'.

Jilly Cooper

picks her top seven

1. The Duke of Beaufort
Still the handsomest man in England, and a mega-giggler. I like the way he feeds the most wonderful food to his springer spaniels during dinner parties.

2. Anthony Powell
Charming and modest, despite being one of the funniest writers of the 20th century. Also terrific to giggle with.

3. Godfrey Smith
Another wonderful writer and the best lunchtime companion in the world.

4. Byron
Ideal toy-boy material. Drop-dead handsome, sexually depraved and wonderfully funny. I prefer him without his turban.

5. Horatius who kept the bridge
The bravest in history. Being Roman he was probably gay, but I always hope that when he saw 'the white porch of his home' and decided to chance swimming across the Tiber, he was thinking of getting back to a wife he adored.

6. William Franklyn
Witty and handsome. I cannot imagine why he hasn't been cast in a series as the older man whom all the girls want to harass sexually.

7. Andrew Parker-Bowles
Intensely glamorous. Having had a blue-eyed brigadier for a father, I have a thing about blue-eyed brigadiers. As head of the Royal Veterinary Corps, he also takes good care of the Army animals.

PIN-UPS

THE MAN *in the* Snow

A true ghost story by TOM POCOCK

On Boxing Day of 1962, it began to snow. By the time I had seen my elderly aunt leave Victoria by coach for Gloucestershire, traffic was disappearing from the streets of London and the snow lay unmarked on the roads.

There was a sense of freedom from family duty and exhilaration in anticipating the week ahead. To savour this freedom, I decided to walk back to my bachelor flat in Chelsea, so, pulling my hat over my eyes and turning up the collar of my coat, I set out. Walking down the middle of the empty streets, my shoes squeaked in the fresh snow and fluffy flakes drifted in the lamplight.

I had taken to the backstreets, where Belgravia becomes Chelsea, and glowing fanlights and lighted windows hinted at cosiness indoors. It was at a crossroads that I spotted Jimmy. He was approaching with his quick, jerky gait, his big chin sunk into his chest in thought. As he wore no greatcoat I assumed he was on the way from one smart party to another.

I did not want to meet him tonight and break my own reverie. He was walking diagonally across my intended path, so I slowed my pace and he passed me without looking up. Out of the corner of my eye, I saw him disappear past my left shoulder. I did not want to talk to him for fear of another unburdening and because I was going to telephone him next day. In any case, he was an acquaintance rather than a friend. Jimmy was in public relations, a familiar figure in Fleet Street and Mayfair, always pouring champagne for journalists. Big and handsome in an Irish way, with crinkled dark hair, expensively, slightly flashily dressed, he had always been bursting with bonhomie – until I had met him three days before.

On the way home from Fleet Street I had seen him in the King's Road, looking so miserable that I had suggested a drink in a pub named The Commercial (now The Chelsea Potter). I had asked him what was wrong. Everything, he said – business, marriage, money. He had had to give up his house. As his lament continued I was only half-listening until he said, 'There's only one thing left and that's the coward's way out.'

What nonsense, I said, suddenly alert. He had plenty of friends. He knew everybody. There would be new and exciting opportunities. He shook his heavy head. Searching for a specific suggestion, I said that my own newspaper, the *Evening Standard*, might well have something for him, perhaps as some sort of social consultant to the news desk, or on the Londoner's Diary. Having promised to talk to them about him in the morning, I noted the telephone number of his lodgings in Sidney Street.

Next morning I told the news editor, whose suave figure was familiar at Jimmy's parties, about his plight. 'We might be able to help somehow,' he said. But today was Christmas Eve

and we would discuss possible rescue plans after the holiday.

My own Christmas, that year, was not festive as I spent it with my great-aunt, a mild, eccentric and genteel bohemian, who wore amber beads, painted still-life watercolours of pewter and peacock feathers and wrote verse about bluebells in Cotswold woods. On Christmas Day, I wondered what Jimmy was doing but decided against inviting him to join us for fear that we might depress him further. He had plenty of friends and anyway I was going to telephone him in a couple of days.

I presumed it was these friends he was visiting in Belgravia when we passed in the snow on Boxing Day. Then remorse clapped a hand on my shoulder. That man had talked to me of suicide only three days before and I could not even call out a greeting. I only had to tell him that I had talked to the news editor about him and that we would telephone him in the morning. Yet I had passed by on the other side.

I stopped and turned to call out. But there was nobody there. The big snowflakes drifted on to the empty, lamp-lit street and no front door was closing on a warm welcome for him. I ran back to the next turning but that street was empty, too.

I did not think of looking for footprints, only that he had been there one moment and not the next. That was odd. But I had just managed to clear my own conscience and so walked on with thoughts of future parties and girls.

Next day, when the bustle of the newspaper office subsided, I approached the news desk. Before I could speak, the news editor looked up from a sheaf of agency copy and said, 'Sad about our old friend'.

What and which old friend? I felt cold. 'Poor old Jimmy committed suicide on Christmas Eve.'

NOVEMBER 1992

My Father
AND OTHER ANIMALS

Harry and Edward Enfield
at The Oldie of the Year
Awards, 1993

In 1992 TV comedian **HARRY ENFIELD** *introduced us to another larger-than-life character – his father Edward Enfield, who was then signed up as a regular Oldie columnist*

My father was born into the educated middle class. His father was a senior civil servant and his mother on the fringes of the Bloomsbury set. He grew up surrounded by the Good, the Great and the Slightly Odd.

My grandmother had a couple of books published by the Woolfs, even though Virginia Woolf detested her. She wrote in her diaries, upon hearing that the Stracheys were spending the afternoon with my grandparents: 'I would rather be dead in a field than have tea with the Enfields.'

In this atmosphere Dad was, I suspect, an ideal son – away a lot of the time. He was evacuated to Canada for the war, then went to Westminster and Oxford, where he read Classics. After Oxford he was about to take his Civil Service examinations when his mother

died. He withdrew and took a job abroad, travelling the world and eventually meeting my mother in the Far East. They returned to England, my mother pregnant with my sister, in 1959.

Now with an embryonic family to support, he took a job with a pharmaceutical firm, where he remained for several years, my younger sister and I being born in the meantime. In 1967 he left his job, determined to become a lawyer, doing a correspondence course from home while we lived off his meagre savings. However, by September of that year he was forced to concede that the grinning little twits that interrupted him as he studied were a lot more expensive to rear than he had hoped, and reluctantly he gave up his studies and took a post in the local education department, where he remained until he retired last year.

Not only did my father give up his chosen career, but also most luxuries.

We lived comparatively frugally, with every spare penny being spent on our education. It was his great hope that he would be able to give us the best possible start, so that we could have the type of fulfilment in our working lives that, by our premature existence, we had denied him. In this he was fully supported by my mother, whose childhood had been coloured by being constantly on the move as her father was posted round the world by the army. With a safe stable homelife and the best education they could afford, their dream was that we would all become successful and financially secure professionals.

By 1976 it looked as if this dream would come to pass. My elder sister was soon to follow her father at Oxford, I had just turned fifteen, and had taken and passed my O' levels a year earlier than is normal, and my younger sisters were at the top of their classes in school. Fifteen years on, my elder sister is a hippy living in a hut with a tribal husband and two babies in one of those West African countries you won't have heard of. My younger sister is a slightly bewildered semi-employed radio journalist. My youngest sister has recently embarked on a career making deceitful promotional videos for lost causes – her current one revolves around the daft idea that Scotland is a nice place to visit and the Scots are in some way civilised.

As for myself, the son and heir, I used my expensive education to charm and cajole the successors of Lord Reith into giving me my own television programme, and now earn a tidy living from old age pensioners' licence fees by making people as idiotic as myself laugh, generally through the comic devices of swearing, shouting and pretending to break wind.

I am extremely mean and happy to see my family reduced to grinding poverty as my bank balance grows

Although now in their mid-twenties and thirties, none of my sisters have any financial security, and frequently nowhere to live either. Being comparatively well off myself, it would be simple for me to help them out, but unfortunately, as is the rule with nouveau riche comedians, I am extremely mean and am happy to see my family reduced to grinding poverty as I watch my bank balance grow too large for the paper it is printed on.

At the start of this year my father noticed that, along with my mean-ness, my vanity had also grown to new heights, causing me to shed two stone from the frame that until then I had been adorning with the flab of a thou-sand pointlessly expensive meals at the many vulgar restaurants which cater for London's upstarts.

He gingerly suggested that he would be prepared to spend many months ghost-writing a 'Harry Enfield's Diet Book' which he was sure my 'excellent reputation' (I insist on flattery at all times nowadays) 'would make highly marketable', the proceeds going to my sisters to pay for their housing needs. All I had to do was agree to turn up for a day to have a few pictures of my beautiful self taken, and give his work to a publisher. Naturally my first thoughts were that I wasn't going to make a penny out of this arrangement, so I refused.

His next idea came from a discussion we had about Auberon Waugh's autobiography. He made the comment that many people who write their autobiographies spend a generous amount of time saying how awful their fathers were, and how they ruined their offspring's lives. He suggested that he would very much like to write about how awful his offspring were and how we ruined his life. He wished to give the world an insight into the horrors of trying to bring up middle-class children in a civilised fashion, and seeing all one's efforts come to worse than nothing.

All four of us are a source of con-stant worry and embarrassment to our parents – 'What interesting children you have' is the veiled insult hurled at them daily by their friends.

If there's one thing my father seeks to avoid more than his children, it is rows and confrontation. He has very rarely raised his voice to us. The last time I remember him doing so was fifteen years ago when he came into my room to inform me, more in exas-peration than anger, that my mother had been worried by the police coming round that day and recovering some property I happened to have stolen from a local shop. I met his enquiry by calling him and my mother every four-letter word I knew, over and over again, until he stormed out of my room. A few minutes later he came back in and apologised for raising his voice to me. Quite right too.

Now he seems to think he'll be able to exercise his pent-up feelings of resentment through his pen. My natural reaction is to scoff at this idea. It seems to me that as none of his family have the slightest interest in anything he ever has to say, why should anyone else? Also, as age takes its toll, he is rapidly losing his grip on reality, and I doubt that there will be a shred of truth in anything he writes.

Nevertheless, to humour the old chap, I sent some of his stuff to Richard Ingrams who, purely to oblige me, said he'd find a space for it in these pages. I have arranged to intercept the greater part of his fee as my commission. So there's a little bit of extra drink money in it for me, and enough left over for him to buy me a passable Christmas present for a change.

The Thoughts of Enfield Senior

'THE ENFIELDS have achieved greatness, or more recently notoriety, in alternate generations. Both Dr William Enfield and his grandson Edward appear in the *Dictionary of National Biography*; my father in *Who's Who*; and my son in the *TV Times*. I am of the generation that slumbers.

'I believe my son to be what is com-monly called an Achiever, and also, I fear, he nurtures a desire one day to go into politics. When it comes, it may be wise to emigrate.

'I would not wish it to be thought that I habitually watch programmes like *Saturday Live*. It is just that my son was on it, and we felt obliged to see it. We do not have a remote con-trol device on our TV, and once we had realised how terrible it was I was always jumping up to turn the sound down when Harry was off, and up again to turn it up when he was on. This was the only way we could bear it, but later Harry gave us a video so that we could record it without watching it, and then skip over the rest of it and just watch him. His bits were often bad enough, and the rest of it was unspeakable.'

See page 91 for more Enfield Snr

'Careful! You could put an eye out with that thing'

WINTER IN VENICE

American novelist **PATRICIA HIGHSMITH** *was also an enthusiastic artist. Here she turns her eye and pen to Venice in December*

By now I can't count how many times I have been to Venice, and I don't care to. Other cities like Rome, even Paris, can become familiar, not particularly exciting on an umpty-umpth visit, but Venice never. Venice is always a surprise, a shock, a miracle, unreal and yet real. And this city built on water does us the favour of staying the same. No high-rises, no neon lettering, no hoardings and, best of all, no cars.

A few minutes after disembarking from a train or a plane at Marco Polo airport, one is gliding along in a *vaporetto* at house and palace-steps level, keeping an eye on the luggage at one's feet, while gazing also at the arched and pointed windows so near, the façades of faded pinks and yellows, each edifice of a different design and colour. Bridges, canal traffic, shouts. A gondolier with two passengers is trying to cross the canal on uneven water.

> *Venice is always a surprise, a shock, a miracle, unreal and yet real*

The Germans translated one of the titles of my books as 'Venice Can Be Very Cold'. I am glad that I have seen Venice in winter, when it is a different city from in summer. I felt I was seeing the real Venetians, the year-round inhabitants who are squashed to near invisibility by tourists, the fair-weather friends of Venice, in summer months. Venice is darkish, cold, damp and serious at six in the morning in December. Lucky people on their way to work get a seat inside the closed part of the *vaporetto*, out of the chill spray. The waters can be rough, and on deck it is sometimes not easy to keep one's balance. Men in sombre overcoats and mufflers, carrying briefcases, their faces paler than those of summer tourists, stare ahead, awaiting their stops, maybe pondering a problem that lies on their desks. Here are the secretaries, plumbers, shopkeepers who haven't the good fortune to live over their shops, bank officers, artisans who work in leather and metal, technicians who repair television sets and refrigerators. Venice functions as a city, of course, as does Paris or London.

In winter Venice tries to recover after suffering the hordes of tourists, the weight of sandals, sneakers and bare feet on its pavements and curved bridges. Venice sweeps up sandwich boxes, candy wrappers and ice-cream sticks, and assesses the damage done to frescoes due to human exhalation and sweat. And how are the bridges holding up? Another tiny crack has appeared?

Was it in summer or winter that I discovered the Trattoria della Città? Its name is written small in black letters on a

lantern that overhangs the doorway. It is in one of the 'ordinary' streets or lanes of Venice, the kind that one wanders into by mistake and stays with, because it is fascinating. One glimpses through an open door a workshop with an open fire going for the heating of metal, dark interiors where tools hang that seem not to have changed since the days of apprentices like Palladio. But the trattoria – it was a find, I thought when I stumbled on it, a serious place for regulars and businessmen, not for

tourists who like to see and be seen. White tablecloths, a newspaper rack, a couple of potted palms for decor, and a superb, fresh, *fritto misto* with parsley and a generous hunk of lemon. Prices moderate. A few years later, with a friend, I tried to find this restaurant and couldn't. Typical of Venice or typical of myself. One day I'll find it again.

To walk in Venice without a map is to get lost soon in a maze of left and right turnings. The two hundred or so *palazzi* on the big canals are just that, highly visible mansions (often empty). The majority of Venetians live in walk-ups four and five storeys high, in labyrinths where washing hangs on lines across the street, often across a narrow canal which is the street without pavements, where dogs and cats know where they're going and where they live, but you don't. Even if you've brought a map, has the street you are in got a name written visibly on a corner house wall? Probably not.

An artist whom I met in Positano recommended the Pensione Seguso to me. 'Accademia is the stop,' he said. 'Demi-pension, if you like.' I tried it. Address: Fundamento della Zattere 779. It is a hostelry with homely atmosphere, no chrome or aluminium when I saw it last. One breakfasts in a communal room with sufficient quietude and space, and it is possible by prearrangement to take a lunch in a sturdy sack before setting off for the Lido, for instance, in the morning.

It must have been the friendliness of the manager and staff that prompted me to install Ray, hero of my Venice novel, in the Seguso, while he had his

dangerous adventure with father-in-law Coleman. Ray had a room, but was absent without a word to the pensione for several days, out of necessity. When he returned to collect his suitcase, the Seguso was sympathetic, had moved his things and kept them secure, for which Ray was grateful. I've heard that I have a 'plaque' on a wall in the Pensione Seguso for my good word for the establishment and literary effort.

A hotel of which I have good memories is the Monaco e Grand Canale with

> **❝I am glad that I have seen Venice in winter when it is a different city from in summer: darkish, cold, damp and serious at six in the morning❞**

its sunny terrace almost at water level for dining and taking tea. And Harry's Bar is two metres away, across the lane that ends in a small pier, stop number eight for the *vaporetti*. At Harry's Bar, one might see a couple of celebrities, but it is less and less likely as summer and tourists set in, the latter looking for the people they have crowded out. The drinks are good if expensive, the canapés often hot, and costly.

Lord Byron wrote:

*'Oh Venice! Venice! when thy
           marble walls
Are level with the waters, there shall be
A cry of nation o'er thy sunken halls,
A loud lament along the sweeping sea.'*

Even then, Byron and others gave thought to the lagoon's waters lapping at low and high tide against the mossy steps, the wooden and stone foundations – pile-like supports rather – of palaces and blocks of houses.

One hears moans and groans, anxious speculations. How long can Venice last? What happened to the big balloon dam that was supposed to rise up in the lagoon at dangerously high tides and protect to some extent the mainland? Specifically the Doge's Palace and the Piazzetta? Only a few months ago, or so it seems, wasn't there a picture in the newspapers of Venetians carrying shoes and wading knee-deep across San Marco's plaza? Aren't things worse than they were five years ago? Logically, yes.

Maybe Venice is running on faith, as is the entire Italian economy, which ought to collapse and never does, completely.

An Orthodox Voice

The Mystery of the Unknown Master Artist
JOHN MICHELL

As editor of *The Cereologist*, the prestigious, low-circulation Journal for Crop Circle Studies, I would like to share with you the truth about crop circles – and if I could I would. As it is, I have not the slightest idea about the cause of these mysterious rings, circles and large, symbolic patterns that appear, year after year, as flattened areas of cereal crops in various parts of the world, but especially in Wiltshire.

This area is full of watchful farmers, keen to discover who or what is laying low their crops, and every year it is flooded by enthusiasts dedicated to the same purpose. Yet nothing definite has been found out. The mystery flourishes.

The greatest concentration of circles last summer was in the ancient temple sanctuary around Avebury and, a few miles to the south, at Alton Barnes, where the famous pictogram appeared in 1990. From early in the season this whole area was staked out by enthusiasts. They patrolled fields by night and watched out from hilltops, but apart from strange lights and UFO-like effects, nothing significant was seen. Meanwhile, revealed in the light of dawn, elaborate circle formations were created under their very noses.

Frustration was followed by paranoia. Watchers began to suspect that some among them had a grudge against the circles and were using their inside knowledge to fake them so as

JOHN MICHELL

The writer, philosopher and radical traditionalist, John Michell, wrote *The Oldie*'s Orthodox Voice column from 1992 until his death in 2009.

to discredit the whole phenomenon. One leading researcher went the whole hog, announced his discovery of an international conspiracy against the circles, promoted by the Vatican, the CIA and the usual cast of bugbears, and stormed off on a lecture tour of America to spread the news.

He is not the only one to have been sadly affected by circle-mania. The worst sufferers have been the explainers, whose theories have all been upset by the contrary, unpredictable behaviour of the phenomenon. Those whose minds are stuck on the primitive level of Opinion – an inevitable result of watching television – can believe at random that the circles are caused by a type of whirlwind, that they are messages from Above or that the whole thing is someone's idea of a good joke. These notions are furiously argued between the rival schools of believers, but none of them is supported by the evidence as a whole. This is one of those subjects which, the nearer you get to it, becomes all the more puzzling.

Man-made or not, the circles are obviously the product of intelligence, and that qualifies them as works of art. Reviewing them on that level, the art critic John McEwen judged that 'whoever or whatever made them is

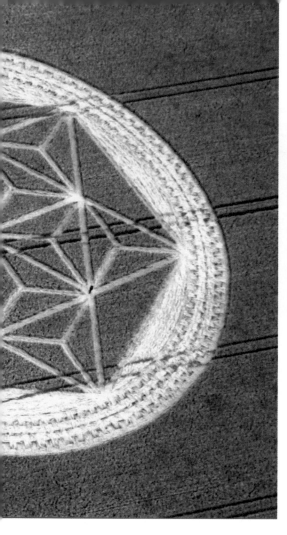

an artist of genius – in its most literal sense'. In an article in *The Cereologist* he chided the art world for praising up the likes of Richard Long ('a plodder by crop-circle standards') while ignoring the anonymous but far more subtle and accomplished works of the cornfield artist(s). That surely is the only useful approach to the subject: to bypass the explainers, clear the mind of vain speculations about causes and messages, and contemplate directly, on their own given terms, these masterpieces of land-artistry. That is how a true artist communicates, immediately through the eye to the mind, not by words or hidden clues within his compositions.

It is a wonderful show and in the finest of all galleries, framed by the rolling hills of Wiltshire – but it will not go on for ever, and those who can should see it while it is still running. But beware of the crop circle experts. They are just as confused and dogmatic as the pretentious frauds who run the modern art racket.

CROP CIRCLES:
Above: Etchilhampton, Wiltshire, 2011
Right top: East Kennett, Wiltshire, 2011
Middle: Ogbourne Down, Wiltshire, 2009
Bottom: Silbury, Wiltshire, 2009

OFF THE RAILS

MOST OF US, I suspect, play that game of spotting the celebrity on the train. The first variation of it is to attach a well-known name to someone who has a passing resemblance to the person with that name. A remark like 'I didn't know Sylvester Stallone got on at Colchester' may raise a smile from a fellow traveller, and if you're really fortunate, the game will degenerate into something giggly. The other version is, of course, spotting the real thing. The trouble is that, while you may be dying to know why Gerald Kaufman is going to Stowmarket, you also feel that any

> **'Celebrities are two-a-penny on this train, for heaven's sake, and who gives a toss for Gerald Kaufman anyway'**

overt recognition is not really on: celebrities are two-a-penny on this train, for heaven's sake, and who gives a toss for Gerald Kaufman anyway.

No sane person can relish the thought of going up to someone like Jeffrey Archer on the train and saying 'Good evening, Mr Archer. I did so enjoy *First Among Equals*. May I have your autograph, please?' But I got involved in something rather like it a little time ago. I was deputed to escort the then Zimbabwean Minister for Energy and Water Resources to Aberthaw Power Station in South Wales. I was accompanied by my firm's marketing director, who happened to be a German. So there we were, a Zimbabwean, a German and an Englishman sitting on the 125 out of Paddington. After a while, when we had exhausted the small talk about British Rail, I spotted Lord Tonypandy, formerly Speaker Thomas, sitting further down the carriage.

'Minister,' I said, 'I see the former Speaker of our House of Commons is on this train. Do you know him, by any chance?' 'Of course I do,' said the Minister. 'What parliamentarian does not know Speaker Thomas?' Suppressing uncharitable thoughts about the health of parliamentarians in a one-party state, I said, 'Would

you like to speak to him?' 'Indeed, I would,' he replied.

Speaker Thomas greeted the Minister like a long-lost friend. My marketing director was bursting with pride at being in such elevated company. After we had discussed the health of Mr and Mrs Mugabe, and other hangers-on in Zimbabwe, and conversation was flagging once more, Speaker Thomas announced he was going to Cardiff to preach a sermon in Charles Wesley's founding chapel, on that very day, which was the two hundredth anniversary of the great man's death.

'I heard something about the Wesley bi-centenary on the radio this morning,' I said. 'They played one of his hymns.' 'Which one?' said Speaker Thomas, his eyes bright with excitement. 'I can't remember the words,' I replied, 'but I know the tune. It's one we used to call "the wobbly" at my church, and we sang it to "While Shepherds Watched".' 'Sing it, boy! Sing it!' cried the Speaker.

My marketing director looked at me imploringly. So, off I went: 'While shepherds wa-a-aa-aa-aa-a-tched their flo-ho-hocks by...'

'I KNOW IT BOYO!' yelled Mr Speaker triumphantly. 'It's a wonderful tune!'

He got to his feet and began to sing 'While Shepherds Watched' to my 'wobbly' tune, urging everyone to join in. The train arrived in Cardiff just as the whole carriage finished the last verse.

It's a bit corny to say such a thing could only happen on a trip to Wales, but the fact is, it did. Thank God it didn't happen on my line. There's not much to sing about travelling between Ipswich and Liverpool Street, and you never know whom you might bump into.

DAVID RANSOM

OFF THE WALL

THE OLDER YOU grow, the fewer opportunities occur to be surprised and to have a hitherto unknown experience. I gained a first on both counts through obscene phone calls.

I would know nothing about this problem at first hand if the directory had not misprinted my name V C Wyndham. I rang up British Telecom to demand a rebate for being three years virtually ex-directory, and made the suggestion that my name should be printed in full. BT's representative was horrified: 'We cannot do that, madam, you would run the risk of obscene phone calls!' I pointed out that that was my problem. His was to see that I was correctly represented in the telephone book. I then sat back to wait for that rare thing, a new experience.

I had to wait two years before a caller, with an immature male voice, asked me the colour of my knickers. It was a bitter disappointment. It came naturally to respond to him as a schoolmistress would to a tiresome member of her class.

'What is your name?' I demanded peremptorily, 'and where are you calling from? Hurry up and tell me. I am not accustomed to being kept waiting.' He replaced his receiver. It had all been entirely satisfactory and the lesson learnt appeared to be to frighten them before they frighten you.

It was eighteen months before the next call came. The voice was more adult, more confident. The speaker wished to know whether I would like him to come round and kiss my twat. I had had no previous knowledge of this approach. 'Not today,' I told him, 'and certainly not you. You are not

handsome enough.' I replaced the receiver, convinced I had handled this one as successfully as the first. When the telephone rang again, I presumed it was a friend calling.

The same male voice announced solicitously: 'If we did it doggy fashion you would not have to look at me.' I had great difficulty preventing myself laughing, which would obviously be fatal. I sat until I had regained my composure, and then, as quietly as possible, replaced it.

He did not ring back. He had no need to. It was game, set and match to him.

Women tell me that having only their initials quoted in the directory does not make them immune from such calls. Since it offers no protection, could we not go back to being recorded as Annie, Betsy and Carol instead of having to toil through pages of As and Bs and Cs in order to find a name?

URSULA WYNDHAM

OFF THE CUFF

I WAS THE THIRD of four brothers, which meant a low profile and handed-down clothes at home and the *-mus* enclitic at prep-school. Then – in the Easter term it was, and, I learnt later, when our armies in France had their backs to the wall – the prep-school found it had more boys in the San than in the class rooms, and it sent its remaining fit ones, including Usbornes *ma*, *mi* and *mus*, back to their homes. We were hardly back in Sussex when the influenza scythed us all down, including Mama, the cook and the gardener. Doctor Brough said I had it worst: 104 degrees, pain in my side when I laughed or coughed, the whimpers – in fact, pleurisy. I became the top patient.

Mama got it comparatively lightly.

A connoisseuse of tonics, she swigged Wincarnis thinking there was no alcohol in it. It reddened her noble nose

before evening, but it made her giggle, and she thought it a splendid tonic. She bossed the household in her dressing gown. She left my brothers in their own beds and put me in the spare-room double bed and had a fire lit in its grate. She sent for Aunt Helen, one of the three spinster 'Aunts at Bath' sisters, to help her carrying trays, feeding dog and cat, and sitting with me through the nights in a creaky wicker armchair in the firelight.

She must have had a bed somewhere in the house, but to me, feverish in the big bed and occasionally floating a foot or two above it, she was a kindly figure in black, with pince-nez spectacles and a distinct whistle in her breathing when she was asleep. She never caught the bug.

Eventually my temperature came down in a night, my pyjamas soaked in sweat, and no more imagined aero-batics. Dr Brough let me listen through his stethoscope to hear that my lungs, though still rubbing together, were doing it less noisily. I was cool and hungry. My brothers were up and about. Aunt Helen had gone back to Bath, and Dr Brough sent us round a family-sized flagon of a special tonic put up in his dispensary.

It was colourless and nameless, to be taken morning and evening. It proved to be viscous rather than liquid, and when poured into a hand-held spoon, it poured itself back as soon as the flagon was returned to upright. I tell the truth: we could only get a dollop of it to stay on the spoon by cutting the flow off with scissors at the right moment, a dollop for the spoon and the rest slithering back upwards to source.

We are, and were then in 1918, a fairly agelast family, but this apparition had us as near rolling on the floor as I've ever seen. Mama, her nose redder than ever, said the laughing alone had done her more good than even Wincarnis.

Dr Brough's final prescription for us was a day of sea air. Mama hired Mr Vickery and his station taxi to drive us all to Hastings and thence along the coast road to Rye and home to Battle. It was a lovely crisp-cold day, and we could hear the guns across the Channel. Since I was almost always sick in vehicles, and today was no exception, I was hung out of the back of the taxi over the folded-down hood, with Mama holding my ankles. The trip must have cost her a pretty penny. I never knew what the exact bill from Mr Vickery was, but I do know it was more than a pound, with tip.

RICHARD USBORNE

'Remember, lads, next week: staff appraisals'

Beyond the **Brown Curtain**

Few people know exactly what happens after the farewell ceremony at the crematorium. **PAUL PICKERING** *witnessed the final journey of Babs, into the incinerator and beyond... (Editor's warning: readers of a squeamish nature may find this feature distressing)*

Illustration by MARTIN HONEYSETT

'I never knew Babs,' begins the vicar with professional enthusiasm. 'However, I understand she was very active in the bowls club, which explains why there are so many glum faces on what really should be a joyous occasion. Babs is rolling along to a better place!'

Babs's friends ignore the empty sales pitch. Sadness continues to rise like steam from the anoraks and car

coats in the congregation. We are in Southend-on-Sea crematorium, the last resting place of Essex man and woman. Babs's soul may be off to a leafy suburban paradise behind sturdy neo-Georgian pearly gates, but her relatives and friends can have no idea what is planned for the body. Indeed, even though more than eighty-three per cent of us eventually go up the chimney, most have no inkling exactly what happens to

our loved ones at the municipal fiery furnace. Or to ourselves.

At Southend-on-Sea a brown curtain silently engulfs the coffin at the end of the service. 'We stopped ours disappearing on mechanical rollers when people believed they could see the flames and smell burning. You don't want that,' chuckles forty-seven-year-old Reggie Barton, the crematorium supervisor and former ballroom dancing medal winner, who in certain lights resembles the late Eric Morecambe.

'And descending coffins were worse. They gave the unwanted impression the loved one is dropping straight to hell.' Reggie stops to examine a floral tribute. 'If folk watch a comic turn they will have forgotten him the next day. But you always remember a cremation.'

I will never forget Babs's. When the final rheumatic fellow bowler is out of the dismal 1960s chapel, her coffin is slid through a hatch in the wall into a waiting area. Here she is loaded on to a trolley and rolled along to shiny aluminium doors very like the ovens at a Pizza Express, set in two banks of three. After Babs's identity has been checked she is pushed into one of the cremators, swept so clean of the last body's ashes one could safely cook an American Hot with extra cheese. At less well-run establishments turkeys have been roasted. One of the staff is whistling the Beatles' song 'Love Me Do'.

Round at the front of the cremator is an armoured glass window, dubbed 'stiff TV' by the visiting undertakers, all strangely small and wizened like jockeys, who pop in the back door for a cup of tea and a biscuit. I open the viewing port to see how Babs is doing. Horribly well, quips Reggie. After ten minutes the coffin has burnt away and the flesh crackles and spirals off Babs's skull in the intense heat. I feel I am intruding on something extremely private.

An alarm sounds on the Swedish-made TABO cremator, the Volvo of the incineration game. Babs is giving off too much smoke and Derek Taylor, an assistant who is disabled, presses complex buttons and brings her under control, much like Mr Scottie on the Starship Enterprise. Babs's bowling chums are in the garden of remembrance poking at the neon-bright displays of forced chrysanthemums, and a foot-high wreath from a loving grandchild spells out GA-GA. Hopefully, they will not get a whiff of Babs before the prawn vol-au-vents at her funeral tea.

'We do not call them ovens. It can have associations with Nazi concentration camps,' says Reggie, who is chairman of the Essex Koi Carp Society and has filled the crematorium pond with a host of

golden orfe and common carp, while mourners have added the occasional common rudd or, on one rowdy occasion, a herring. 'Freddie Mercury had koi carp. And he was cremated,' Reggie muses, as if there is some metaphysical connection. 'It's nice to continue your hobby at work.'

I step back to watch Babs. Her arms have fallen away. The entire top of the coffin has gone and Babs's intestines have reared up nearly a foot above her pelvis, a Gorgon's head with a terrible life of its own. The rib cage is visible and the

the legs pop up at right angles to the body,' explains Allan, aged forty, a former lorry driver, who likes the job as it gives him more time to spend with his second wife and his hobby, not carp, but collecting a poisonous species of tropical sea fish. 'We do get the odd explosion though if a pacemaker is left in. But we have all got a sense of humour.'

At the viewing port I check on Babs. Her intestines have vaporised. Her skull has split open and the brains are oozing out through the fissures. I wonder what she laughed at. What

'You're not cut out for our business,' sniffs Reggie. 'We just regard the bodies as the deceased. If you didn't you could go mad. People have'

lungs and organs beneath flicker with yellow flame. Babs's legs have started to spread and rise eerily off the floor. The flesh on them appears to evaporate. This spectacle must be too much after the cornflakes every morning. One understands why Reggie and Co need the carp.

'We get all sorts of myths,' beams Reggie as the gas is turned up and the cremator approaches one thousand degrees centigrade. 'People say we do not burn the coffin. But we actually need the coffin for fuel. They claim we take the handles off. However, the handles are a special plastic and are combustible. Whatever is in the coffin we cannot touch, by law. One woman had her budgie put down specially so it could be buried with her.'

Allan Mitchell, another assistant with long curly hair, nods. 'Yes, friends stick in whisky bottles. Cans of beer. Very Egyptian. An old dear even had the ashes of two dogs in the coffin. We get told by the undertakers.' Reggie is at pains to point out that the corporation does not cremate animals. They are all very concerned the ritual should be extremely proper. A woman recently phoned to see if he could 'do' her horse.

To ask about the ritual of cremation made me feel rather adolescent, like inquiring about sex. I admit that I have heard tales that bodies sit up, but everyone shakes their head and sniggers knowingly. They are educating another crematorium virgin. 'Sometimes, as I think you can see,

passions coursed through that skull. You cannot help but speculate. Flames crackle, bones shift. A vision which came back for days. Everything has a reddish glow. Another alarm sounds.

The body is burning too quickly. They have to slow it down to make sure the oven stays hot for the next customer. Babs will thus take longer than the usual hour and a half. Suddenly there is a smell. A smell of charcoal grill at a Greek kebabist. Allan opens the front of the cremator and a piece of Babs's skull, not yet calcified, bounces out onto the floor. I step on the fragment. It is hot and makes a hole in the leather. 'We all wear safety shoes,' laughs Reggie.

Babs is slowly becoming a pile of glowing ashes. So we go and watch Reggie's carp at his house which is within walking distance of the 'Crem'. Bobby, his wife, is in the neat sitting-room frowning at a knitting machine with a friend. 'Reggie loves his work,' she says, over a cup of milky tea. 'He is always talking about it. Or carp. They are his hobbies. Nice when your work is your hobby. We had my mother cremated there. She is in the grounds. It is such a friendly sort of place. I tell Reggie that I want his ashes for an egg-timer.'

Outside, the carp, some of them one-and-a-half feet long and coloured white and red and black, glide under the five-foot-deep Japanese-style pond. I am still talking about Babs. 'You are not cut out for our business,' sniffs Reggie. 'We just regard the bodies as the deceased. If you didn't, you could go mad. People have.'

We call in at the Mitsubishi service station on the way back, to buy our lunch. Reggie is considering installing a café at the crematorium. I draw his attention to an article in *Pharos*, the Cremation Society magazine, which reports that a crematorium in Hainan, China, was selling 'cheap and delicious' spicy dumplings made of human flesh. Reggie is amused. I go for a Big Bite cheese roll. Reggie chooses smoked ham. A lunchtime favourite is barbecue Pot Noodles, redolent of when the cremator goes wrong. The gardener has brought beetroot sandwiches for the last five years. In an effort to be one of the Hancockian posse of 'lads', I force down my Big Bite.

'It's not affected your appetite because you do not know the deceased personally,' observes Reggie. In fact, to watch the disintegration of the body does not give one any further clues as to the mystery of life and death, only the tissue-thin nature of human dignity. Our own death is what really scares us, agrees Reggie. We all know that sooner or later, like Babs, we will have to cope with life's Big Bite.

Back at cremator number three Babs has been scraped into a little bin by the oven door for her ashes to cool. Every last calcified bone of her. 'We get ninety-nine point nine per cent,' says Allan. The tag showing her name and age is then moved to her metal bin, while another coffin is pushed into the cremator and the process begins again.

Two more bodies are burning 'nicely' as Reggie shows me around the garden of remembrance, which is a mixed blessing due to the hole in my shoe made by the piece of Babs's hot skull. 'This place will be packed with relatives at Christmas. You would be amazed at the mushrooms we get here. The lads cook them up.'

In the tea-break room in front of the warm cremators, I have a cup of decaffeinated coffee. Under the breasts of Gorgeous Justine in the *Sun* is a story that 'Russian fellas are falling over themselves to find an Essex girl...' Next to the paper is a neat list containing Babs's name and that of several other octogenarian Essex girls. Tom McBride, a sixty-one-year-old former Canadian

seaman, who first got a 'taste for the job' when working the winter in Toronto hospital, nervously rolls cigarettes. Someone is trying to make Eileen Neath, the seventy-four-year-old deputy organist, play 'Great Balls of Fire'. 'I came here after my parents died. Talk about one door closing and another opening,' she smiles. Derek, who also collects koi carp, and at fifty-three has worked in the crematorium for thirty-five years, laughs and shows large canine teeth. A normal day, says Reggie.

Soon Babs is cool enough for the ultimate process. Her ashes are tipped on to a tray. Allan picks carefully through the remnants of bone and removes the coffin nails and other metal fragments. 'Look at that,' he says, holding up a piece of melted silver. 'That was a brooch. Gold evaporates. This here is a pin for a leg. We get hip joints sometimes. Made out of

'Aren't there any concessions for the elderly?'

titanium. But nothing is recycled. All this is buried separately in a grave.'

Allan switches on the Dowson and Mason Cremulator Mark Two and the heavy steel balls grind Babs up to powder. Dust is everywhere. Here, you take your work home with you.

But it does not seem to worry anyone. No one sees ghosties flitting around their Japanese cars at the traffic lights. Allan inserts an elec-

tromagnet into the cremulator to get out more metal bone pins which held Babs together on the bowling green. She is then poured into a plastic bag with the brown tag attached which has followed her through every step of the process. Her ashes weigh about three kilograms. 'Make a good fish tank filter,' Allan remarks.

Do they ever get, well, a trifle down? 'Suicides tend to upset the staff, know what I mean? It's so final.

> **'Whatever is in the coffin we cannot touch, by law. One woman had her budgie put down specially so it could be buried with her'**

From our end,' Reggie admits, patting a plastic urn. 'If they could only see what happens here...'

Babs's family have not decided what to do with her. Perhaps they are trying to get permission to scatter her across a bowling green. The cremation only costs £132 but is extra if you are very big. 'We did a thirty-eight-stone man once and now they have to be buried, he made so much smoke. They can damage the ovens,' warns Allan. He adds proudly that they could easily manage a Robert Maxwell on a not too busy day. Crematoriums are great levellers.

The lads have recommended I stay at the Roslin Hotel on the sea front, which Allan informs me is in Southend's red-light district. Reggie held the Christmas dinner of the Koi Carp Society there last year. 'My vice chairman resigned, all on account of what we were doing with this rubber blow-up doll.'

I do not have much of an appetite for dinner. I don't choose meat on purpose, but keep finding morsels in my Fisherman's Broth that remind me too closely of Babs. So I go round to see Reggie for a cup of tea.

To cheer me up Reggie relates tales of his previous employment as a funeral director. Of Mercedes hearse races on the A11. Of turning up at a house to be ordered to 'Fuck off' repeatedly from what seemed to be the coffin, only to discover that the voice was from a mynah bird. Of the stray dog that mated with an elaborate Gates of Heaven floral display at the funeral of a leading

Southend-on-Sea dignitary. His wife beams. 'I have never laughed so much as when I have been out with a bunch of undertakers. Dealing with death, they really want to live it up.'

The next day Reggie checks the paperwork on Babs. I ask him what most people do with the ashes. He ponders for a moment. 'Many are buried here. But throwing them in the sea is very fashionable with the young. Only about one per cent go on the mantelpiece. A lot chuck them from the end of Southend pier. You are meant to have the harbour master's permission to do that but most don't. Of course, it doesn't matter what you do beyond the three-mile limit...' Being fired into the heavens by rocket is another local whim.

'If only folk realised,' concludes Reggie. 'Life is too short to fall out. Eighty years is not long. A day soon goes...' We discover that Babs's relatives have opted for an ornamental shrub so her remains can go into the grounds. Reggie is rather partial to the idea of having memorial carp in the fishpond.

'Don't take the mickey,' warns Tom, as I leave. I wouldn't. An infernal regiment of Reggies is always around to open that little armoured glass window one day and have the last laugh.

My First Job

by **MARY ELLIS**, *actress and singer (1897–2003)*

IT WAS SPRINGTIME in New York City, 1918. At twenty-one I had been studying music, drama and, of course, singing for four years. I was a very ambitious student, encouraged by teachers and my parents. I studied for two years with Fernando Tanara, the opera coach from Milan. A dear tubby man with a beard, he insisted that I learn at least six operas (vocally ridiculous at my age, but marvellous training for what was to come). Then he suggested that I sing for his friend, the director of the Metropolitan Opera, in order to get advice as to where I should be sent in Italy – some little opera house, 'now that the war was over'. These opera houses were greenhouses really, where singers learned and blossomed – or failed. After several years, some lucky ones would be good enough to get to the big cities of the world. And so end at the pinnacle, the Opera in New York, Paris or Milan.

One May morning in 1918 it happened. Of course I knew the inside of the Metropolitan – its red and gold baroque magnificence – but now I saw it for the first time from the stage. It seemed a black infinity – a nowhere, awe-inspiring, frightening. Somewhere near the stage five shadows were huddled in their seats, murmuring in Italian. One electric light bulb on a metal stalk stood by the piano, a spot of deliverance in the distance of that huge stage, soaring up to the sky. Dear maestro Tanara sat on the piano-stool, waiting. A sickening silence. Then I heard my own voice, disembodied, asking the black emptiness if I might have a table and a chair, to act my scene from Massenet's *Manon*. A deadly pause, before a loud, rasping Italian voice from the stalls asked an invisible stage hand to bring the requested items. He also brought another rehearsal light and planted it near me, and gave me a wink and a thumbs-up sign. I was thrilled. I had wings! (No nerves – that would come later.) A deep breath, and I was away! Acting and singing 'Adieu, notre petite table' and enjoying every minute. How I

did it, I will never know. At the end, I was trembling, and ready to faint.

Signor Tanara told me to sit down and wait. The light by the piano was switched off. An almost palpable silence cloaked me. I saw Tanara leave the stage, looking grim. He joined the Italian ghosts in the stalls. After an eternity, it seemed, he came back. The tears were running down his face into his beard. My heart gave a lurch. I must have failed him so miserably. He hugged me and his voice was choked with tears. All I could say was, 'Maestro, I'm sorry, so sorry.' Then it came – the shock: 'But *cara*, listen. They gave no advice. They offer you a four-year contract, here!'

Four years! To sing all the established 'young' roles – a debut in the première of Puccini's *Triptych*; Mytyl in the new French opera of *The Blue Bird*; and particularly Giannetta in *L'elisir d'amore* with Caruso, Scotti and Barrientos (the dream of every young singer was to sing with Caruso); Siébel in *Faust* with Farrar – and so on. I gathered up enough voice to go to the edge of the stage and say 'Thank you, thank you' and had just enough strength to walk off the stage without falling down. I heard their soft laughter following me.

My long life in the theatre (because it came to pass that after those first four magical years I defected to the real theatre) started as Nerissa in *The Merchant of Venice*. But music is still in my bloodstream – and every new 'job' still has the thrill of that first one. The magic persists – even at ninety-six.

THE OLDIE
22 JUL 1994

The **Oldie**
YOU CAN TAKE IT WITH YOU FORTNIGHTLY

ISSUE 64
£1·60

WILLIE RUSHTON *(1937–1996), a lifelong collaborator with Richard Ingrams since their schooldays, was a regular contributor during The Oldie's first years. He worked almost always in colour using felt-tipped pens. His sudden death in 1996 came as a blow to his countless admirers.*

RAGE

I DO NOT KNOW how many readers of *The Oldie* drew the proper conclusions from the case of a popular and respected widow in Rye, sixty-two-year-old Mrs Sheila Bowler, who grew so fed up with the cost of a retirement home for the eighty-nine-year-old aunt of her late husband that she drove the old lady to the banks of the nearby River Brede and pushed her in. Mrs Bowler received life imprisonment for what was described as a 'cruel and callous' murder, which means that taxpayers will be paying £500 a week to keep her.

Some may judge that it makes Mrs Bowler's posture even more unattractive that she was not paying the old lady's lodging fees herself. The aunt, Mrs Florence Jackson, had a flat in Rye, which she sold for £36,000, and the Sussex social services ruled that she should pay £252 a week towards the nursing home fees. Mrs Bowler had hoped to inherit the money.

It is all very easy to take Mrs Jackson's side against her niece, and say what a wicked and terrible thing it was for Mrs Bowler to push the old lady into the river. This is obviously not the way to treat old people, however much of a problem they may be, but before we identify too closely with the late Mrs Jackson we might reflect that Mrs Bowler, at sixty-two, is already an oldie, and the problem she faced will be more familiar, and more immediate to many readers, than that of her Aunt Flo:

Oh, Jemima, look at your Uncle Jim,
He's in the duckpond,
learning how to swim.

By the turn of the century – that is to say, in less than six and a half years' time – there will be a million people over the age of eighty-five. Their number has more than doubled in the last ten years. Half of them will be immobile like the late Mrs Jackson – that is to say, unable to walk without assistance. Most will be incontinent and confused, about one in five will be so affected by Alzheimer's disease or senile dementia as to need intensive nursing.

A government which is already overspending its income by £50 billion

AUBERON WAUGH

Auberon Waugh (1939–2001) wrote the Rage column in *The Oldie* from the first issue until 1996, before becoming wine correspondent in 2000.

a year will never be able to take on the additional burden of paying for all these super-oldies. It is no good putting on a smug socialist face and saying that of course the government must pay 'even if it means the wealthier may have to pay a little more in taxes'. The whole concept of rolling back the Welfare State arose from an awareness of the huge demands of an ageing population which would place an unacceptable strain on people at work, even before we start to consider the implications of an unemployable, largely criminal and welfare-oriented generation of younger 'workers'.

I have a solution to all these problems, but it is as well to set them out first. It is most unlikely, with all the officious new legislation setting impossibly expensive standards for old people's homes, that any place in any of them will cost less than £500 a week by the year 2000. What we are going to see is an end to all inheritance. According to Maggie Drummond in the *Telegraph*, £2.5 billion disappears each year from family inheritance because of the need to pay for long-term care of the elderly. I should put it much higher. If one looks at the over eighty-fives alone, a million of them at £500 a week works out at £26 billion a year. Whether the government screws

that sum out of the working population – it represents 13p in the pound on the standard rate of income tax – or whether it is paid for by a sale of all your life's savings, acquired possessions and the house or flat in which you live, it comes to the same thing. As this government-imposed longevity begins to bite, prolonging the misery of extreme old age, the temptation to bump off these super-oldies will grow.

A further misery of early old age or late middle-age is that with the collapse of law and order and the rise of the lawless, unemployable generation, anybody who owns anything is liable not only to lose it to burglars and squatters, but also to be beaten up, possibly murdered, at the same time. It is no good railing against the police, who have disappeared behind their computers, or judges or juries. We simply cannot afford to keep the greater part of the younger generation in prison any more than we can keep the older generation in geriatric nursing homes. The only gratuitous element in all this is the law's insistence that private citizens are not permitted to have weapons with which to defend themselves against the young.

As soon as citizens reach the age of sixty, they should be permitted to wear a sword out of doors

Here, then, is the solution to all these problems. As soon as citizens reach the age of sixty without a prison sentence, they should be permitted to keep a firearm in the home and wear a sword out of doors for their protection. They would not be allowed to take the firearm out of the house under any circumstances, nor, under pain of a heavy fine, could they draw their swords out of doors unless attacked by a stranger. In their homes, they would be permitted to shoot any stranger carrying a weapon or obviously intent on burglary who refused to lie on the floor when told to do so.

How, people will ask, would this affect the problems of senility and inheritance? Work it out. America's experience teaches that where firearms are kept in a house, the risk of accidental discharge is very high. But any death is preferable to being drowned, like a kitten, in the nearest river.

KITTY

There is one maid in particular who stands out in novelist **WILLIAM TREVOR**'s *childhood memories*

Illustration by Peter Bailey

'Why have you shut the door, Kitty?' 'Because of the boys, ma'am.' 'What have they been doing, Kitty?' 'Setting the house on fire, ma'am.'

Kitty wasn't young any more, or seemed not to be, and she'd never been pretty. She had eyes that were always blinking and teeth my brother called 'stormy' – a mouthful of enormous white crags, constantly bared in laughter or anger. When I was eight and my brother six we particularly enjoyed lighting fires and would indulge this inclination on the kitchen floor when Kitty was left in charge of us. While she was changing into her afternoon black we would carefully arrange newspaper and kindling before putting a match to them, and she'd return to the kitchen to find it full of smoke and flames. Later she'd stand terrified in the hall while we paraded through the house with lengths of flaring bog-wood held triumphantly above our heads, as often as not dressed up in some of her clothes. When we couldn't afford Woodbines in Mrs O'Brien's shop just down the road we rolled up damp paper and smoked it instead. Kitty's only weapon was to shut the kitchen door. The kitchen door was never shut as a rule.

Severe punishment followed, but we never learned a lesson from it. The day my father drove the fifty-two miles to Cork to have his teeth out he made us promise we'd be good, hinting at a reward. My mother, who could never resist Cork, went with him, and when they returned he came into our bedroom and asked us if we'd behaved well. We replied that we had. He produced two gold-coloured metal pencil-sharpeners, but before he could give them to us Kitty appeared in the doorway.

'Indeed they haven't, sir,' she contradicted shrilly. 'They've never been worse, sir. They called names over the wall at Mr Hayes, sir. They took raisins and syrup, sir.'

'Oh, now,' my father began.

'They brought tinkers into the kitchen, sir. They had them sitting down in the drawing-room.'

The pencil-sharpeners were withdrawn and were never given to us. My father looked at us without saying anything.

Kitty was the nearest we ever came to having an old retainer. For the time she was with us she was part of the family, yet her life – as the life of any general maid tended to be at that time – was solitary. She was permitted liberties: when she bought new clothes, which wasn't often, she ordered a selection to be sent to the house from three or four drapers' shops. Vast piles of coats, skirts or hats would accumulate on the dining-room table and Kitty would try on garment after garment while my mother – gratefully killing an empty morning or afternoon – helped her to choose.

But in spite of all that the two were not companions in any close sense, for no matter what confidences were shared, there remained the gulf that inevitably separates mistress and servant. Kitty was there to work – in the kitchen and the bedrooms, the dining-room, the drawing-room, in the hall and on the stairs and landings. It is hardly an exaggeration to say that, in return for modest wages, she gave the greater part of her being.

The lone general maid was a familiar fixture in any household that could afford one. She was to be found above stairs in public houses and grocers' shops, in the terraced dwellings of clerks and small-time bookmakers. 'Have they a maid?' was a question often asked, the answer supplying instant social status. Maids' uniforms were illustrated in drapers' catalogues, blue or pink for the mornings, black or brown for later on. 'Is she clean?' was a query made of previous employers, and: 'Is she honest?' Smarter households had more than one, called parlourmaids, and a cook, and a weekly woman for the floors and washing. All that made a difference, not just where status was concerned, but to the maids themselves. There was companionship in the kitchen, meals taken together, the foibles of the family whispered over.

'Is it a fast-day for you, Kitty?' my mother would enquire and if it was, Kitty would fry herself an egg, her isolation again compounded. She went to Mass, we to church. Yet she never hung a holy picture in her bedroom: that would have been presumptuous.

Her existence was lightened by bits of gossip. Awestruck, she would repeat the latest about Jack Doyle and Movita when they'd visited Bantry or Dunmanway. Doyle was a once-renowned boxer, now a general entertainer on small-town stages. Movita was declared to be a 'film star' and certainly dressed like one. They were mild hell-raisers, one story being that finding a hotel full when they wished to spend a night in it, Doyle drove a honeymoon couple from their bed and pursued them in their night clothes through the streets.

Recalled with equal pleasure was the night the French hypnotist reduced a hardware merchant's assistant to a state of unconsciousness and couldn't bring him back. 'The poor fellow went home thinking he was a chicken,' Kitty never tired of repeating, tears of delight streaming on her roughened

cheeks. In the end a medical hypnotist from Dublin had to rescue the youth from the tower of the Protestant church, where his confusion had led him. But even though he later managed to shake off the delusion that he was a chicken, he was never, according to Kitty, the same again.

church when she tried to ignore him. She afterwards retailed the episode in detail, stuttering through her laughter, her huge teeth stormier than ever. 'The commotion there was, ma'am! Father Tracy with the Host, and Dano rampaging, and the men at the back whistling to get him out!'

a sunset, she would laugh wildly.

She had a friend, another maid in the town. On Sunday afternoons they would cycle out on the Cork road for a couple of miles and then cycle back again. They went together to Women's Cofraternity, once a year to Piper's Travelling Entertainments, occasionally to the pictures. No man ever took Kitty out: she didn't have the looks for dancehalls, or for courting in hedges; the housepainter who tried something on was a married man in his fifties, father of nine.

> **While Kitty was changing into her afternoon black, we would carefully arrange newspaper and kindling before putting a match to them, and she'd return to the kitchen to find it full of smoke and flames**

A wrestler called O'Mahoney, whom she confessed she'd never seen in the flesh, was her hero, but for the most part her interests and her preferences went unmentioned. She instigated little in her life: experience was what happened to her. Our dog Dano once followed Kitty to Mass, barking at her in the

She courted such embarrassment. At Duffy's Circus one of the clowns sat in her lap while everyone applauded. A man who came to paint the hall tried to kiss her, putting his arms around her under a ladder. A drunk sang to her when she was buying chops in Bridge Street. Her reaction in these awkward moments was always the same: red as

'These days I do most of my shoplifting online...'

Had she not become our maid she would have remained at home, in a cottage near Bally-cotton, an extra mouth to feed. Meagre though it was, the money she earned was something, and at least when she closed the door of her attic room she was private while she slept. A chipped, white-painted wash-stand, with a narrow cupboard and dressing-table to match, a single discarded hearthrug on the boards of the floor, constituted

> ## Had she not become our maid, she would have remained at home in Ballycotton, an extra mouth to feed

that bedroom world, where rosary beads were told and Hail Marys repeated, and all Kitty's washing of herself took place. She was woken at half past six by the rattle of the alarm clock that summoned her to the first of her tasks – the lighting of the range. The kitchen became hers only in the evenings, when the day's work was done, after earthenware hot-water jars had been placed in every bed, and the fire in the range had been damped down after the day's last meal. One of the armless wooden chairs was drawn out from the table and Kitty darned or read *Ireland's Own*, or just sat there with Dano and the cat.

Eventually she gave notice and returned to her family in Ballycotton. My mother said the obstreperousness of my brother and myself had unhinged her. There followed a long procession of unsatisfactory maids. One of them didn't return after a night's dancing at a roadside platform, another wouldn't get up in the mornings, others couldn't be trained. 'Well, I'd better go out and look for a maid,' my mother used to say when she found herself without one, and would set off at random into the countryside to see what the cottages had to offer.

Years later, Kitty was written to in Ballycotton and informed that my brother and myself had at last acquired sense. We were older and would soon be going away to boarding-school. So Kitty made the long journey to where we now lived, and my brother and I met her at the railway station. I wheeled her bicycle through the streets, my brother balanced her brown cardboard suitcase on the carrier. It seemed like a lovely town, Kitty said, blinking excitedly as she looked about her. We said it was a great place.

'Oh, that's a lovely room!' she exclaimed a little later, surveying her bedroom from the door. The same white wash-stand was there, a little more chipped than it had been, the same narrow cupboard and dressing-table, the same discarded hearthrug. From the window there was a view of a turf-merchant's yard.

'Whatever became of your plans for world domination?'

MUSIC
RICHARD OSBORNE

SHURA CHERKASSKY, eighty-two last month, is the last surviving member of a cavalcade of great pianists (Horowitz its latter-day Crown Prince and standard-bearer) who instinctively knew how to temper virtuosity with caprice. In fact, you could probably argue that Cherkassky is himself the king of caprice – and not just when he is playing the piano. He is both Pan and Peter Pan, a musical mesmerist who has never quite grown up. A denizen of airport lounges, recital rooms, and the Never-Never Land that is music.

On the subject of music his evasiveness is legendary, which is why I travelled light when I called on him at The White House (The White House, Regent's Park, that is, where he has a famously small shambles of a suite, more like a student squat than an executive penthouse). I took no tape-recorder, no bulky file of press clippings, no questions along the lines of 'And how many hours a day do you practise, Mr Cherkassky?' (Four hours a day is the official figure, but don't tell him I told you.)

He had arrived back from Geneva, slightly jet-lagged, only minutes before our scheduled tryst, but he was in peak condition on the evasion front.

'You knew Stravinsky?'

'He was *terribly* pedantic.' (The 'terribly' dragged out in the coy Russo-American drawl that is another of Cherkassky's trade marks.)

'Rachmaninov? You went to him for lessons.'

'He wanted me to stop appearing in public for two years, but I was too impatient. I never had any patience. That's why I hate restaurants. All that waiting around, it's so boring. I prefer room service.'

Cherkassky was more interested in talking about sex than about music. 'Do you remember an English actress called Celia Johnson? I was crazy about her.' (I also noticed several books about Bette Davis spreadeagled on a bookshelf beside the hotel television.) The other day in Switzerland Cherkassky struck it lucky in a TV studio. Expecting to be confronted by some balding central-European music

Pan and Peter Pan: Shura Cherkassky, the last of the great Romantic concert pianists

buff, he found himself instead in the presence of a rampant Swiss Delilah.

'Mr Cherkassky,' she oozed. 'Do you analyse your dreams?'

'I don't remember my dreams.'

'You must write them down.'

'Is that what you do?'

'I don't have to. I have a wonderful lover. He writes them down for me.'

Cherkassky adored Delilah. Telling me about her, he confided, was very naughty. I gave him my solemn assurance I wouldn't mention it to a soul.

Cherkassky is an extremely short man. Which is perhaps just as well. One day in the autumn of 1917, while he was standing on the balcony of his father's house in Odessa, a bullet grazed his scalp, bedding itself in the building behind. The mother of this would-be victim of the October Revolution was the musician in the family (she is said to have played for Tchaikovsky), though it was Cherkassky's father who actually taught him to read music. Cherkassky *père* was a dentist. After young Shura had been to the opera, visitors to the house got accustomed to 'Paraphrases on Themes from Gounod's *Faust*' being mixed in with the chloroform.

If Cherkassky has a musical god it is Anton Rubinstein (1829–94), Russia's answer to Franz Liszt. Hanging by Cherkassky's piano in The White House are concert schedules written out in Rubinstein's own hand. Until recently, he even had a cast of the hand itself. But it got stolen.

'Who stole it?'

'I don't know, but I have my *suspicions*.' Cherkassky is clearly a man who relishes a good suspicion.

Next year he will record Rubinstein's Piano Concerto, Ashkenazy conducting. Ever the intelligent child, he loves learning new music. For his electrifying eightieth-birthday recital at Carnegie Hall (winner of the 1993 Gramophone Instrumental Award) he learnt Charles Ives's 'Three-page Sonata'. Recently he has been playing two preludes and a polka by Lennox Berkeley.

One of Horowitz's pipe-dreams was moving to London so that he could play duets of an evening with his friend Shura. It was Horowitz's bad luck that New York scares Cherkassky rigid. He also told me

how lonely and down-at-heart he had been during the Second World War in New York. At thirty he was the prodigy no one wanted to know.

With very few exceptions, Cherkassky's best playing, and best records, have all been done 'live'. The only company that has successfully lured Cherkassky into the recording studio is Nimbus, with its policy of long takes and minimal editing. Their Cherkassky Edition includes a lot of fascinating repertory – the Grieg Sonata, Bernstein's *Touches*, Stravinsky's *Petrouchka*, the Berg Sonata.

Cherkassky himself is far readier to endorse the series of CDs assembled from live concerts for Decca by the late Peter Wadland (the producer who also helped create Jorge Bolet's Indian summer on record). The eightieth-birthday recital, mentioned above, is Cherkassky at his extraordinary best in an astonishing programme: Bach/Busoni, Schumann's *Symphonic Studies*, the Ives, a Tchaikovsky paraphrase (*Eugene Onegin*: shades of the dentist's surgery in Odessa), Chopin, and a *Boogie Woogie Étude* by Morton Gould. Decca also do an entire and unmissable CD of Cherkassky encores, all 'live', several of the performances reducing the audience to audible gasps and guffaws of pleasure.

Cherkassky was at the Dorchester Hotel for the Gramophone Awards on the 7th October, the day of his eighty-second birthday. The speeches went on so long lunch wasn't served until 3.30 pm. For a man with the world's lowest boredom threshold he was sphinx-like throughout, a model of rectitude. When his turn came to speak, he uttered just one sentence: 'I play the piano better than I talk.' And with that, he was off back to Essen. Or was it Geneva, for more advice on how to write down those dreams?

'The obese one on the end can't possibly be famine...'

45

JOHN O'CONNOR

1913–2004

John O'Connor, the distinguished engraver who studied with Eric Ravilious and John Nash, contributed regularly to *The Oldie*, almost until his death aged ninety in 2004. He illustrated Germaine Greer's Stump Cross column, then the column by *The Oldie*'s gardening correspondent Patricia Morison, and finally Candida Lycett Green's Unwrecked England feature.

A book of his *Oldie* engravings, *People and Places*, was published by Whittington Press in 1999.

TOP: Chatsworth, issue 71. MIDDLE ROW: Ightham Moat, issue 77 (left); Mushrooms, issue 18 (right)
BOTTOM ROW: Somersby, Lincolnshire, issue 73 (left); Cat in greenhouse, issue 27 (right)

TOP ROW: Bishop's Palace, Wells, issue 80 (left); Craster, Northumberland, issue 95 (right)
BOTTOM ROW: Southend Pier, issue 68 (left); Whitby, issue 121 (right)

'The Oldie engravings usually take me four or five hours. Before starting on the block, I draw the design on a piece of paper. I whiten the block (made of boxwood or pear) so that I can see what I'm doing, and draw the design onto it in pencil. If it's of an actual building, I have to reverse the picture by holding it up in front of a mirror. I engrave over the pencil lines using thin cutters to begin with, then gradually work into the wood with thicker cutters, like small chisels. There are various engraving instruments. One of my favourites is the multiple cutter, whose design hasn't changed since the mid-nineteenth century. It cuts several lines at once and is useful for quick cross-hatching. The principle of engraving is straightforward enough – the uncut areas will come out black, the thin lines and cross-hatching grey, and the deeply cut areas white.

'I bought my press, an 1864 Albion Harold, from a garage in 1947 for thirty shillings. It's worth about £1,000 now and it prints as clean as a whistle. The block goes on, I roll over the block with Lawrence ink, put the paper on and pull the press down. It doesn't take a moment. The paper has to be pulled off slowly – and there's the picture. And that's the most rewarding part of all, seeing it finished, thinking, "There's the moon, there's the cat". I never cease to be astonished that it works at all.'

JOHN O'CONNOR, JUNE 1998

A MASTER *in the House*

When novelist **JANE GARDAM** *was having trouble with her maths homework,*
she would immediately turn to her father – a brilliant, eccentric schoolmaster
who once claimed he could get a cow into Cambridge   **Illustration by PETER BAILEY**

All my teachers at school were as the walking dead compared to my father who, though he did all my maths homework for me for five years, was not my official teacher at all. He was what is called 'a famous schoolmaster', a housemaster of Sir William Turner's, a seventeenth-century grammar school turned public school in the late nineteenth century which I did not attend, being a girl. It had great pretensions and was famed for its 'Results'.

A dreadful headmaster of my father's first years had remorselessly sacked any master who could not produce ninety-eight per cent passes in the School Certificate. He paid them almost nothing. There were few jobs about. It was *Decline and Fall* time. The stress was awful.

For seventeen years boys passed through my life in multitudes, and through our house, which was across the road from the school itself. Every evening and at the weekends for several hours my father's voice could be heard ringing out from behind the dining-room door, where he gave extra coaching in maths and physics. He did this for forty-seven years, dying at ninety-two. To his funeral came old, old men in floods of tears who had been golden lads just after the first war.

My father taught eccentrically. 'I could get a cow into Cambridge' was his cry. 'I have a little girl at home who can do quadratic equations and she's only five.' (Oh, what a lie.) Across at the school he would begin his lesson at the foot of the main stone staircase, chanting mathematical rules, the classroom above falling utterly but expectantly silent by the time he reached it. Long before I was born he had stopped the very thought of any boy cribbing by jumping from desk-top to desk-top about the room, which he found excellent exercise. Gales of laughter issued from his classrooms and floated down corridors.

Every form was always the worst he had ever had. There was 'no hope for any of them' and he marked their books in a way that would nowadays ensure instant dismissal by order of the parent. 'FOOL!' he wrote, 'DROP DEAD! Do you want to be KILLED?' A life-long opponent of capital punishment – one of the servants on his father's Cumbrian farm had been executed for murder in 1919 – he would sometimes write 'YOU DESERVE TO HANG'. Everyone always passed, but if very occasionally there was a failure my father was silent for a week. In the Second World War some of his boys taken prisoner in Burma survived, they said, only because they re-taught themselves physics from his remembered voice.

It was a Cumbrian voice to the end – easy to mimic. He was a tiny man, a mixture of Chaplin and Woody Allen but with Celtic blue eyes. He also was said to have a Celtic sixth sense and could guess the next year's public examinations' questions with ease.

His speciality was with thick boys. 'I heal the thick,' he said, and was very successful with those who needed a mathematical qualification to reach

medical school. 'God knows how many people I've killed,' he said. He was adored.

My brother and I were his two failures. Mathematical paralytics. My brother now runs his own farm successfully – a difficult arithmetical job – and I coped with logic and Latin at the university, so we can't really be dim-witted, but our father could not comprehend our numerical terror before his lightning mind. Even now, four years after his death, I can't read my bank balance or my royalty statements without shaking

He stopped the very thought of any boy cribbing by jumping from desk-top to desk-top

and, whatever I know I've paid in, I always expect my card to be confiscated by the machine. My father kept note of every farthing, halfpenny and sixpence – though he had few enough – all his life, and was in endless consultation with his bank.

He was atrociously mean – the result of an anxious childhood and a cruel father – and was never known to give a present; but he gave me more than a present when he had me privately coached in Latin for

university entrance. Still afraid of his own father, he was particularly gentle with us as children. I believe that his childhood insecurity went very deep. When I later won a small postgraduate award he said that he was pleased because it had 'done him good in the staffroom' where he had been a respected fixture for over thirty years.

When I began to write fiction he was utterly mystified ('Why couldn't you be a teacher?') and couldn't get on with my books at all, except for the bits about Cumberland ('You're not as good as that fellow Bragg, though mind you he's more of a misery – very slow') and one short story about a repentant daughter, which he said was wonderful.

He sank into terrible depression in old age. We grew further and further apart and only found common cause in his last years when he took to growing roses. (He'd always been a chrysanthemum man – I had not dared compete.) Once he even asked my advice on pruning, and before he died gave me £100 for my ailing rose garden, 'In my memory,' he said.

It was a staggering sum, but I resented the reason for it. I didn't want to see his critical face among the black spot and the thrips, and I bought a hundred pounds-worth of manure instead, planning to buy new roses of my own. Needless to say it was the manure that at once did the trick.

'Well at least we've got you two talking'

Ronnie Barker

picks his top six

1. Tommy Cooper
Funny.

2. Eric Morecambe
Funnier.

3. Wilson, Keppel and Betty
Funniest.

4. Ingrid Bergman
My first love.

5. Lynda Baron
Much favoured in the
Bristol area.

6. My Aunt Louisa
What a gal!

PIN-UPS

Country Life

*Nature writer **RICHARD MABEY**, author of Flora Britannica and biographer of Gilbert White, wrote The Oldie's Country Life column for a year from October 1996*

For decades the British tended to regard trees as a kind of cross between outdoor furniture and domestic staff, all the better for being spruced up and standing obediently in rows. Undisciplined oaks and raggle-taggle ashes with wills of their own were not what we wanted cluttering our countryside. But suddenly this straitlaced attitude has started to soften. All over Scotland, the knobbly, contorted, indigenous Scots pine is being encouraged to spread at the expense of cultivated conifers. In Milton Keynes, of all places, there is a breathtakingly ambitious scheme to establish a wild, flood-plain forest at the edge of the city. And a campaign has been launched to save Britain's 'veteran trees', culminating a few weeks ago in one of the biggest conferences ever for a forestry symposium.

'Veteran trees' is a serendipitous phrase. Only a few years ago these hoary giants, sporting burrs and gaunt grey branches, were disparagingly referred to as 'senile' or 'derelict'. 'Veteran' has a distinctly more respectful ring, and is a sign of the changing times. It is also usefully vague. No one can unequivocally define a veteran tree, but you know one when you see it. It's not a matter purely of age, or architecture, but of character, a sense that this particular individual has lived a bit.

Many of the veterans are, understandably, oaks. The Milking Oak in Northants, for instance, acquired its name from having a crown so vast that cows were milked under it on very hot or rainy days. An oak at Castle Malwood in the New Forest, first recorded in the 1650s, produces new leaves at Christmas and a second crop in spring. But lesser species can acquire the patina of veterans too, like the Witch of Hethel in Norfolk, a seven-hundred-year-old meeting place

hawthorn, and the Tortworth Chestnut (a thousand-plus years) in Gloucestershire, now virtually a small grove in its own right. The thing about all veterans is that they are individuals, recognisable by their cracks and bosses and idiosyncrasies. They are also – stretching a point – places. They have their own nooks and crannies (sometimes even airborne ponds and second-storey woodlets growing in rot-holes) inhabited by bespoke collections of insects and epiphytic plants. Ancient trees don't age and degenerate in the same irrevocable way as humans. What we may describe as 'damage' may be nothing of the kind. A large branch torn off may be a chink for fungal spores to enter, but is just as likely to reduce the tree's top-heaviness and actually prolong its life. And even the

most ancient trees repair their wounds in rounded, conciliatory ways. They adjust their budgets, too, disposing of costly top branching and unnecessary heartwood. The fact that these cast-off bits very occasionally land on houses or people is one reason veteran trees aren't always popular, especially with local authorities and curmudgeonly members of the Country Landowners Association. But, as was amply demonstrated during the storms of 1987 and 1990, old hollow trees, with low centres of gravity, are virtually immovable by the wind. It is young, tall, whippy plantation trees that are vulnerable to weather.

The remarkable thing is that despite having one of the lowest areas of woodland in Europe, we probably have more veterans than the rest of the continent put together. There is barely a parish that doesn't have a venerable boundary tree, or a gnarled pollard on its common, or a thousand-year-old yew in its churchyard. No wonder that, now we are growing out of that misplaced desire to have a neat and fussy countryside, we want to prolong their lives as much as possible, even if one of the best ways of doing this (it generates better regrowth and a more gothic look than sawing) is to blow off any top-heavy bits with gunpowder.

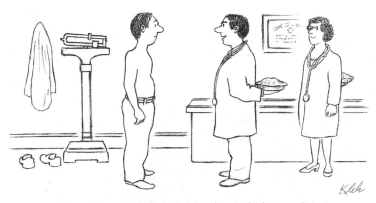

'Around here we believe that laughter is the best medicine'

Island of THE SAVED

Travel writer **DEA BIRKETT** was a rare visitor to the remote and almost inaccessible island of Pitcairn

Lost in the swells of the South Pacific is a speck of volcanic rock which should be paradise. This mile-by-mile-and-a-half island is home to forty half-Tahitian, half-British men and women whose race, culture and country arose from a historical hiccup – the 1789 mutiny on HMS *Bounty*. Two hundred years ago, a handful of British mutineers, with their Tahitian women and followers, landed on Pitcairn seeking a haven from the gallows. Today, their island at the uttermost end of the earth is the image of escape. Each year the Pitcairners receive thousands of letters from those who yearn to live 'far from the madding crowd' on an island without cars, banks, TV, taxes, roads, and with the lowest crime rate in the world.

An estimated 2,500 books and articles, and three Hollywood movies, have been produced about this Garden of Eden. But if Pitcairn is the most imagined, it is the least known place on earth. It is rarely visited. Only a handful of applicants for the Licence to Land are accepted by the Island Council each year.

Pitcairn is the last British colony in the South Pacific, lying just below the tropic of Capricorn, with New Zealand 3,300 miles to the southwest, Tahiti 1,910 miles to the northwest, and Antarctica over 6,000 miles south. The coast seethes with a white ruff of surf – there are no beaches, just cliffs and craggy rockfaces battered by an untempered ocean. Steep bare ridges and deep crevices make the island sit up in the water like a crumpled sheet of steel. Less than a tenth of the land is flat. The few white houses which form the only settlement, Adamstown, are faintly discernible among the banana trees and coconut palms.

The islanders are a bizarre hybrid race: tall like Europeans but with Polynesian jet-black hair; dark eyes but fair skin. Their language is a blend of eighteenth-century English and Polynesian. They still call their guns 'muskets'. Once they wore bark cloth, but today the tribal costume is sponsored T-shirts and baseball caps which arrive from well-wishers in every post: 'Bora Bora Yacht Club', 'His and Her Tournament Chub Cay 1983'.

Like characters in a child's game, all the twenty-four adults on the island wear several hats. Dennis Christian, sixth-generation descendant of the mutinous Master's Mate Fletcher Christian, is not only Postmaster, but Rubbish Collector and Tractor Driver Number Three. He lives in a bungalow constructed out of weather boards with a tin roof for catching the rain. His simple home is cluttered with modern appliances – a food processor, blender, electric fryer, two cookers, four industrial freezers, two VCRs. His mother Irma heats up the Pitcairn dish 'pilhi', made from grated sweet potato wrapped in banana leaves, in her microwave. Irma, an avid radio ham, has five electric kettles donated by contacts.

Bounty mania ensures that overseas devotees send a never-ending supply of often useless artefacts, as if hoping they could buy a piece of paradise with them. One charitable consignment contained enough dresses for each girl to receive twenty. When an American Adventist congregation saw a video of the barefoot islanders, they shipped out fifty pairs of Reeboks.

With its hotchpotch of donations from outside, and rich red volcanic soil, Pitcairn appears a land of plenty. Orange, mango, plantain, grapefruit, avocado and banana trees flourish alongside the ubiquitous coconut. Fresh vegetables are grown in small family plots scattered all over the island. The earth is rampantly fertile. Lettuce and beans which I sowed from seed were ready to eat within two months. Breadfruit are knocked from the trees with live bullets.

But if you need a can of tomatoes, a battery or a light bulb; if you run out of writing paper; or if, heaven forbid, the clutch goes on your three-wheeled motorbike, then Pitcairn's situation is brought starkly home to you. You must wait for a passing ship.

Pitcairn lies on the Panama Canal–New Zealand shipping route, and a vessel working that passage will pass within a few miles of the island. But it is not certain when the next ship will call; it might be tomorrow, next week, next month, or not for several months.

A family of Pitcairners pose on the cliff edge

PHOTO COURTESY OF REX FEATURES

In April 1988 twenty-seven ships passed Pitcairn. In the same month three years later, only one ship stopped.

When a ship is sighted offshore, the bell in Adamstown's square is rung five times and the whole island hurries down to Bounty Bay to help launch the long-boats, *Tin* and *Tub*. The bay is no more than a slight dent in the iron-bound coastline and provides no natural harbour. Even a few yards from the shore, the water is treacherous, and there have been accidents and deaths. One islander broke his jaw only a few feet from the jetty when the longboat hit a swell.

The forty-foot boat is packed with people and goods for trade. The men's baskets are heavy with fruit, vegetables and fish which they exchange with the chief steward for prized provisions – oil, eggs, flour. The women carry carvings, stamps, baskets, and Pitcairn T-shirts, which they sell to the visiting crew for US dollars. A model of the *Bounty*, copied from a video of the movie, will fetch $150.

But the islanders' most pressing shortage is not cash, but opportunity. Questions we ask our own children – What would you like to do as a career? What are your ambitions? What do you want to be? – are totally inappropriate on Pitcairn. Betty Christian's two elder daughters have left for further education in New Zealand. It is unlikely they will return. 'The more educated the children are, the fewer opportunities there are for them here,' says Betty. 'In most cases they move away. We're just left with the old fuddy duddies and the very young, and nothing in between.'

The vast chasm of ocean has sealed Pitcairn's destiny. There is no place where you cannot hear the crash of surf. I soon learnt of the awesome nature of this watery isolation. The long boats were returning in convoy from a trip to uninhabited Henderson Island, where the Pitcairners collect wood for their carvings. It was rough sea and *Tin* was heavily laden with logs, but the night was clear, we had a compass to steer by, and Pitcairn was only ten hours away. Then there was an almighty crash. A freak wave had broken over our bow and flooded the boat. The engine, submerged beneath the swirling water, spluttered and stopped. We began to sink.

Around us the dark ocean stretched for three thousand miles, utterly empty except for *Tub*. We flashed our torches

frantically towards her. There was no reply; the long boats must have drifted apart in the heavy seas. Everyone was very quiet and very still; if we moved we might sink the boat. We sent up a flare.

The red light exploded in the sky, illuminating the black water. In the far distance, only showing when the swell lifted her higher than our boat, we spotted a tiny *Tub*. Soon we saw the helmsman's face and knew we were safe. At a service in the Seventh Day Adventist church on the following Sabbath, we thanked God for our safe return. Half the Pitcairn population would have been lost.

The islanders were converted to Adventism by an itinerant American missionary in 1887, and no other faith has been practised since. The pigs, considered unclean meat, were pushed off the edge of the cliffs. Dancing was forbidden, and it became illegal to import cigarettes or alcohol. Any remnants of Polynesian culture, in which suckling pig is the favourite dish and dancing a part of life, were wiped out.

> **The vast chasm of ocean has sealed Pitcairn's destiny. I soon learnt the awesome nature of this isolation**

The Pastor is one of two outsiders employed on the island; the other is a Government Adviser and School-teacher. There are twelve pupils at his school; they cannot play a soccer match and school plays have to be adapted. 'Snow White and a Handful of Dwarfs' is one of their favourites.

In such a small place, the good of one is subservient to the good of all. If what is best for an individual is not best for the island, then that individual does best to forget it and try to fit in. 'Here everyone has been the same, always,' says Kari Young, whose two children attend the one-room school.

Such is the fear of creating differences that no one person is promoted above another. Although the Postmaster has three Assistant Postmistresses, the Forester has two Assistant Foresters, and the Radio Operator has three other operators under him, no head of department will issue orders to a junior.

Betty Christian, like all the islanders, believes this absence of reproach holds the community together. 'Nobody likes to tell somebody else what to do, or

say "I don't think you're doing your job right." That's a good thing.'

But, in practice, incompetence is allowed to flourish. Strong personalities can hold sway unchecked, and crimes are overlooked. Domestic violence, although well testified, goes unprosecuted. Beneath the community spirit seethes a savage undercurrent of frustrated ambitions and justice denied. Disputes are settled in unconventional, often violent ways. When one islander cut down another's banana tree, he was greeted next morning with three-inch nails planted in the mud path outside his home. Police officer Nigger Brown has never made an arrest.

Social censure is expressed through an ancient, effective and most deadly weapon – gossip. One older islander did not approve of a teenage girl smoking, yet she never complained directly to the girl herself. When the girl came to visit, she laid out an ashtray especially. But behind the teenager's back, the older islander gossiped – the girl was ruining her health, her boyfriend had caught a horrible cough – hoping this disapproval would filter back. In such a closed community, rumours reach the culprit within hours.

Solitude, privacy, independence – the things we may strive for – are as foreign to Pitcairn as supermarkets and subways. Anyone can listen in to your phone calls on the party line, or tune into your radio contacts on the ham radios. They can be at your consultations with the nurse; the dispensary is just one room. Personal business is considered such public property that the Pitcairnese greeting when you meet on the road is 'About you gwen?' (Where are you going?)

For the children of the *Bounty*, existence on a lonesome rock is not enchanting. Their country, where fewer people live than on a single floor of an average block of flats, is distinctive and extraordinary, but not as the outside world romanticises. Their lives are framed by two unrelenting and unalterable facts: the island is absolutely tiny and utterly remote. It is more crucible than melting-pot.

'There's no perfect people, no perfect community,' says Betty Christian. 'Here you have to live up to some kind of standard. You have to be something you're not. It's sort of like the Garden of Eden. There was a serpent even there, which ruined a perfect place.'

Miles Kington

1941–2008

RICHARD INGRAMS *salutes a faithful contributor and friend*

We had known for some time that Miles was very ill, but he was the last person to make any kind of drama about it. He seemed determined to carry on writing until the end and that is what he did.

It was typical of Miles. He had written for *The Oldie* from the very beginning and in all that time I can't remember a single occasion when he missed a deadline, complained about misprints or cuts, demanded more money or did any of those things that have been known to vex me over the years. In other words, Miles was an editor's dream.

He wrote quite effortlessly, so that a monthly column for *The Oldie* seemed like a doddle when he was writing a daily column for the *Independent*. Other journalists would have been reduced to repeating themselves, or merely waffling if given an assignment like that, but Miles had not just an extraordinary memory but a ceaseless curiosity about his fellow humans which meant that he was never short of original subject matter.

He was always getting into conversations with taxi drivers or strangers on a train and would invariably come across some strange coincidence or curious piece of information which would inspire a column. He thrived on out-of-the-way characters and books, forgotten jazz musicians, cartoonists (a special love) and railway journeys. But there wasn't much nostalgia involved. Everything he wrote was as fresh and tasty as the loaves he used to bake.

Miles was an editor's dream. He wrote quite effortlessly – a monthly column for The Oldie seemed like a doddle

Looking through his *Oldie* columns – which incidentally would furnish more than enough stuff for a most entertaining book – I came across a piece that seemed to epitomise the Kington world. It began by relating how he had tried to discover if a book by Byron Rogers called *An Audience with an Elephant* was still in print, only to be told by Rogers's publisher that

they were about to bring out a new book of his about J L Carr. It was typical of Miles to get very excited about a book by one obscure writer about another one, equally obscure. But what he went on to write about Byron Rogers could just as well be applied to himself: 'He writes very plainly but evocatively about the odd things and odd people in life. The small oddities that is. He would never write about the Leaning Tower of Pisa or Stephen Hawking...'

It is tempting to follow the example of the *Independent* and reprint, month-by-month, a number of Miles's *Oldie* columns, but I don't think he would have approved. There would still be so many things in the world that weren't the Leaning Tower of Pisa or Stephen Hawking. Now it would be up to someone else to write about them all.

I have, however, chosen one of Miles's earlier columns [*see opposite*] to remind everyone of his supreme skill as a humorous columnist.

April 2008

TOP: Willie Rushton's illustration for Miles's *Oldie* page.

Entertaining Lines of Conversation

MILES KINGTON

'So, who did you talk to on the train today?' says my wife when I come back from a railway journey.

It's true. I talk to people on trains. I don't always mean to. There are lots of people on trains I don't talk to. But if I am sitting next to or opposite someone, I generally start chatting, and before long I start finding out that they are interesting people. Is this because everyone is interesting if you talk to them long enough, or because interesting people make a habit of sitting with me?

Do they even feel, deep down, that I need material for an article, and get drawn to my journalistic wants? Well, let's examine the evidence from the last month alone.

Exhibit 1. This is a woman I met on the train between Salisbury and Cardiff. She works as a supply officer at an MoD office in South Wales and lives in Wiltshire. She had risen in her hierarchy until she had twenty people under her, and she was now in a position of some authority. But she was sick of it. The trouble was, as far as I could make out, that she had little power to go with the authority. She could often see that the MoD was ordering the wrong stuff, and the wrong quantities of it, but she couldn't stop it happening, and this made her miserable. 'I hate my job,' she said, as we got into Bristol. She was not an especially interesting person, perhaps, yet it is always thrilling when a stranger confesses an inner secret. 'I hate my job' may not be as compelling as 'I hate my husband,' as you can change a job more easily, but it is still exciting to be confided in.

Exhibit 2. A girl I met on the train to Newport. I hardly noticed her sitting opposite me for some time, as she was still and pale, and young enough still to have the remains of embarrassing acne. But she had rather a sweet, noble face, and once or twice she smiled at me, so I asked where she was going. She was a bit lonely, it turned out. She was French, fresh out of college in Rennes in Britanny, and had landed at Portsmouth that very morning for her first glimpse of Britain. She was heading off to Herefordshire for a working holiday picking raspberries – and, *bien entendu*, to practise her English. I thought I should practise my French on her instead, if only to convince her that at least one person in Britain could speak a bit of French, but I am not sure that was the impression I gave. At one point I was floundering because I couldn't remember the French for 'homesick'. I explained that it was the state of missing your family... '*quand votre famille vous manque...*' She smiled and said, in English, 'But I don't miss my family.' The other thing I remember her saying was, 'Do you know how good the buses are between Hereford and Leominster?' I was flummoxed, I can tell you.

Exhibit 3. A man going, like me, from Bath to Cardiff. He dealt in watches, was in his fifties, was German by origin and had lived in Switzerland for a while before settling in Bath.

'Where did you live in Switzerland?' I asked.

'Nowhere you would know,' he said. 'A tiny village above Lake Geneva called Chexbres.'

But I did know it! I had not only been there, but I had spent my holidays there as a boy in the Fifties. My Dad, for a while, always took us on holidays to hotels owned by ex-mates of his from the War. So my brother Stewart and I went there for our hols when we were about ten and twelve. I still have firm images of the lake, of the mountains, of a restaurant in Evian, of the jars of Maggi sauce on the table and of the portrait of Christ in our bedroom (hideous, with thorns, blood and tears).

'I still go to the edges of Switzerland for my holidays,' said the man, 'but usually on the Italian side. The lakes, you know. Lugano, Maggiore, Como...'

The only one I have ever been to is Lake Como, and for a very curious reason. I am related distantly to the Cardew family, and was once present at a far-flung family reunion. I sat next to a distant English cousin called June, who turned out to run a hotel in Bellagio, the Hotel du Lac. This seemed like a good hint for a holiday, so two years later we went and stayed there. And very nice it was, too.

'I have been to Lake Como, but not the others,' I said.

'I stayed in Bellagio,' he said, 'at the Hotel du Lac. And do you know – the woman who owns it, who is English, is related to the people we stayed with in Lugano! Don't you think that is amazing?'

'Not as amazing as the fact that she is also related to me,' I said.

Exhibit 4. Two men opposite me at a table on the London–Bath line. They were coming home from work, and were joshing each other – taking each other's crisps, insulting each other creatively, in the way the British do – so I assumed they were workmates or old friends. Not a bit of it. They were train companions. They had met on the train and now sat together about once a week, and their companionship was entirely train-oriented. Neither of them knew what the other did, or even what the other's name was. Under the catalyst of my curiosity they winkled each other's name out of the other (Roy and John), and then their jobs. One was a carpenter. The other a lecturer in architecture.

'I used to work in Bath,' said the architect, when I confessed where I was from, 'but then I went to New York for four years.'

'What were you doing there?'

'Working on a cathedral.'

'A cathedral?'

'St John the Divine, on 112th Street and Amsterdam. I call it St John the Divine and Unfinished. It was started in 1892 and it's going to be the biggest in the world when finished, but the money keeps running out. As it is, it is already the second largest in the world.'

'Which is the largest?'

'St Peter's in Rome, I think.'

'And what were you doing there?'

'Well, I'm quite good on Gothic detail and masonry, so I was brought over to do a couple of 400-foot-high towers. If you ever go there, have a look at the West Front. They are my towers.'

'I'm going to New York this Wednesday, as it happens.'

'Then you must go and have a look.'

And so I shall.

I wonder if I will meet anyone interesting on the subway.

My *Crossman* Diary

As a close aide **JOHN DELAFONS** *saw the human side of a famous political figure*

I was sent to work as Richard Crossman's Principal Private Secretary in March 1965. He had become Minister for Housing and Local Government in the new Labour administration in October 1964. It was his first ministerial appointment, but not the job he wanted or expected. His main interest during his first twenty years in Parliament had been foreign affairs, and more recently he had been a front-bench spokesman on social security. But he loved his new department: on leaving it two years later he said it had been the happiest time of his life. His officials were not so enamoured of him. He had no idea of how a minister should behave towards his civil servants. At first he bullied, mistrusted and offended them at every turn. He had already got through two private secretaries before I was sent to him. The Permanent Secretary, Dame Evelyn Sharp, said to me: 'You'll have to make a go of it: we can't go on like this.' Crossman himself said to me: 'What I want is a sparring partner; everyone here is too deferential.'

Our relationship was a bit stormy at times. Once, at home, my wife heard me shouting angrily at someone on the telephone and was surprised to learn that I had been speaking to Crossman. She said: 'I thought you were talking to the builder.' But Crossman and I settled into a reasonably good working relationship. He realised that he needed an efficient private office, and Dame Evelyn had made it clear to me that the department needed to establish sensible relations with the minister. I never liked him much but I enjoyed his intellectual energy, indiscretion and informality. It was certainly the most entertaining period of my forty years in Whitehall.

One of my earliest recollections is of being summoned over to his flat in Vincent Square to deliver some urgent papers. Crossman was in his bath, talking loudly to Tam Dalyell (his Parliamentary Private Secretary) who was sitting on the lid of the lavatory. I waited with Mrs Crossman in the living room. Crossman then emerged in a cloud of steam, still talking, with a towel round his neck and otherwise naked. He was a large man. Mrs Crossman remonstrated: 'Oh, Dick! Don't come in here like that.' Crossman looked down at himself and, somewhat nonplussed, stopped talking and retreated to the bathroom.

I sometimes went down to stay at Crossman's house near Banbury. It was part of a small farm that had belonged to Mrs Crossman's father. On the first occasion I met his two children, who happened to be the same age as mine. After tea we all had to play a game called, I think, Dragons. One person was the dragon and he or she had to find the others, who were hiding around the house, and take them to his cave – which was a gloomy lumber room full of old cupboards and wardrobes. Those captured would be released by others, if they could evade the dragon. I was caught by Patrick Crossman almost immediately and deposited in the cave. After a few minutes one of the wardrobes started wobbling violently and Crossman burst out shouting 'Free, free!' and thus released me.

I often accompanied him on visits around the country to local authorities or to official speaking engagements. On one occasion he had agreed (reluctantly) to give an after-dinner talk at Ditchley, which is a rather grand country house that seems to exist for no better purpose than to host 'top level' conferences and seminars, chiefly on defence and foreign affairs. I have no idea who pays for it, but it is supposed to be very posh and, in those days at least, guests were required to wear dinner jackets in the evening. It was a rule with Crossman that he would never dress for dinner, so he did not on this occasion. We were delayed on our journey and arrived late. The front door was opened by an imposing butler who had been there for many years and was reputed to rule the establishment with a rod of iron. Crossman asked to visit the gents'. The butler led the way down a wide corridor and threw open a huge door inside which was a rather small WC with a mahogany seat. I hesitated outside and Crossman said over his shoulder 'Come on, John, don't be shy'. So we both peed into the bowl with the door open, under the astonished gaze of the butler.

There was a famous occasion when Crossman left some official papers under his chair after dining on his own late one evening at Prunier's. Someone picked the papers up after Crossman had left and, instead of returning them, took them to the *Daily Express*, which resulted in a front-page scandal. George Wigg, who was the Prime Minister's self-appointed security expert, at once learnt of this from his Fleet Street sources and spent most of that night trying to trace me so that he could blame me for letting my minister take papers out of the office, not in an official box. In fact this happened while I was out of the office and Crossman had failed to tell the staff what he was taking. What seemed to infuriate Wigg was that I had not been at my post at 10 pm and could not be contacted at my home address. 'Where were you?' he roared. 'I was at the theatre,' I replied. I suspect it suited Wigg (and the *Express*) to let it be thought that the papers Crossman had left in Prunier's were 'Top Secret'. In fact they were a set of out-of-date housing statistics which Crossman had wanted to use for a speech he was due to make later that week.

The Oldie

THE OLDIE
SEPT 1995

THERE'S ONE BORN EVERY MONTH

ISSUE 78
£1·80

Artist-reporter and one-time Communist sympathiser **PAUL HOGARTH** first volunteered his services to The Oldie with an illustrated account of his chance meeting with John Paul Getty (later owner of the magazine). Subsequently he became a regular contributor of articles, illustrations and a number of memorably colourful covers. He died in 2001 aged eighty-four.

Douglas Bader

*It was with some trepidation that **EVE LUCAS** met her RAF hero – but she found him to be very jolly indeed*

The year was 1982, and Sir Douglas Bader was to be interviewed by Michael Parkinson. A young researcher was sent to talk to him in his mews house near the Albert Hall. Within half an hour Sir Douglas phoned to say he was sending her back as she knew nothing about him. I was asked to go in her place. 'Do you mind?' The producer asked. Mind! I'd have paid for the privilege.

I knew all about him, of course. A biography had just been written by his friend 'Laddie' Lucas and I asked for an hour or two to skim through it. Somehow, I managed to grasp the fundamentals of Bader's views on how the Battle of Britain should have been fought, what the Duxford Wing was, why there were differences of opinion between 11 and 12 Fighter Groups, pilot shortage and Lord Dowding's strengths and weaknesses.

Nevertheless it was not without trepidation that I rang his doorbell. My hero opened the door and beamed. 'Thank God they didn't send a young researcher.' I laughed. 'Come in, my dear. I can only give you forty-five minutes because I have to pick up the old duck.' I daringly asked who that was. 'My wife, Joan. And God help me if I'm late.'

I asked him if he'd be able to come down the steps leading to the TV interview area. 'No problem, my dear. If I fall down, Parky can come and pick me up. That'll be a laugh to start with.'

He said he only had a problem with his legs if he had to kneel. When he went to receive his knighthood, 'old' Dicky Gillette (everybody was referred to as 'old' this or that) worried in case he overbalanced and decided they'd better have a rehearsal. 'Good idea, old boy,' Sir Douglas had said. 'Don't want me falling flat on my face and bringing HER down, do we?' Fortunately 'old' Johnny Mills and another chum, 'old' Neil Cameron, were also there. They both pretended they had tin legs, and fell about all over the place. Altogether they had 'a good giggle'. I soon discovered that Sir Douglas's main aim in life was to have a good giggle.

'If I fall going down the steps, Parky can come and pick me up. That'll be a laugh to start with'

Sir Douglas didn't want to talk about flying, the Battle of Britain, or being a PoW. 'Oh forget about that. Everybody knows about it. They've seen the film and think I'm Kenneth More.' He laughed uproariously.

We talked about sport, and the joy of still being able to compete, with or without legs. He was full of admiration for the chaps who played wheelchair basketball. He nearly fell off his chair with laughter recalling a game he'd watched in Canada. The referee was unpopular, so the participants ran him down and he had to be carried off.

His philosophy regarding loss of limbs was that the younger you lost them the better! He meant that it is much easier to adapt when young. He was tremendously enthusiastic about the work he did talking to other disabled people.

Inevitably the conversation came round to golf. He'd had one of his artificial limbs shortened to improve his stroke and hit the ball much further. 'Old Henry Longhurst could never understand the principle of this. Said I'd had the wrong leg shortened. Ha, ha, ha.'

He secretly enjoyed a spot of fortune-telling. A couple of years later he and his wife Joan went to a fête near Banbury. Noticing a booth marked 'Fortune Teller', he popped in. The lady inside said that she wasn't really a fortune-teller, but was in touch with 'the other side'. She told him, 'Someone called Henry wants to tell you that he went to sleep for a little while and then woke up. He's now doing exactly as he wants, and he'd like you to know that the grass is a great deal greener this side than it ever was over your side.' Sir Douglas was adamant Henry had sent a promised message.

Sir Douglas often went to Scotland to play golf with his good friend, Jan Collins, the publisher. Jan always arranged for Sir Douglas to have one particular caddie, Andy Anderson, a dour Scotsman. 'He's long since gone up there to join Henry, where the fairways are greener. Ha, ha, ha, ha!' One day, as they were completing a round of golf at Troon, Jan told him about a lovely course called Machrihanish, over the water on the Mull of Kintyre. 'Let's go over,' said Sir Douglas. 'I've got my aeroplane at Prestwick. It'll only take us twenty minutes to fly.' As they finished the game, he said to Andy, 'I'll pick you up in the morning in my car, drive you to Prestwick and we'll fly over there.' Andy stopped dead in his tracks, and banged Sir Douglas's bag of clubs onto the ground with a determined thump: 'I'll no fly with ye, ye mad bugger,' he said, and they never did play at Machrihanish.

Andy's description of Sir Douglas

prompted me to say that I'd heard his language when flying was very colourful, and that the RT had to be turned off so that the WAAF in the ops room couldn't hear him. 'Nonsense,' he said. 'I can't remember saying anything worse than "My eyes are hanging out like dogs' balls, and I can't see a bloody thing." The girls loved it. Ha, ha, ha, ha.'

His philosophy regarding loss of limbs was that the younger you lost them the better

I asked him whether he thought youngsters today would be prepared to fight and die for this country, as he and all his contemporaries had been. 'Of course they would. People don't change. The country doesn't change. Our parents thought we were a bunch of bums in our wide trousers with long scarves wrapped round our necks.'

All the time we'd been talking, Sir Douglas had been lighting his pipe, puffing it, knocking it out, or re-filling it. Suddenly he knocked it out again, without re-filling it. There was a certain finality about it. My forty-five minutes had gone in a flash.

'Well there you are, my dear! Can I give you a lift anywhere?' he asked. 'I'm going to Hyde Park Corner.' I was going in the opposite direction. 'Oh, thank you,' I said. 'Hyde Park Corner will be wonderful.' Anything for a few more minutes with my hero.

I asked if I could use his bathroom. 'Yes, but hurry. I daren't be late for the old duck.' I'd hardly got up the stairs when I heard him revving up. 'Bang the door behind you and leap in,' he said, the Mini already on the move. The mews became a runway, and I was in a Spitfire, taking off down the narrow cobbled lane. He darted between cars on Kensington Gore – I swear we were airborne. We screamed to a halt just in time, as Lady Bader walked up from the other direction. She took my place, and the Spitfire zoomed away.

He'd told me that, during the War, he'd been able to park his aeroplane outside his hut – no running out to it like you see on the films. So I arranged for him to park his Mini right outside TV Centre for the programme. Vera Lynn was one of the other guests, and sang 'We'll Meet Again'. When Sir Douglas was ready to leave I took him down to his car. He gave me a kiss and said 'We will meet again, Eve.' I was thrilled, although I couldn't quite see how. A few weeks later he died. Now it would have to be on the other side, where the grass is greener.

'Who plumbed this in?!'

Mortimer's Goan Adventure

Rumpole author **JOHN MORTIMER** *meets ageing hippies and is disowned by his children on holiday in India*

It was sunset, a few days before Christmas, and we were sitting on the wide verandah of a cool house, built by a Portuguese landowner, now owned by our friends Denis Forman and his wife Moni. The sun was setting over the paddy field and rare birds were settling down for the night, when a cart came trundling down the road, drawn by two white oxen with proud horns and sagging chins, driven by a boy wearing nothing but a loincloth. And then, capering in the twilight, came eight or ten figures, some in saris, some in grotesque Father Christmas masks with white beards, some carrying sticks with lanterns, singing at the tops of their voices 'Rudolph the Red-Nosed Reindeer'. They crossed the garden and pranced up the steps to the house. They gave us 'God Rest Ye Merry Gentlemen' and we gave them money and Indian champagne.

It was just one of the religious festivals of north Goa, where Epiphany is celebrated by three boys wearing brocaded silk and crowns, who ride to a hilltop on white horses; where the Bandeira festival is marked by returned emigrant workers marching through the village firing pea-shooters, and Shiva's wedding is celebrated by the drinking of a mixture of milk, sugar and ground cannabis leaves. It's the country conquered by Portugal for the Catholic Church, where glistening white churches, like baroque wedding cakes, stand next to brightly coloured Hindu temples. Goa's first Bishop was a Franciscan friar; it suffered under the Inquisition and now the church, about half a mile from Denis and Moni's house, calls the faithful to mass at dawn, not with a gentle bell but with taped music of the sort which can be described as Hollywood devout, played at an ear-splitting volume for an hour between six and seven. It fills the landscape like thunder, wakens the exotic birds

John Mortimer in front of the sign to 'the old farts' retirement spot' in Goa

and sends the children scurrying for the school bus with their ears ringing: sitting on the terrace trying to write, I find myself concentrating entirely on 'Mary's Boy Child', 'A Winter Wonderland', 'White Christmas' and a no longer appropriate rendering of 'Silent Night'.

We were a large party setting out from England, where religion manages to pass almost unnoticed: Bill, my father-in-law, and I, both in wheelchairs (by far the most comfortable way to travel), he because of a replaced knee and I from a failure to see steps and judge distances, my wife as commander-in-chief, our daughter Emily who exhibits signs of uncontrolled terror as soon as she hears the distant sound of an aeroplane, and Rosie our younger daughter. At 2 am we were among the crowds in the baggage arrival at Bombay airport, having waited more than two hours for our suitcases. Emily, her fear mercifully blocked out by tranquillisers, was asleep. I was reading the small Oxford India-paper edition of Trollope's novel *The Prime Minister* and my wheelchair pusher said, 'That is right, you go on reading your Bible, sir. And pray that

the luggage will not be delayed very much longer.' God must have mistaken Trollope for the Bible because he sent our luggage and a mini-bus to take us to a hotel where we could spend four hours until we had to set out for Goa.

At Goa airport Denis was waiting, smiling and endlessly hospitable. Having found room for a detailed map of north Goa in his head – which already contains all the Beethoven symphonies, the Mozart piano concertos, most operas and the accumulated wisdom of a man who was responsible for the best years of British television at Granada – he had worked out a number of trips in the land of Christmas and Shiva which turned out to have an unforgettable magic about it.

Driving in Goa is enormously exciting. Stuck behind a bus, a bursting-at-the-seams taxi or a lorry full of goats, the driver twists the wheel and is out on the wrong side of the road with another bus or taxi, or a loose water buffalo charging towards us. Death is missed always, if not by a particularly wide margin. It's a pity if your attention is diverted from the roadside notices, some of which contain dire warnings such as 'DO NOT ACCUSE ANYONE FALSELY

IN THE COURT OF LAW JUDGES ARE VERY BUSY THERE IS A TIME FOR SOWING/REAPING GOD TO MANKIND. WHO CARES WHO!'

At the end of the road a notice pointing to the old farts' retirement spot says, 'Home for the beautiful aged'. Bill and I read it with satisfaction and felt inclined to book in.

The hippy era may be over and all those headbands, beads and Afghan waistcoats that set off to find the Holy Bagwash, or danced to the full moon on the beaches of Goa, have no doubt become accountants or computer programmers. But there are still ageing hippies on huge motorbikes among the straying oxen and the wandering elephants, one of which had 'Welcome to Goa' written on its vast rump. Some of the motorbikes bump down the paths of a mini jungle towards a clearing where the 'German Bakery' welcomes hippies in exile. There's an *As You Like It* feeling about the place, with bright scarves and shawls hanging from the trees instead of Orlando's love poetry, and fresh fruit juice and vegetarian samosas instead of ale and venison. But melancholy old Jacques, pierced and long-haired, sits on his own and similarly dressed German or Scandinavian lovers hold hands in silence.

There's a noisier, dirtier, more strident hippy beach at Arambol, with sands crowded with fishing boats, wooden shacks and tourist bars. In search of genuine, up-to-date hippies, I found two young men, stripped to the waist, skirted in bright sarongs, with shoulder-length hair, nose rings and numerous tattoos. I asked them how long they had been living the free, care-less and lotus life of Arambol.

'Just a week,' said one. 'Actually we're window cleaners from High Wycombe on a package tour. But it's great fun here, isn't it?'

'Wonderful,' I said. 'Where are you staying?'

'In a shack on the beach. We're hoping to find some girls to shack up with us. We've asked about two hundred so far and we hope to get lucky before we have to go back to High Wycombe.'

Notices on the beach at Arambol threaten 'ten years rigorous imprisonment' to those found taking drugs, a threat probably as effective as health warnings on cigarette packets. Denis took us to Holywood beach, a huge, empty stretch of golden sand where the palm trees grow down to the breakers of the Arabian Sea. On Holywood the shacks are closed down, with orders from the High Court of Bombay to shut them, pending trial, pinned to their walls. Some might have been used for drug dealing. We called at one shack and a carpet, table and chairs were pulled out of some recess. The carpet was spread on the sand and bottles of cold Kingfisher beer appeared on the table. We were about to drink gratefully when a police patrol was seen approaching. Like the magic meal in *The Tempest* the tables, chairs, carpet and Kingfisher disappeared and

> **I ignored the red flag and was immediately knocked over by a huge wave. A fierce undertow dragged off my Marks & Spencer shorts**

the police were engaged in friendly conversation with the shack's owners. We stood gazing casually at a group of children on the edge of the water who ran away, screaming with laughter, at the sight of flying fish. Then the police patrol moved on down Holywood and, by another blessed stroke of magic, the Kingfisher and the carpet returned.

On one beach where we went for lunch, nuns in fluttering white habits congregated on the edge of the water like seagulls and schoolgirls in blue uniforms paddled. An old man, another wheelchair rider, was pushed to the water's edge and an umbrella was put up over him; but umbrellas are not allowed and it had to be put down again. I ignored the red flag and plunged into the sea, where I was immediately knocked over by a huge wave and a fierce undertow dragged off my Marks & Spencer's shorts. I tried to remember stories of drowned writers and felt sure that Shelley never lost his Marks & Spencer's shorts in the undertow. My children disowned me and left the beach. Finally I and my shorts were rescued by the old man's wheelchair attendant – another proof, if proof is needed, of the value of that form of transport.

'Ramshackle Mapusa,' says the *Rough Guide* to Goa, 'is the state's third largest town. Other than to shop, the only reason you may want to visit Mapusa is to arrange onward transport.'

We didn't want to arrange onward transport and I didn't want to shop. The others vanished into the ramshackle town, which seemed to contain at least half a million inhabitants jammed together, with acres of fish, miles of meat, hectares of vegetables, old iron, second-hand clothing, small statues of the Buddha and religious pictures for sale. Off they went and I was left alone in a sweltering car park, sitting on a stool and trying to write a story about life in the Thames Valley.

Later Denis came to rescue me. He took me to a chemist's shop where he bought a small bottle of artificial sweetener, not because he particularly wanted it but so that he could borrow the chemist's padded bench, which the obliging shopkeeper brought out and stood on the pavement for us to sit on. So we sat among the jostling crowds, the hooting cars and gasping motorbikes, the swift, evasive bicycles and pecking chickens, the lost tourists and wandering oxen, and chatted of this and that as the others tried to find a pay phone, or a lavatory, or bought saris, shirts and Buddhas carved out of fishbone. Later we were joined by a youngish Goanese man who was on holiday from Australia where he programmed computers. I was grateful for the company and the bench and resolved to leave the story until next morning when I would get up before Bing Crosby's singing took over the sky.

But what I remember most are the rusty ferry boats, chugging across the broad, sluggish, khaki-coloured river, past mangrove swamps, towards a Portuguese fort on a high cliff, put there for a defence against the British, or the Dutch, or the army of the Hindu Maratha from central India. There were old vans on the ferry, and bicycles, and a tall, hawk-faced hippy dressed in yellow with his motorbike (later we saw him on the beach with two beautiful women and a baby). There was an old woman with a jewel fastened to her forehead with Sellotape, and a boy who carefully wrapped betel in a palm leaf to chew. An Australian girl in a long white dress with a rucksack stood at the rail, impeccably clean on the rusty boat, on the oily river beside which the turtles were nesting. It was a moment to remember in the early darkness of an English February, when the talk is all about the sex lives of pallid politicians in suits.

Theories of RELATIVITY

Once she was one of Leicester's four beatnik teenagers, then the bestselling author of Adrian Mole, now she wears a long fleecy nightgown, pickles cucumber and indoctrinates little children: **SUE TOWNSEND** *is a grandmother*

Illustrations by ARTHUR ROBINS

I am writing this at ten minutes to three on the morning of 14th September, which is the copy deadline I have been given by *The Oldie*. Please don't feel sorry for me. It was three years ago that Richard Ingrams first asked me to write about being a grandmother. Three years ago I had four grandchildren, I now have five. Three of them visited me this afternoon. I was lying in bed, eating grapes and reading the Sunday papers. When I heard them come thundering up the stairs I hurriedly put my lipstick on and modestly pulled the sheets over my Knickerbox satin shorts'n'camisole bed wear. After kisses all round, the seven-year-old gave me an excited account of the Spice Girls concert

she'd attended in Sheffield the night before. 'They changed their clothes six times,' she said, admiringly, 'and Emma was the best.' Meanwhile, the three-year-old fell upon the bunch of grapes, ignoring her sister's stern warning that, 'If you eat the pips you'll *die*'. I noticed that when there were only stalks left in the bowl, the little one went to a mirror in the bedroom and studied herself closely. Was she searching for signs of imminent pip-induced death? Who knows? All three-year-olds are mad. It's pointless to speculate on what goes on inside their heads.

My husband gave the eleven-year-old boy a balsa-wood aeroplane that he'd constructed the night before, and this techno-whiz of a child went

into the garden and marvelled that something without batteries or remote control could fly and dip so elegantly, using only the low-tech breeze.

None of the children asked me why I was in bed in the afternoon. They are used to seeing me lying around. I have six sofas in the house and one hammock in the garden for that very purpose. I was reminded that my own grandmother always went to bed on Sunday afternoons. She took the *News of the World* and a half-pint of dark brown tea with her. It was probably the high spot of her hard working week.

She was called Lillian (my middle name) and she looked after my granddad, Jack, two grown-up children, two lodgers, and various visiting grandchildren. She worked full-time and kept her small terraced house immaculately clean. There was a back-breaking routine of housework starting at seven o'clock in the morning, when she would empty the urine from the pot under the beds into an enamel bucket, ending at eleven o'clock at night, when she would bank up the coal fire in the back room, in the hope that it would last until morning.

I was one of the first teenagers. We were invented so that our 'never had it so good' prosperity could be exploited by the teen-based industries that were springing up. We were told by the American generation above us that teenagers were rebellious, moody and difficult. So we became those things, though not in the house, because it wasn't allowed. In the house you didn't answer back, and you did as you were told, though you wore an outrageous teenage uniform which shrieked rebellion.

My own grandma was soberly dressed at all times. Sometimes I shared a bed with her, and in the morning I watched through half-closed eyes as she dressed – large brassiere, *directoire* knickers, vest, corset, full-length petticoat, stockings, dress, cardigan, wrap-around apron and slippers.

Just before she died I saw her bare legs for the first time. They had never been exposed to the sun. They were as purely white as the underside of a swan's neck. Her hair was steel grey and crimped into waves by the metal curlers she wore during sleep. There were no cosmetics of any kind in the bathroom.

In fact, there was no bathroom.

Her word was law. If she had told her grandchildren to throw themselves into the canal we would have done so immediately, without stopping to remove our shoes.

I went to meet her from work, late one Saturday afternoon. The sun was streaming through the high factory windows. The air was full of floating white fibres from the white cotton socks that she helped to make, eight hours a day, six days a week. At the time I was enchanted. It seemed to me that my grandmother worked in a perpetual internal snowstorm.

> **All three-year-olds are mad. It's pointless speculating on what goes on inside their heads**

Much to her alarm I turned down one of the roads marked 'beatnik' in the subdivision of the teenage highway which eventually opened up. 'Beatnik' incorporated most of the things I was interested in: jazz, cigarettes, Russian books, French films. There were very few beatniks in Leicester. I was one of four.

I bought the *Manchester Guardian* and read it secretly, with a dictionary to hand. I knew that one day I would be able to understand it.

I'm writing about my grandmother because, I think, I'm slowly turning into her. I've started to bake bread and cakes, and I steep cucumber slices in malt vinegar like she used to. When my husband is away I wear a long fleecy nightgown and bed socks. After years of prevarication I am now developing certain fixed opinions.

The turning point came when I was forced to take to my bed for six months in August of last year. Disc trouble and sciatica brought me down as violently as a rugby tackle. The pain was dreadful; it felt like a family of particularly

sharp-toothed beavers was gnawing at my back and legs. Pain-killers and tranquillisers became grandma's little helpers. These pills dull the wits and allow one to watch junk TV day and night. (Are the programme makers on the same pills, I wonder?)

On the few occasions when I left my bed, I was assisted by a stick. When my grandchildren saw me hobbling towards the lavatory, stick in hand, wearing a sensible nightgown and bedsocks, hair in need of a cut and dye, I think for the first time I became a *proper* grandma to them. And, when I briefly lost control of my bladder and bowels – incontinence is a dirty word, but double incontinence is even dirtier – I was entirely sympathetic to my two-year-old granddaughter's struggle with toilet training.

I've taken it upon myself to inform my grandchildren about the natural world. These children are entirely modern – skilful with the video, the computer, the microwave and the mobile phone. But they are not totally seduced by technology. They are still full of wonderment that a dull-looking grey bean can transmogrify six weeks later into a beanstalk as tall as the house. And they are thrilled that they can actually *eat* the lettuces they have sown themselves.

Breadmaking is another satisfying activity (we like our food in this family). When we're pounding the dough we talk to each other and I take the opportunity to indoctrinate them with my beliefs: *kindness* is the most important thing in the world, and *good manners* are a form of kindness. *Socialism* is good. *Capitalism* is bad. I am a shameless propagandist. I also play music while we bake. I am currently obsessed with Bach's suites for cello, and the children seem to enjoy the sonorous sounds echoing around the kitchen.

I act as a buffer between their harassed, busy parents. If there is a dispute I am usually on the side of the child.

I am haunted by the feeling that I didn't do the best I could have done for my own children. Though in my own defence, I remember shouting up the stairs to them, 'Will you please stop *laughing*!'

Being a grandmother is giving me another chance to love and be loved by children. Last week I took a row of previously despised pearls from their box, and fastened them round my neck. When I looked into the mirror I saw Lillian my grandmother looking back.

Great DAMES

Theatrical writer and raconteur **PATRICK NEWLEY** arranged for Dougie Byng and Billy Milton to perform together in Bournemouth – and found no love lost between the old luvvies

I didn't start it. The phone rang in the early 1980s. It was a nice lady in Bournemouth. 'We want a Thirties' star to be in our forthcoming summer festival – can you supply one?' 'Douglas Byng,' I replied sharply. 'Who's he?' she asked. 'Look him up in *Who's Who in the Theatre*,' I said, more sharply. 'He's got three pages.'

Douglas Byng – or Dougie, as he was affectionately known – was a great panto dame and revue artiste who scored notable hits with his risqué songs in the Thirties, for instance 'I'm Millie a Messy Old Mermaid' and 'Doris, the Goddess of Wind' ('My life's been one long blow from morning till night'), and was championed in later life by George Melly and John Betjeman. He'd long since retired but even in his late eighties could easily be coaxed out for an appearance. The lure of an audience proved irresistible.

The nice lady from Bournemouth phoned again the next day. 'I had no idea that Douglas Byng was so famous. We'd like him for two weeks, twice daily.'

The telephone nearly dropped from my mouth. 'You do realise he's nearly ninety?' I spluttered. 'Will that be a problem?' came the reply. 'Not really, but he'll need somebody to work with him. May I suggest the performer and pianist Billy Milton?' 'Who's he?' 'Look him up in *Who's Who in the Theatre*. He's got three pages.'

Dougie was excited. So was Billy, and he was only eighty-three. We all met up at the National Film Theatre before taking our first-class train from Waterloo to Bournemouth. Dougie arrived in a hired limousine and Billy came on the bus. Each was dressed immacu-

'Is he saying something, dearie?' said Dougie. 'If she goes on like this any longer, I'm getting off at the next stop,' said Billy

lately. Dougie had brought five suitcases and Billy a small holdall with his toiletries and a pile of sheet music. We had a splendid compartment to ourselves and excellent service. It was then that I discovered that they hated each other. And always had.

I sat next to Dougie, who was somewhat deaf, and Billy sat facing us.

Dougie (shouting at me): 'You know, dearie, I'm very surprised they booked Billy – he was never a star. You don't mean he's going to do an act?'

Billy (turning to me): 'I can't really bear the thought of two weeks with Dougie. You will keep him out of my way, won't you?'

Dougie: 'Is he saying something about me, dearie? Tell him to speak up, will you?'

Billy: 'If she goes on like this any

longer, I'm getting off at the next stop.'

We arrived at Bournemouth and were greeted like visiting royalty by the theatre's management. Happiness prevailed until we were shown backstage to the dressing-rooms. Dougie insisted on the number one and Billy ended up in the number two. Later that afternoon he placed a note on the door which read 'Number one dressing room – Billy Milton'.

The show opened to a large audience including the Mayor of Bournemouth and a gaggle of seaside landladies, all on free tickets. Billy played the piano to perfection, interspersing his own compositions with anecdotes about Noël Coward, Mistinguett and Maurice Chevalier. The audience loved him. But Dougie did not. 'Why does he go on and on?' he asked me in the dressing-room, where he could hear the show on the Tannoy. 'I mean, are they really interested in all those old stories?'

When Dougie went on, some members of the audience gave him a standing ovation. He told some ex-

tremely risqué gags and sang some of his best-known songs. He overran by fifteen minutes, and the audience couldn't get enough of him. Except Billy. 'Why oh why does she go on and on?' he asked me in the dressing-room. 'I mean, who's interested in all those old stories?'

This went on for the whole two weeks, but worse still were the evenings when fans came backstage clutching books and records to be signed. If there were more fans in Dougie's dressing-room there would be a loud shout from Billy: 'Why are people going in there? They've come to see me!' When an admirer went into Billy's dressing-room, Dougie went white and screamed, 'He's gone to the wrong room! Quick, tell him I'm in here!'

They rarely spoke off-stage, despite staying in the same hotel and in next door rooms. The walls were paper-thin, so they could hear each other's telephone conversations. 'You wouldn't think that Billy had any friends,' Dougie once remarked.

There was an exception when, one Sunday, we were invited to afternoon tea at the Royal Bath Hotel. The three of us sat in the sunshine in the gardens, drinking champagne at Dougie's insistence. There was no arguing, and they began to remember past glories. They fell asleep, and when the afternoon became chilly Billy woke up, patted Dougie on the hand and said, 'Dougie dear, we've a show to do tonight.' Dougie stirred and muttered, 'Oh, I suppose we should be getting along, dearie.' They helped each other up and as they walked through the hotel Dougie said to Billy, 'You know, it's been a long time. We must be the oldest performers in the business and still working. No one can criticise us anymore.'

Dougie Byng died at the age of ninety-four. Shortly before he died I visited him at the actors' rest home, Denville Hall in Middlesex. He was by then frail and confined to his bed. He turned to me brightly on this occasion and said loudly, 'You know, I wouldn't mind doing another show with Billy. I mean, he's not that bad really.' Billy Milton died a few years later, after writing me a letter in which he said, 'Do you think we could do another of those shows with Dougie? He's bloody difficult, but not that bad.'

Left: Douglas Byng
Right: Billy Milton

He should have stopped

Author and playwright **NELL DUNN** met a brave woman on the number 14 bus

I AM ON the number 14 bus riding up the Fulham Road, sitting downstairs front left (the one I try and get if I am carrying too much to go upstairs front left, my favourite). We approach a request stop and a black woman holds up her hand. She realises the bus is not slowing and steps out into the road, her hand held high to hail the driver. He drives straight past her but is forced to stop at the lights fifty yards on. She belts up the road. She is thin and wiry and about fifty years old. And just makes it to leap on to the platform as he pulls away.

'Why didn't he stop for me?' she asks the long-haired, laid-back white conductor. He shrugs and points to his temple. She marches up the aisle and knocks, rapperty-tap, on the glass partition behind the driver. He turns around.

'Why didn't you stop for me?' she asks.

'You didn't put your hand up,' he says, turning back. She raps again, harder this time. He turns around.

'Why didn't you stop for me?' she asks again.

He stops the bus, jumps down from his cab, goes round, gets on the platform and hurtles up the aisle to where she is sitting. He is ugly, fat and white.

'Get off this bus,' he says.

'Why didn't you stop for me?' she says.

He leans over her, almost drooling in fury. The conductor stays on his platform.

'Get off now,' he shouts.

'No,' she says, 'this is a public bus. I'm not getting off.'

He pushes his face still closer. 'Get off,' he shouts.

'I'm not frightened of you,' she coolly says.

Almost crazy with rage now, 'If you don't get off this bus now I'll make everyone get off,' he yells.

'I don't care,' she lightly returns.

'You don't care?' he screams.

'No,' she says, 'I don't care. Why didn't you stop for me?'

To my amazement he is defeated. He turns and stomps back down the aisle, gets back into his cab and drives on.

'You were very brave,' I say.

'He should have stopped for me,' she says.

A DESERT SEDUCTION

Allah looked kindly on **LYNNE REID BANKS** *when she placed her
trust in Arab hospitality...*

Illustration by LARRY

After we'd finished with the pyramids and the sphinx, Imud, my guide, asked me if I could ride. A good question; he'd already seen me on a camel (well you have to, don't you, and it's more fun than walking between pyramids) and I suppose he wanted another bit of quiet entertainment.

On receiving a qualified assent, he drove me to a sort of shed on that scruffy street where Cairo ends as abruptly as a knife-cut, and the desert begins. There he introduced me to his Uncle Fouad, who rents out horses and camels for a living. Fouad was a rotund Bedouin of fifty, with a smiling sun-darkened face and better English than his nephew, whose eccentric pronun-

ciation had rendered our tour of the Egyptian Museum that morning more confusing than enlightening.

Fouad and I shared a glass of tea and a chat, and he asked me if I'd like to go riding in the desert at night. I said I hadn't ridden in some years and that perhaps a trial run by daylight might be a good idea.

So a nice little Arab pony was brought out, Fouad twisted a white headscarf round my head against sun and dust, and I had a ride, after which he said I'd passed and, if I liked, we could go riding that night. I could watch the *son et lumière* on the pyramids from the desert side, and we'd have a picnic. Sounded good... How much?

'How much? Let's not talk of

money! Give what your heart tells you.' My heart told me $10 now (broad smiles) and, I thought, another $20 later. I returned to my hotel, the Cleopatra Palace (if that's Cleopatra's palace, I'm Nefertiti), had a shower and a rest, put on 'riding clothes' (some thick socks), and thought about what I might be letting myself in for.

Nothing to worry about. I'm old enough to be his mother. Never turn down an adventure. Besides, it's my last night in Egypt and there's a full moon. Yes. Go for it.

I left Fouad's card on my bed just in case I didn't come back and took a taxi to the Mina Hotel, a very grand establishment where nobody looked anything like Fouad (or me either, come to that). Just as I was deciding it wasn't going to happen, he came swanning up the drive in his black robes with his fat tummy preceding him, and swept me off in a beat-up old car which he hadn't dared bring onto hotel premises.

The pony wasn't ready and the *son et lumière* was starting, so he led me to a recumbent camel and I perched on its soft, commodious saddle. Behind me the moon rose over the city. The camel grumbled and belched and shifted under me while the French commentary wafted over the darkening sands ('*La p'tite reine, couchant pour l'éternité...*')

The pony arrived and I mounted with some help from a rock. There's dismayingly little of an Arab pony. Accustomed to quite a lot of horse in front of the saddle, I felt as if I were on an edge, but this didn't faze me after the camel ride that afternoon. There's a moment in camel-riding when the camel alarmingly vanishes. When it's time to dismount, he sinks, gurgling mutinously, to his knees and just isn't there any more – for a moment you are left at a one-in-two gradient still far from the ground, held in place entirely by the strength of your grip on the pommel.

'Would you like to sit closer to me?'

I have heard that line before, though not for a number of years, and my previous 'oh-oh' suddenly didn't seem so unthinkable.

'I'm fine where I am, thank you. Pass the beer.'

Pause. Then, in a definitely lecherous tone: 'Aren't you afraid to be out alone in the desert with me?'

'Not in the very least.'

'Why not?' (rather peevishly).

'Because,' I said pleasantly, 'I know a gentleman when I meet one, in whatever part of the world.'

'And if I am not so gentleman, and I try to hug you and kiss you, will you kill me?'

There's a thought! How would I do it? No doubt he has one of those curved daggers in a sheath at his waist. Snatch it out as he pounces, scream loudly, plunge it in, the beautiful Persian rug soaked with blood, my honour saved...

'Kill you, Fouad? Possibly, but you're not going to, so I won't need to.'

'Why I'm not going to?'

'Well,' I said, 'for three reasons. One, you're a gentleman, as I said, whom I trust, or I wouldn't have dreamt of coming out here alone with you. Two,

'I am wearing, as you may have noticed, my medallion on which is inscribed a prayer in Arabic to Allah. Allah is watching us and he will not allow you to show me the slightest disrespect.'

Since Fouad was swigging back the beer, I knew he couldn't be a very strict Muslim, but I thought this would carry the day if the other two points were weak.

Happily, I was right – or possibly the deciding factor was when I proved that I was older than he took me for. Luckily, the satellite child returned after what was perhaps planned as an enabling interval, bringing pots of delicious hot food and pitta and more beer, and we had a feast in the moonlight and watched the delicate play of lights on the pyramids while I described my happy marriage, my three grown sons, my hordes of (imaginary) grandchildren, though he seemed to have lost interest by then. Afterwards we remounted and rode for an hour through the desert. It was heavenly.

As we rode back he said plaintively, 'Your husband is how old?' I told him, over seventy. 'And can he still, er, does he still...?'

'Fouad,' I said kindly, 'don't worry. You've got twenty good years ahead of you.'

It's great being old. One really does feel so safe.

I ought to add that the idyll ended on a somewhat sour note. When I handed over the $20 bill he let out a roar of disappointment. 'But this is not enough!' he yelled. 'You said what my heart told me to give,' I said feebly. But to no avail: he sent a cohort back to Cleopatra's Palace with me to collect another $30. I couldn't help wondering if $20 would have been enough, if...

It would be rather fun to think that my ageing favours could be worth at least half a ride in the desert.

> '**Would you like to sit closer to me?' Fouad asked.**
> **I have heard that line before, though not for years, and**
> **my 'oh-oh' feeling suddenly didn't seem so unthinkable**

Off we rode. Fouad on his camel, looking every inch a desert wanderer, and in his orbit a little satellite child on a donkey with a rolled-up carpet across its rump. I looked at the carpet, and an 'oh-oh' did cross my mind, but I banished it. Unthinkable, surely.

We rode for about fifteen minutes straight into the Sahara, till the city passed from sight and we arrived at a point from which we could still see the pyramids peeping over the dunes. There we dismounted, and the carpet, a beautiful Persian one, was spread out on the sand. Cold beer was produced. While we were washing the dust out of our throats, the little boy silently vanished into the night, taking with him horse, donkey and camel.

We watched the play of lights on the pyramids and listened to the music while the moon climbed the sky. It was really rather wonderful. Then Fouad spoke.

I am well aware of the Arabs' respect for age, and for women.' (This was an outrageous lie. It has not been my experience that Arabs have much respect for women, and the present situation bore out my impression that a lot of them will shag anything that moves.)

'And third,' I continued smoothly,

Modern life

What is...
Kumbaya?

THEY'D HAVE YOU believe it was African. Well of *course* they would. Were it European, it would be merely maudlin, sub-literate, a parodic infantile whine for unspecified assistance, more appropriate to some ill-digested cargo cult than one of the most complex and mystical religions in the history of mankind.

But *African*, African is just *fine*. If 'Kumbaya' is *African*, then it's innocent, almost prelapsarian, noble in its simplicity and, gosh darn it, *moving* – thousands upon thousands of black faces turned with child-like trust to the White Man come to lead them from benighted paganism into the Light of Christ, their eyes rolling ecstatically, their bodies swaying with that natural sense of rhythm, little piccaninnies scrabbling in the dust... and so it plays beautifully into the lily-white, innately

racist hands of the maundering classes.

And so they perpetuate the myth. A quick trawl around the world wide web produced, within ten seconds, this fine and juicy example: 'It originated in Africa among the native peoples who saw missionaries floating down the river in a boat. The natives were hungry to know about the Lord and they wanted the missionaries to "come by here", but their pronunciation made it sound like "Kum-by-ya". The words of the song are the natives' invitation to the Lord: "Come by here, my Lord, come by here"' (©1998 by Galen C Dalrymple). (And, no, I am not making that up.)

Isn't that *sweet*? And isn't it touching that here and now, with all the advantages of two thousand years of Christendom, surrounded by the apparatus of our intelligence and sophistication, we can still become

'Someone's crying, Lord...' Someone? My money's on several million outraged African Christians

as little children each time the vicar – oops, Team Ministry Leader – Ken invites his good friend Roz to bring her guitar up to the sanctuary and strike up the drear, thudding chords of this, like, really meaningful song which, you know, would be a real favourite of Jezza's if He were here among us today, which in a very real sense He is...

> Someone's crying, Lord, Kumbaya;
> Someone's crying, Lord, Kumbaya;
> Someone's crying, Lord, Kumbaya;
> O Lord, Kumbaya

Someone? My money's on several million outraged African Christians, by and large a far more stern, orthodox, theologically unyielding and mystical bunch than any old rattle-bag of hangdog Western apologists; and one day they will rise up in a new Reformation, demanding a return to right thinking and decorum on the sanctuary and an end to patronising ethnocentricity. It will be the snake-pit for graspingly sentimental American fundamentalist preachers ('I prayed to GAWD! And GAWD! gave me a condo and a low mileage T-Bird and a twenty-three-year-old HELPMEET with candyfloss hair and BIG TITS!

And GAWD will do the same for YOU!') and the burning fiery furnace for the Holy Trinity Brompton crowd ('Jezza's having a drinks party, yah? and you're all invited to come, yah? I mean, doncha think Jezza's the most apsley *brilliant* chum?'); the guitars will be driven off the sanctuary, the laity will be flogged for desecrating the Host with unclean hands, and the acquiescent, favour-currying clergy will be driven into the sadomasochistic servitude they so richly deserve for having turned the church into a branch of New Labour.

And then will be the moment to reveal the truth about Kumbaya. African? Phooey. It's not African at all. It's not even anything to do with religion, let alone Jesus. Kumbaya is Welsh.

Yes. Would I lie? It's *Welsh*. Try it and you'll see what I mean, as in: 'Halloa, Mrs M, can you tell Griff to kumbaya on his way hoame and I'll give him that tinner paint he were after,' or 'I doan know what happened to our Lil, I told her to kumbaya but she musta gonbythur.' That an entire myth should have been built on such a simple misunderstanding is embarrassing; that millions of innocent, harmless worshippers should have had their liturgy disrupted with such inappropriate maunderings is lamentable; that the people of an entire continent should have been traduced by having it laid at their door is unforgivable. But none of it is surprising. It's been going on for millennia now, and if you don't believe me, I have one word to say to you, and that word is παρθενος. That little catchphrase may have caused a great deal more difficulty, but at least the tunes are better and nobody ever blamed it on the Africans.

MICHAEL BYWATER

'Look at that poor excuse for a moustache'

TOP CHUMPS

MADONNA

CHUMPFILE ▶

★ Conical bras	97%
★ Kabbalah membership	100%
★ Adopted babies	97%
★ Crap Wallis Simpson film	100%
★ Brazilian toy boy	90%
★ Yoga addict	88%

RUN, RABBIT, RUN

As a schoolboy, sports writer **JOHN MOYNIHAN** *met his hero, runner Sydney Wooderson, whose exploits cheered postwar Britain*

Alone in a thick, vaporous Essex mist, I awaited the arrival of the champion runner Sydney Wooderson – one of my sporting gods during those austere, immediate postwar years. Others included the Chelsea and England footballer Tommy Lawton and the heavyweight boxing champion Bruce Woodcock.

We frozen, bullied second-formers at Felsted School had been detailed to act as markers for a cross-country race meeting between our lot and Blackheath Harriers. There was a great excitement because Wooderson had agreed to take part.

He may have looked like a spindly, bespectacled articled clerk, but once he donned the all-black running strip of his club there was no disputing who was going to win the race.

We all knew Sydney could run very fast: he had become a national hero before the war by breaking the world mile record, running 4 minutes 6.4 seconds, and the world 800 metres record a year later. But we were not prepared for the pace he set around our turgid ploughed fields.

Out in the murky countryside, I had taken up my place as a marker by a gnarled oak tree not far from the River Chelmer. It was difficult to see through an enveloping mist, but suddenly there was Syd, emerging like Omar Sharif in black, arms pumping, his legs pounding over the mud like steam pistons. For one magic moment, he stopped, having hardly raised a sweat.

'I'm a bit lost,' he said, putting his hands on his hips. 'Where next?'

'Across the ploughed fields, and you'll find another marker,' I replied, pointing vaguely in the right direction. 'Not far to go now, sir.'

'Thank you.' Just as he belted off, I mentioned I had seen him run the mile against the giant Swede Arne Andersson at the White City two years

before. Wooderson had lost by inches. 'Quite a race. Andersson was very strong and quick.'

The great runner went on to win the race by miles in the centre of the school cricket ground. The other runners came in dribs and drabs, my laconic house prefect Cox asking where 'Woody' was. 'Almost an hour ahead,' I ventured.

My first sighting of Wooderson at the White City, a few days before the atom bomb was dropped on Hiroshima, helped ignite my devotion to top-class sport. Wooderson and Andersson could not have looked more different: the Englishman had lived on wartime rations and resembled an undernourished rabbit beside the Swede, who had been able to train on a far more exciting diet in a neutral country. What chance had Wooderson got against this muscular Nordic stallion?

My parents had taken me to this inter-service meeting. It was a dull, humid evening, and we craned for a proper view, surrounded by thousands of men and women in uniform. The Yanks yelled for Sydney to beat the

'big Swedish bum' as the pair veered away for the first lap. Wooderson, running for the British Army, hung onto his man, glasses glinting, his face contorted, his slim, firm legs moving smoothly behind the bouncing bottom of the Swede. Wooderson suddenly acquired the stature of a Spitfire.

The crowd roared him on until the final bell, and they roared even more when Wooderson went ahead of the Swede down the back straight. He tried to kill off Andersson's reserves, but the Swede's constitution was made of steaks and fresh air. When he swung round the last bend and made his final dash towards the tape he seemed to draw on unknown strengths, and away he came to pass Wooderson's shoulder and win by a nose.

It wasn't fair, of course, and the crowd fell back in despair, but then the cheering came again as Andersson congratulated Sydney, who stood modestly by the track after putting on his track suit.

Sydney lost, but it was obvious he had a lot in store. A year or two later he beat the Swede on his own soil – sweet revenge before his own retirement.

Wooderson was unlucky to miss two Olympic Games – he was injured before the 1936 games in Berlin, and retired before the 1948 Olympics in London. Now in his late eighties, he can browse through his cuttings at his home in Helston, Cornwall, with pride. Great middle-distance runners were waiting to beat his own outstanding records – Sir Roger Bannister breaking the four-minute barrier in 1954 and earning a special cheer from one of his chief mentors.

Wooderson attended a special dinner for mile champions in London in 1994 to celebrate Sir Roger's achievement. I'm sure Bannister reminded Sydney of that special meeting at the White City which, like me, he watched as a schoolboy. Wooderson lost by a nose. Some nose.

PHOTOGRAPHS COURTESY: ASSOCIATED NEWSPAPERS /REX FEATURES

The Wink

A chilling short story by crime novelist
RUTH RENDELL

Illustrations by
ROBERT GEARY

The woman in reception gave her directions. Go through the day-room, then the double doors at the back, turn left and Elsie's room is the third on the right. Unless she's in the day-room.

Elsie wasn't but the beast was. Jean always called him that, she had never known his name. He was sitting with the others watching television. A semi-circle of chairs was arranged in front of the television, mostly armchairs but some wheelchairs, and some of the old people had fallen asleep. He was in a wheelchair and he was awake, staring at the screen where celebrities were taking part in a game show.

It was at least ten years since she had last seen him but she knew him, changed and aged though he was. He must be well over eighty. Seeing him was always a shock but seeing him in here was a surprise. A not unpleasant surprise. He must be in that chair because he couldn't walk. He had been brought low, his life was coming to an end.

She knew what he would do when he saw her. He always did. But possibly he wouldn't see her, he wouldn't turn round. The game show would continue to hold his attention. She walked as softly as she could, short of tip-toeing, round the edge of the semi-circle. Her mistake was to look back just before she reached the double doors. His eyes were on her and he did what he always did. He winked.

Jean turned sharply away. She went down the corridor and found Elsie's room, the third on the right. Elsie too was asleep, sitting in an armchair by the window. Jean put the flowers she had brought on the bed and sat down

on the only other chair, an upright one without arms. Then she got up again and drew the curtain a little way across to keep the sunshine off Elsie's face.

Elsie had been at Sweetling Manor for two weeks and Jean knew she would never come out again. She would die here – and why not? It was clean and comfortable and everything was done for you and probably it was ridiculous to feel as Jean did, that she would prefer anything to being here, including being helpless and cold and starving and finally dying alone.

They were the same age, she and Elsie, but she felt younger and thought she looked it. They had always known each other, had been at school together, had been each other's bridesmaids. Well, Elsie had been her matron-of-honour, having been married a year by then. It was Elsie she had gone to the pictures with that evening, Elsie and another girl whose name she couldn't remember. She remembered the film, though. It had been Deanna Durbin in *Three Smart Girls*. Sixty years ago – well, fifty-nine.

When Elsie woke up she would

ask her what the other girl was called. Christine? Kathleen? Never mind. Did Elsie know the beast was in here? Jean remembered then that Elsie didn't know him, had never heard what happened that night, no one had. She had told no one. It was different in those days: you couldn't tell because you would get the blame. Somehow, ignorant though she had been, she had known that even then.

Ignorant. They all were, she and Elsie and the girl called Christine or Kathleen. Or perhaps they were just afraid. Afraid of what people would say, would think of them. Those were the days of blame, of good behaviour expected from everyone, of taking responsibility, and often punishment, for one's own actions. You put up with things and you got on with things. Complaining got you nowhere.

Over the years there had been extraordinary changes. You were no longer blamed or punished, you got something called empathy. What the beast did would have been her fault then. Now it was a crime. She read about it in the papers, saw things called helplines on television, and counselling and specially trained women police officers. This was to avoid your being marked for life, your whole life ruined, though you could never forget.

That was true, that last part, though she had forgotten for weeks on end, months. And then, always, she had seen him again. It came of living in the country, in a small town, it came of her living there and his going on living there. Once she saw him in a shop, once out in the street, another time he got on a bus as she was getting off it. He always winked. He didn't say anything, just looked at her and winked.

Elsie had looked like Deanna Durbin. The resemblance was quite marked. They were about the same age, both born in 1921. Jean remembered how they had talked about it, she and Elsie and Christine-Kathleen, as they left the cinema and the others walked with her to the bus stop. Elsie wanted to know what you had to do to get a screen test and the other girl said it would help to be in Hollywood, not Yorkshire. Both of them lived in the town, five minutes walk away, and Elsie said she could stay the night if she wanted. But there was no way of letting her parents know. Elsie's had a phone but hers didn't.

Deanna Durbin was still alive, Jean had read somewhere. She wondered if she still looked like Elsie or if she had had her face lifted and her hair dyed and gone on diets. Elsie's face was plump and soft, very wrinkled about the eyes, and her hair was white and thin. She smiled faintly in her sleep and gave a little snore. Jean moved her chair closer and took hold of Elsie's hand. That made the smile come back but Elsie didn't wake.

The beast had come along in his car about ten minutes after the girls had gone and Jean was certain the bus wasn't coming. It was the last bus and she hadn't known what to do. This had happened before, the driver just hadn't turned up and had got the sack for it, but that hadn't made the bus come. On that occasion she had gone to Elsie's and Elsie's mother had phoned her parents' next-door neighbours. She thought that if she did that for a second time and put Mr and Mrs Rawlings to that sort of trouble, her dad would probably stop her ever going to the pictures again.

It wasn't dark. At midsummer it

wouldn't get dark till after ten. If it had been she mightn't have gone with the beast. Of course he didn't seem a beast then, but young, a boy really, and handsome and quite nice. And it was only five miles. Mr Rawlings was always saying five miles was nothing, he used to walk five miles to school every day and five miles back. But she couldn't face the walk and besides, she wanted a ride in a car. It would only be the third time she had ever been in one. Still, she would have refused his offer if he hadn't said what he had when she told him where she lived.

'You'll know the Rawlings then. Mrs Rawlings is my sister.'

It wasn't true but it sounded true. She got in beside him. The car wasn't really his, it belonged to the man he worked for, he was a chauffeur, but she found that out a lot later.

'Lovely evening,' he said. 'You been gallivanting?'

'I've been to the pictures,' she said.

After a couple of miles he turned a little way down a lane and stopped the car outside a derelict cottage. It looked as if no one could possibly live there but he said he had to see someone, it would only take a minute and she could come too. By now it was dusk but there were no lights on in the cottage. She remembered he was Mrs Rawlings's brother. There must have been a good ten years between them but that hadn't bothered her. Her own sister was ten years older than she was.

She followed him up the path which was overgrown with weeds and brambles. Instead of going to the front door he led her round the back where old apple trees grew among waist-high grass. The back of the house was a ruin, half its rear wall tumbled down.

'There's no one here,' she said.

He didn't say anything. He took hold of her and pulled her down into the long grass, one hand pressed hard down over her mouth. She hadn't known anyone could be so strong. He took his hand away to pull her clothes off and she screamed then, but the screaming was just a reflex, a release of fear, and otherwise useless for there was no one to hear.

What he did was rape. She knew that now – well, had known it soon after it happened, only no one called it that then. No one spoke of it. Nowadays the word was on

everyone's lips. It seemed to her that nine out of ten police serials on television were about it. Rape, the crime against women. Rape, that these days you went into court and talked about. You went to self-defence classes to stop it happening to you. You attended groups and shared your experience with other victims.

At first she had been most concerned to find out if he had injured her. Torn her, broken bones. But there was nothing like that. Because she was all right, whole, and he was gone, she stopped crying. She heard the car start up and then move away. Walking home wasn't exactly painful, more a stiff achy business, rather the way she had felt the day after she and Elsie had been learning to do the splits. She had to do it, anyway, she had no choice. As it was, her father was in a rage, wanting to know what time she thought this was.

'Anything could have happened to you,' her mother said.

Something had. She had been raped. She went up to bed so that they wouldn't see she couldn't stop shivering. She didn't sleep at all that night. In the morning she told herself it could have been worse, at least she wasn't dead. It never crossed her mind to say anything to anyone about what had happened, she was too ashamed, too afraid of what they would think. It was past, she kept telling herself, it was all over.

One thing worried her most. A baby. Suppose she had a baby. Never in all her life was she so relieved about anything, so happy, as when she saw that first drop of blood run down the

71

inside of her leg a day early. She shouted for joy. She was all right, the blood cleansed her of it, and now no one need ever know.

Trauma? That was the word they used nowadays. It meant a scar. There was no scar that you could see and no scar she could feel in her body, but it was years before she would let a man come near her. Afterwards she was glad about that, glad that she had waited, that she hadn't met someone else before Kenneth. But at the time she thought about what had happened every day, she re-lived what had happened, the shock and the pain and the fear, and she called the man who had done that to her the beast.

Eight years went by before she saw him again. She was out with Kenneth; he had just been demobbed from the Air Force and they were walking down the High Street arm-in-arm. Kenneth had asked her to marry him and they were going to buy the engagement ring. It was a big jewellers with several aisles and the beast was quite a long way away, on some errand for his employer, she supposed, but she saw him and he saw her. He winked.

He winked just as he had just now in the day-room. Jean shut her eyes. When she opened them again Elsie was awake.

'How long have you been there, dear?'

'About half an hour,' Jean said.

'Are those flowers for me? You know how I love freesias. We'll get someone to put them in water. I don't have to do a thing in here, don't lift a finger, I'm a lady of leisure.'

'Elsie,' said Jean, 'what was the name of that girl we went to the pictures with when we saw *Three Smart Girls*?'

'What?'

'It was 1938. In the summer.'

'I don't know, I shall have to think. My memory's not what it was. Bob used to say I looked like Deanna Durbin.'

'We all said you did.'

'Constance, her name was. We called her Connie.'

'So we did,' said Jean.

Elsie began talking of the girls they had been to school with. She could remember all their Christian names and most of their surnames. Jean found a vase, filled it with water and put the freesias into it because they showed signs of wilting. Her engagement ring still fitted on her finger, though it was a shade tighter. How worried she had

been that Kenneth would be able to tell she wasn't a virgin! They said men could always tell. But of course, when the time came, he couldn't. It was just another old wives' tale.

Elsie, who already had her first baby, had worn rose-coloured taffeta at their wedding. And her husband had been Kenneth's best man. John was born nine months later and the twins eighteen months after that. She had had her hands full. That was the time, when the children were little, that she thought less about the beast and what had happened than at any other time in her life. She forgot him for months on end. Anne, her youngest, was just five when she saw him again.

> ## His eyes were on her and he did what he always did. He winked

She was meeting the other children from school. They hadn't got a car then, it was years before they had a car. On the way to the school they were going to the shoe shop to buy Anne a new pair of shoes. The Red Lion was just closing for the afternoon. He came out of the public bar, not too steady on his feet, and he almost bumped into her. She said, 'Do you mind?' before she saw who it was. He stepped back, looked into her face and winked. She was outraged. For two pins she'd have told Kenneth the whole tale that evening.

But of course she couldn't. Not now.

'I don't know what you mean about your memory,' she said to Elsie. 'You've got a wonderful memory.'

Elsie smiled. It was the same pretty teenager's smile, only they didn't use that word then. You were just a person between twelve and twenty.

'What do you think of this place, then?'

'It's lovely,' said Jean. 'I'm sure you've done the right thing.'

She kissed Elsie goodbye and said she'd come back next week.

'Use the shortcut next time,' said Elsie. 'Through the garden and in by the French windows next-door.'

'I'll remember.'

She wasn't going to leave that way, though. She went back down the corridor and hesitated outside the day-room door. The last time she'd seen the beast, up till an hour ago, they were both growing old. Kenneth was

dead. John was a grandfather himself, though a young one, the twins were joint directors of a prosperous business in Australia, and Anne was a surgeon in London. Jean had never learned to drive and the car was given up when Kenneth died. She was waiting at that very bus stop, the one where he had picked her up all those years before. The bus came and he got off it, an old man with white hair, his face yellowish and wrinkled. But she knew him, she would have known him anywhere. He gave her one of his rude stares and he winked. This time it was an exaggerated, calculated wink, the whole side of his face screwed up and he squeezed his eye shut.

She pushed open the day-room door. The television was still on but he wasn't there. His wheelchair was empty. Then she saw him. He was being brought back from the bathroom, she supposed. A nurse held him tightly by one arm and he leaned on her. His other arm rested, it seemed just as heavily, on the padded top of a crutch. His legs, in pyjama trousers, were half-buckled, and on his face was an expression of torment as, with the nurse's help and to the nurse's whispered encouragement, he took small tottering steps.

Jean looked at him. She stared at him and his eyes met hers. Then she winked. She saw what she had never thought to see happen to an old person. A rich dark blush spread across his face. He turned away his eyes. Jean tripped across the room towards the outer door, like a sixteen-year-old.

Nuptial bliss?

SAM TAYLOR *watches the wedding of the year unravel...*

IT CAME AS A GREAT SURPRISE to his long-suffering friends when they discovered that someone had actually agreed to marry Fungus Friend, the man who claims to be supernaturally attuned to female *parfum* of any kind yet douses himself in athlete's-foot powder every day – and an even greater shock that this deluded creature was none other than a stunning beauty, a member of the Scottish aristocracy with a long list of letters after her name. After much discussion, it was generally agreed that she had been drugged into submission and that eventually she would come to her senses. But by then it was probably going to be too late.

As she gracefully glided down the aisle to meet her fate, there were silent murmurs of 'Run, run' from women unable to contain their sisterhood instincts. Her relatives sat expectantly on the right-hand side of the church. There wasn't a cheap hat or threadbare sporran among them; they had come down from the Highlands in all their finery. Little did they expect to be greeted by the sight of Fungus Friend attired in a nine-piece orange check suit complemented by spats and a fob watch encrusted with a cameo portrait of himself – as anyone who knows him is fully aware, there is nothing Fungus Friend likes more than looking at his own visage, a stance that came as quite a shock to the official photographer, who was eventually reduced to physically abusing the groom in order to squeeze the bride into the rose-tinted photographs. Her hand-woven silk organza gown looked priceless, a fact not wasted on Fungus, who was busy taking orders for cheap copies behind her back, to be delivered by the end of the reception by his trusty Taiwanese tailor. The more he sold, the greater the reduction in his own annual couture bill.

Meanwhile, no expense had been spared by her proud parents. The reception was a lavish affair. A Raj-style banquet was laid on and champagne of the highest quality was quaffed by the bucket-load, particularly by the usher conscripted in to video the event for posterity, with the result that the lens seemed to spend most of its time pointed at the floor filming the warp and weft of the carpet. He was ably accompanied by several other characters from Fungus's nefarious past. On more than one occasion, the more highly educated of the group had to retrieve an extremely inebriated former go-go dancer from underneath the top table where she was boldly attempting to reveal a Scotsman's secret. By the time the father of the bride stood for his speech, there was barely a sober member of the groom's entourage left in the house.

The bride's father gallantly chose to ignore the disintegrating scene and gave a heart-warming speech he had obviously prepared for the day his daughter married an upstanding member of the community. As this had not transpired, he read the speech out anyway. There wasn't a dry eye on their side of the room. 'How much worse can it get?' the increasingly distraught Scots were heard to murmur.

Unfortunately, many of their number had no idea that Fungus Friend had insisted on organising the entertainment himself, with the result that he, personally, was going to sing, for a full forty minutes, at his own wedding, despite a protest petition signed by over two hundred people, including all the residents in the neighbouring area. Small wonder that those who had heard him sing before were currently anaesthetising themselves with anything available.

But first there was the best man's speech, given by a leading member of London's literati, a poor unsuspecting fellow who had agreed to stand only on the understanding that he would be reimbursed his train fare and that he would be able to plug his new book. He had known the groom for a long time, he explained, but only because he was still waiting to get his money back. He thanked the bride's parents profusely for their hospitality, and wondered if they were aware that their new son-in-law had a penchant for dyeing his eyebrows, wearing strange leather garments and fleecing his friends at every available opportunity. Silence, save for the uncontrollable bouts of hysteria emanating from Fungus's more knowing side of the room.

By the time the chairs had been cleared for the first waltz, a large contingent of elder Scotsmen had hurriedly convened in the gentlemen's convenience. Stunned and shell-shocked, the men from the Highlands wanted answers. What had gone wrong? How could this have happened? Who was this nancy? 'We were told he was a millionaire publisher,' they chorused. The peals of uncontrollable laughter were still ringing in their ears as they boarded the train, bound straight for their lawyers' office.

ILLUSTRATION BY CRAMER

DECLARATION OF *Waugh*

How Evelyn Waugh's 'late lunacy' was triggered by a hostile conversation with **ALAN BRIEN** at White's Club

Three in the morning. The telephone rings in my bedroom. My wife groans. It is my employer, Randolph Churchill. He did not hesitate to wake anyone – millionaires, Cabinet ministers, film stars, gangsters, press lords. Accompanying him on his noisy, inflammatory quests and crusades, criss-crossing the globe in private jets and golden trains, linking St Tropez gambling casinos, Westminster lobbies, university libraries and grand country houses, I felt I had been conscripted into a Sherlock Holmes adventure. My blood raced. Some game was afoot!

'It's a postcard,' explained Randolph. 'From the Little Captain. To Annie. About both of us.' I felt a thrill of pleasure. To be the subject of even a line or two passing between the Little Captain (my favourite author, Evelyn Waugh) and his playmate, grand-daughter of the Earl of Wemys, widow of the third Baron O'Neill, later the wife of the 3rd Viscount Rothermere, and now married to Ian Fleming, creator of James Bond – was this not calculated to flatter even the most radical of council-house journalists? Randolph had given me the magic pass to the world of the Establishment. The message ran something like this: 'Off to Ceylon for a sea voyage. All my friends in London appear to have turned against me. Even Randolph, my oldest, hired a Jew to attack me in White's.'

> ## 'All my friends in London appear to have turned against me. Even Randolph hired a Jew to attack me in White's'

Randolph set out to decode it. Not much in the tropical cruise. Not since he left the Army had Waugh failed to escape from the boredom of post-Christmas domesticity every February. The falling away of his friends was a well-known fact of his life, and widely thought to be his own fault for becoming irritatingly predictable. His relations with some of his dearest companions had declined into schoolboy tantrums, silly japes and jests. Even Annie had been provoked to strike back, in public – once dislodging his ear trumpet by the blow of a spoon and another time pushing his face into a pyramid of eclairs. But it was the hiring of the Jew that escalated Randolph's laughter to near hysteria as he spun a fantasy about an agency that supplied the top people not just with cooks and butlers but also rootless, Marxist bravos trained to undermine our best authors even in their own clubs, driving them to the verge of paranoia.

Randolph, who believed a true gentleman always

Evelyn Waugh in 1959 (his ear trumpet can just be seen on the left)

PHOTOGRAPHS COURTESY: ASSOCIATED NEWSPAPERS /REX FEATURES

forgot any conversation after midnight, had suppressed all memories of his introduction of me to the Little Captain only two days before. I was in no doubt this was the origin of the postcard, which sprang from an increasingly hostile conversation between Waugh and me, with some uncharacteristically ineffective umpiring from his old friend.

Contrary to all I had heard about Waugh as a testy figure wearing a purple papier-mâché mask of a face, 'inoffensive' was the word that sprang to mind. I was particularly surprised by the eyes, embarrassed by their own prominence. More than anyone, he recalled Augustus John's portrait of the youthful Dylan Thomas.

It is always difficult to know how to behave when you meet an idol face to face. To say little is to risk losing a chance of a contact that might never occur again. To spill over with compliments he has heard so often is to risk being boringly pushy. For the first half-hour of the afternoon, I chose silence. At last, in a pause, I asked, politely, if Waugh had read a somewhat waspish, anonymous profile of himself in the obscure weekly paper, *Truth*.

'I do not know the publication,' he replied, releasing a flash of irritation as of a diner focusing on a clumsy waiter.

I knocked back a huge drink and intervened again. 'That is rather odd, surely, Mr Waugh,' I said, 'considering there is a brief letter from you in the current issue correcting an error in that profile.'

He turned slowly, the candle-power of his headlamp eyes frighteningly brighter. 'I assume, then, that you must be the author of that miserably ill-informed piece. It is scarcely probable that anyone else would either remember or care about its contents.'

The gage was thrown down. 'It has certainly made its impression on you,' I said, trembling a little. 'It's about time somebody called your bluff and exposed the ghastly snobbery that infects all your writing today.'

From now on, Waugh directed all his remarks through Randolph. 'Who did you say this person was?' he inquired. 'I knew the club had declined but I had not expected to be insulted here by someone so obviously lacking the equipment of a gentleman.'

Randolph looked uneasy in the role of mediator. 'Really, Evelyn, you can't talk like that. Mr Brien is a friend of mine and a guest in the club.'

'I have had occasion to speak to you before about your taste in low companions,' Waugh remarked with cold disdain. 'He is clearly out of place here.'

'I do not want to be a gentleman, thank you. What are your claims to the rank, anyway? Birth? Breeding? You were born in a flat above the dairy in the Finchley Road.'

'Your friend, as you call him, Randolph, continues with his stupidities. I am not at all ashamed of my upbringing. Tell him my family had moved from what he calls "the flat above the dairy" before I was born.'

'Good point,' I said. 'So, you were conceived above the dairy in the Finchley Road.' And I spewed out all the half-truths that I had collected and honed for my profile in *Truth*: Waugh at the dimmest, wettest college in Oxford, running into debt keeping up with the rich, converting to Catholicism as a ladder for social climbing, sneaking into Debrett as a footnote to a second marriage – even here at White's a joke figure. I believed only smidgens of my indictment. We all three drank late, and as we drank my attacks grew more and more exaggerated.

The duel lasted half a day in 1954. When *The Ordeal of Gilbert Pinfold* was published in 1957 Randolph rang me at 3 am to point out the parallels between what I had said and what the persecuting voices had jeered in the autobiographical novel. I did not tell the story until I contributed an obituary of Waugh to the *Spectator* in 1966. Randolph was convinced Mrs Fleming would release the missing postcard as the key to what Waugh himself called 'my late lunacy'. She was a perpetual fountain of gossip and fantasy. But despite several requests, she held on to the evidence of the hired Jew in White's. Pity.

Oscar's Legacy

*For former Oldie wine critic **MERLIN HOLLAND**, 'the love that dared not speak its name' was his grandfather Oscar Wilde's love for his wife and children*

Some years ago when he was commissioned by George Weidenfield to write a biography of Oscar Wilde, Sheridan Morley asked whether it was a good idea when so many had already appeared. 'Maybe,' said the publisher, 'but the story is so moving it needs to be retold every ten years or so.' If one trebles the time-span to a generation, the same, I feel, is true for the book that my father wrote in 1954, *Son of Oscar Wilde*, if only to remind the world that Oscar Wilde was married, had two sons and that the family line continues.

Conditioned as we were in the mid-Fifties (and still are to a great extent) to the either/or of sexual polarities, the idea of Oscar Wilde as a loving father and an intermittently dutiful parent, mending his children's toys and crawling around their nursery floor, was improbable; so improbable, in fact, that it generated more than two hundred letters to my father, Vyvyan, from complete strangers, most of whom were writing to say that they had never imagined Wilde with a wife, let alone children. Oscar Wilde as a warm-hearted, approachable, fallible human being, behaving like the rest of us at home, whatever he got up to in the West End, was quite a new angle. It gave the story added poignancy, especially since it came from his own son, who finally at the age of seventy had found the courage to relive a childhood brought crashing to the ground by the madness of his father.

Those who had known Vyvyan before the War said that the change in him after writing the book was astounding. He had, as it were, laid to rest the bitter memory of those early years by the cathartic effect of recording them for posterity.

However, it is only in the last few years, while researching a book on Wilde's posthumous reputation, that I have realised how the repercussions of Wilde's downfall and disgrace went far beyond my father's childhood and affected the greater part of his adult life. Having to leave England for the Continent with 'a grim and hysterical governess' shortly after Oscar's arrest in April 1895 was something of an adventure; Vyvyan and his elder brother Cyril, respectively ten and eleven, then had no proper schooling for a year and only the minimum necessary adult supervision, the dream of any child of that age; the change of name to Holland on account of a Swiss hotel-keeper, who asked them to leave because he felt that having the wife and children of the infamous Oscar Wilde under his roof would be bad for business, was vaguely disturbing but no more than that. No, the real tragedy started in April 1898, less than a year after Oscar's release, with their mother Constance's death, and with it the single object of love in their fragile world was removed and its place was taken by Victorian self-righteous hypocrisy at its worst.

Letters which have surfaced since my father wrote his book show that Oscar started corresponding with his wife almost as soon as he was released from prison. She in turn wrote to him once a week and sent him photographs of his sons. There was talk of a reunion, but she was dissuaded by family and friends who were concerned that Oscar could be a corrupting influence on his children, so on her death there was no question of his having any hand in their upbringing. They were dispatched back to England, to be remoulded by straitlaced relatives whose principal aim was to brainwash the boys into forgetting their father completely, even suggesting obliquely that he was no longer alive and thus preventing the boys from asking after him.

One of the constant and distressing

Facing page: Constance Wilde and Cyril, 1889
Left: Cyril (left) and Vyvyan in Heidelberg, 1896
Below: Vyvyan Holland and me about the time he wrote *Son of Oscar Wilde*. I was then exactly the same age as my father had been when he last saw Oscar

features of the next nine years in my father's life was to be the sense of uncleanness and contamination which Oscar Wilde's name seemed to evoke with these figures in authority. It was the start of many years of concealment and having to cope with what the outside world perceived as the shame of their family history, which Cyril would take to his grave at the Front in 1915 and would stay with my father until he was sixty.

My father's first marriage, for example, in 1914 made Fleet Street headlines – 'Oscar Wilde's Son To Be Married' – much to his own embarrassment and the fury of his mother's family, who boycotted the wedding. Cyril's application to become a career soldier in the Royal Artillery in 1903 had to be accompanied by a copy of his birth certificate on which he naturally figured as the son of Oscar Wilde, a fact which he also gave on the application form under 'Father's Name' but which was heavily scored through and replaced in another hand with 'Father Dead'. The Civil Service Commission needed to preserve the birth certificate and the documents relating to his change of name for its records, but on the file it states that the Commission was 'specially desired to regard this evidence as confidential'.

Later, in the 1920s, my father was asked by Frank Harris to contribute openly to the corrections in his *Life of Oscar Wilde*, but he refused, saying that he craved anonymity and self-effacement

to the extent of signing his published translations from the French with his initials only, and those reversed as HBV.

If the writing of *Son of Oscar Wilde* helped my father to come to terms with his past, I believe it also prepared important ground for the future. The acceptance of Oscar 'warts and all' was a stage through which the general public needed to pass as much as the son who felt himself so betrayed by what he saw as the self-destructive behaviour of his father. There was a tendency, even as late as 1960, to keep Wilde the man and Wilde the writer at arm's length from one another, the former still tainted with his scandal and unmentionable depravities. All this was changed by the publication of Oscar's collected letters in 1962,

but it needed a further act of courage on Vyvyan's part to allow their unex-purgated publication, especially those from the period after prison which are often unequivocally homosexual in tone. I am certain that the critical acclaim of his autobiography played no small part in the decision to allow his father to appear 'full frontal' to the public, but it is a sobering thought that the law under which Oscar Wilde was convicted in 1895 was not repealed until three months before my father's death in 1967.

DIGNITAS

'Does it contain nuts?'

Nigel Hawthorne

picks his top six

1. Joan Littlewood
A greater influence on me than anyone I have ever met. I frequently dream about her. The theatre sadly misses her cheek and her imagination.

2. Ingrid Bergman
I fell in love with her watching *For Whom the Bell Tolls* and worked with her during her terrible battle with lymph gland cancer. A very courageous, beautiful person. When I came to her trailer during *A Woman Called Golda* I was dressed for my role as King Abdullah of Trans-Jordan. She nearly fell over laughing. It endeared her to me for ever.

3. Mary Poppins
For surviving that really awful film which, for a lot of people, paradoxically, brought her to their attention for the first time.

4. Thelma Holt
My producer with the RSC on *King Lear* and a close friend for thirty-five years. Known affectionately to her staff as Mad Woman, she is loquacious and caring. Perhaps one day she'll be Dame Thelma. For her contribution to the world theatre scene it would not only be appropriate, but would suit her.

5. Joan Collins
For looking as good in her late sixties as most women in their mid-thirties.

6. Gwen Ffrangcon-Davies
We didn't meet until she was in her mid-nineties, though many times I'd seen her on stage. She died when she was 101. We had become close friends. A great and highly intelligent actress with a naughty sense of fun and a phenomenal memory. I miss her very much.

PIN-UPS

Four Foyer Friends

Surprisingly, no-hoper **WILFRED DE'ATH** *actually likes a few of the people he's met in various French foyers*
Illustrations by LARRY

Wilfred

Not all the Frenchmen who do the rounds of the foyers (homeless shelters) are tramps or drunks or hopeless neurotics. Some of them are quite sane. And intelligent. Some have even become my friends...

Jean, sixty-five, is known on the foyer circuit as 'the Professor', because of a didactic way of speaking. He was once a director of a large oil company. He has worked in America and Canada and understands English. The loss of his wife and children (in a car crash) would seem to have traumatised him for, since then, he has lived exclusively in the foyers. A handsome man, whom all the foyer waitresses and cleaners adore, Jean is, in fact, a professional gambler. He once sold me his umbrella for twenty francs (£2) and put the money on a horse that came in at 100–1. Jean spent

Jean

the two thousand francs on a luxury hotel room and a rich meal – quite an easy thing to do in Toulouse – and was back in the foyer the following night.

He says he will retire to an apartment in Cahors one day, but I doubt this. I doubt, too, whether he has a father, aged ninety-two, still living in Alsace, who will one day leave Jean all his fortune. The fact is, Jean just enjoys living in foyers. He is extremely well-read and knows his way round the European political scene. He lectures me occasionally on British

Gérard

politics, about which he knows more than I do. He pays me the compliment of saying that I am the only serious Englishman he has ever met.

Gérard, fifty, is another foyer friend, based in Angers, but constantly on the move. He spends all his days in various municipal libraries reading about the Third Reich, and he knows more about Adolf Hitler than Adolf can have known about himself. Not that Gérard has any fascist tendencies – he is horrified by recent events in Austria and is a genuine French socialist and republican who believes that Britain will not progress unless she gets rid of her royal family. Gérard is the kind of man who would share his last meal with you and can always be relied on for a loan. The only thing that upsets him is when I ask him if he is *au chômage*, i.e. out of work. 'I do not believe in work,' he says with dignity, and has never worked in his life. He has no family. I have met many social outcasts in the French foyers, but Gérard is the real thing. He says he will commit suicide when he reaches sixty-five.

I have made many friends among the foyer staff as well. Michel, the director of the one in Limoges, with his ugly, broken, ex-boxer's nose and his immensely caring attitude towards even his most difficult clients, is almost certainly homosexual. I have to admit that he brings out vague homosexual inclinations in myself, though that may be no more than one of the symptoms of paranoia from which I suffer, all part of the increasing narcissism of old age.

One of Michel's most demanding

clients is not a man at all. Aida, the foyer tart, has lived there for seven years. She was expelled from Morocco after serving two years for a *crime passionnel*. At the foyer, she has been known to give *pipe* (fellatio) for as little at twenty francs (£2). She is always immensely kind to me: indeed, we have struck up a weird kind of friendship. Whenever I am really short of money, which is most of the time, she goes off to the Gare des Bénédictins (the Limoges station) for a couple of hours and returns with a fistful of two-hundred-franc notes for me. What she does to obtain these I have no idea. (Michel once told me that she specialises in sex for the handicapped – whatever it is, it must be extremely well paid.) Yet Aida is old and ugly. It is a mystery I prefer not to penetrate. (I cannot even admit to myself that I am living off the earnings of prostitution.)

The one thing I really cannot bear is to encounter other Englishmen in the French foyers. There was a certain (homosexual) ex-public school boy, a former head boy of Dulwich College, who had drifted into alcoholism, at the foyer in Toulouse. He was one of the most atrocious people I have ever met, though he spoke superb French. Only recently in Limoges I met a young tramp from Fleet, Hampshire, of all places. I didn't like him either. I suppose what I really detest in these people is the mirror image of myself. One never knows who is going to turn up next. An *Oldie* subscriber?

Aida

Belly Fine View

On a trip to China, **FRANCIS KING** *marvelled at the Great Wall... of American flab*

Illustration by MARTIN HONEYSETT

Simultaneously but separately, a psychologist friend of mine and I decided that the time had come for us to pay a visit to the Land of the Long March and the Great Leap Forward. Since John is both more practical and more leisured than I am, I was happy when he proposed that he should be responsible for making the arrangements. I was less happy when he eventually announced that he had booked us on a package with Saga – the acronym, so one is sometimes told, for Send All Grannies Abroad. If I have the choice, I always prefer the company of people less decrepit than I am. To my relief, the other eight English participants proved to be lithe, nippy and – with the exception of one dear old girl fearful of going anywhere, even to a restaurant lavatory, unaccompanied – full of initiative.

> ## I had never in my life seen so many human jumbos corralled together

However, when we arrived at the luxurious Beijing Shangri-La Hotel (each night the maid would place a text from James Hilton's *Lost Horizon* on my pillow instead of the usual chocolate) and met the nineteen Americans also on the tour, I was aghast. They were all courteous, many of them were chummy; but I had never in my life seen so many human jumbos corralled together. At the Peking Opera two of them stood throughout, no doubt fearful that if they jammed themselves into seats, they might be stuck there forever. Having been transported to the Great Wall, some of them declined to mount on foot or even, understandably, to get into the tiny and fragile-looking cable cars, and remained dormant on the coach, a prey to the ubiquitous and importunate sellers of souvenirs.

I was walking beside Bud, a mountainous Texan, at the entrance to the first building of the Summer Palace, when suddenly he fell forward, appeared to bounce upwards on the enormous balloon of his belly, and then lay still. Having

assumed that he had suffered a heart attack, I steeled myself for the unattractive task of giving him the kiss of life. But he then rolled over and assured me: 'It's OK, OK! No problem! Just tripped.' After having lain there for a minute or two, he scrambled to his feet with my assistance. A man less lavishly cushioned might have broken some bones.

Many of these Americans had an insatiable appetite. No doubt to compensate for the expense of our luxurious hotel, we usually ate in Chinese restaurants entirely empty – for reasons at once apparent when the same indifferent food was yet again set out on a number of lazy susans – of any Chinese people, but crammed with tourist parties like our own. Showing an energy conspicuously lacking during our sightseeing, the Americans would at once convert these lazy susans into frenetic ones, whirling them round in their determination to tuck into everything on offer before anyone else could do so. They showed the same energy over shopping, waddling over at a remarkable speed to some stall piled with junk, while the rest of us waited, with mounting impatience, to enter a temple or garden on our group ticket. Not unnaturally, our Chinese guide made no effort to discourage this mania for acquiring 'silk' (i.e. polyester) scarves, blouses and ties, clumsily carved jade animals, and coarsely embroidered doilies and tablecloths. After all, guides all over the world rely on their commissions.

After a day or two, it was interesting to see how almost everyone had been cast in a role by the others, and was prepared to conform to it. John was our graciously patrician pundit. One of the Englishmen was the jokey one; another, the one who could always be relied on to relay our complaints, in a voice of hurt persistence, if things had gone amiss. An American woman was our glamorous grandmother, an American man our loquacious, nervously ingratiating Woody Allen. My role, I soon discovered, was to be 'ironic' – 'Oh, I love your English irony!' I was told more than once by an American woman, in an odd and disquieting variation of the usual 'Oh, I love your English accent!' Usually, such tour groups contain someone who arouses dislike or disapproval in everyone else and is therefore fated to be demonised. But we were fortunate. There was not a single such character among us.

John and I were soon living double lives. There was our Saga one of boarding our coach each morning – no doubt our tough little driver had acquired his impressive muscles through constant pushing of his more mountainous passengers up the steps; of saluting everyone else with, in my case at least, an often weary bonhomie; and of then joining in repeating the elementary Chinese phrases taught to us by our guide before he embarked on a lecture on some such subject as China's centuries-long ownership of Tibet. But soon we also had another, secret, even more interesting life.

Rambling through the thickets of the internet in his search for information about Beijing, John had stumbled on a site created by an individual who was clearly a computer wizard. This man, whom I shall call Ting, told John that he would be delighted to meet us on our visit and to show us his city. We suspected that we might well find that he was a professional guide and that he would charge us accordingly. But, to our amazement, he turned out to be an extremely wealthy businessman, able to write a weirdly stilted English but almost wholly incapable of speaking it. Since he was constantly obliged to rush off to other engagements, he was with us only intermittently. 'What sort of car would you like tomorrow?' he asked at our first meeting. Jokingly, John replied, 'Well, how about a Rolls Royce?' So far from being amused, our new friend looked embarrassed. There was a large Audi, he told us apologetically. When the Audi, with its smoked windows, arrived the next morning, it contained not merely its driver but also an interpreter.

Throughout that day our new friend kept appearing and disappearing. When he was not with us, there were frequent calls by mobile phone. When that evening he took us to a Chinese restaurant, it was not in the least like those that we had visited with our Saga companions. We were even accommodated in a *salle privée*.

In Britain, the one surviving taboo is money. But our host talked about money constantly and with total freedom. When John invited him, along with a scientist friend of his proficient in English, his twelve-year-old daughter and the scientist's nine-year-old son, to dinner at our hotel, he asked at the close of the meal whether it had been expensive. Embarrassed, John replied: 'Well, it wasn't all that cheap.' This answer clearly did not satisfy him. He wanted to know precisely how much John had paid. At a subsequent meal in a Chinese restaurant, he told us that it had cost him only six dollars per person, but that any foreigner would have had to pay far more than that. When he presented us with scroll paintings as farewell gifts, he informed us that each had cost four hundred dollars. Whether Christie's or Sotheby's would confirm that price, I somehow doubt; but I am no expert on modern Chinese scroll painting.

Inevitably, unless the interpreter or the scientist friend was there to help out, conversation was extremely difficult. But two things that our friend said through the medium of the scientist have stuck in my mind. The first was a remark about the different criteria by which we in the West and the Chinese define a good government. People in the West, he told us, ask, 'Is it a democracy?' and if the answer is yes, then, however inefficient or corrupt, they give it their approval. The Chinese ask, 'Is it improving the quality of life for the majority of the population?' and, if the answer is yes, then the government, whether democracy, oligarchy or dictatorship, can be accounted good. A similar thing was said to me a few years ago by the novelist Han Suyin, who added – with what truth I do not know – that for centuries there was no word for democracy in Chinese. The other point that our new friend was eager to get across to us was that Western commentators continued to write about China as it was ten years ago, instead of as it was now. We could see for ourselves, he said, that huge changes had taken place, and that the rate of these changes was constantly accelerating.

What impressed me most in China was precisely what impressed me most in Japan when I arrived to live there for the first time in the early Sixties: boundless energy and a determination not merely to survive but to push constantly upwards and onwards. Whenever our bus stopped, we would be surrounded by laughing, cajoling, clamouring peddlers, male and female, of all ages. Few of them ever made a sale, but their spirits never faltered. I soon found myself comparing them, so full of dauntless, cheerful initiative, with the forlorn, silent young people sitting out begging in our streets, with a placard saying 'Hungry' or 'Homeless' and a dog beside them. The first thing a Chinese would do in similar circumstances would be to eat the dog. Then he would lay siege to any tourist bus in sight with Hard Rock T-shirts, miniature replicas of Big Ben and statues of Princess Diana.

In Japan, in the now distant Sixties, foreigners like myself used to be condescending about the general trashiness of the consumer goods on offer, many of them, such as cars, manufactured under licence from foreign firms. It is easy to be equally condescending about the consumer goods on offer in China today. But a visit to Shanghai, the Hong Kong of the mainland, a maelstrom electric with entrepreneurial vigour, convinced me that, in twenty years, China, no doubt by then united with Taiwan, will be the most powerful commercial power in the world.

'You're not taking the microwave, are you?'

The JOY of SECTS

Following a health crisis, actor and film-maker **KENNETH GRIFFITH** *found comfort among a variety of Christians*

bout nine months ago I confronted a big crisis in my life: I had reason to suspect that I was soon to die – as did my medical advisers. The first intimation that I had taken a wrong direction was when we were filming beside the tragic Boer War battlefield of Paardeberg. It is overlooked by 'Kitchener's Kopje', a high hill topped by massive boulders; Field Marshal Lord Kitchener had chosen it so that he could supervise his brutal bombardment of the four and a half thousand Boers (including women and, no doubt, a few children) who were trapped there. My colleagues tried to dissuade me from climbing it but I suffer an old-fashioned compulsion to fulfil my duties, and up I went, at the age of seventy-seven. Afterwards, the pain developed into excruciating agony, moving from my spine down my right leg and into my right foot.

Back in London I was treated by anxious and caring medical people, but out of hospital, I found myself living in a physical and mental nightmare. Sleep – except through fearful exhaustion – was impossible, and for sanity's sake I discovered that my only escape was to shuffle round the block at, say, 4 am. The cold night air, above all else, shifted the frightening predicament, together with the novelty of a dark and deserted Islington. The shuffle took me about forty minutes, by the end of which I felt a good deal better. Of course, I pondered on the journey, down amongst the flinty reality of poor human life. And then, one night, I stopped by a lamp-post and thought to myself: 'Griffith, if you survive this you had better begin to think deeper...' I have several times wondered if this was, in any way, a prayer.

I am an agnostic. I was brought up, by my beloved paternal grandparents, a Christian, Wesleyan Methodist, but a hardish life – though threaded with good fortune – has forced me to doubt the Resurrection and the water-into-wine, etc. Of course I am ingrained with the Great Man's message; anything decent about me is driven by His principles – even (for the benefit of startled English people) my

support of Irish Republicanism. One of my favourite pieces in the New Testament is about Jesus losing his temper in the Temple and footing the wretched businessmen up the arse. My work always aims to tell the whole truth, as against the practices of our lying political masters. Fair, as far as it goes – but what about God the Father? That was the question that shocked me under the lamp-post at 4 am.

My medical friends had warned me to eat well, and since I live virtually alone, I trekked to the better restaurants in my neighbourhood. The following evening I entered a large and pleasant eating place and selected a secluded corner. I would describe myself – on that occasion – as an old, shabby man, with his back very much to the audience. Soon the manager came to my table to assure himself that all was well with me. It was an extraordinary experience in London in 1999. He was a shade swarthy, so I asked him if he was Italian (I suspected the southern half). 'No, I am an Egyptian.' 'Oh, Coptic!' – having struck a clever strain.

'No,' said the Egyptian, 'I belong to the Brethren,' and I was firmly struck, imagining a busy gathering of Egyptian Oxford Groupers. I asked if it would be possible to meet them. I have a strong compulsion to venture onwards. 'Of course you can,' replied the Brother. 'I can collect you in my car at about 9.30 on Sunday morning.' The Meeting Place was beyond the Blackwall Tunnel, and my kind friend's name was Ehab Nashed. I finally deduced that the Brothers – and Sisters – were Plymouth Brethren, and a nicer congregation of people you are unlikely to find. However, I still have my doubts about the Resurrection.

The next day I was pottering up my road, carrying an East Indian bag (bought in Murshidabad, I think) full of groceries from my dear friend Mr Patel's shop, when a cultivated English voice, just behind me, said: 'What a contemplative figure.' And there was a neighbour from diagonally across my road: Mr Stephen Finch, ex-military officer and later an adviser on communications to an oil company. I began to babble about my Spiritual Tussle. As we made our way to my front gate, Stephen talked to me in his quiet voice. Only an Englishman can be as quiet as that, even when declaring the pedigree of the Lord. I asked him if he would come in and continue his advice, and he did so over a cup of tea. Now he and his gentle wife are ever poised to collect me in their car at 10.30 am each Sunday to drive me to their grand Anglican church, Saint Helen's, in the City of London.

But the following Sunday I accompanied my eldest daughter, Eva, and her son, John, to their simple Roman Catholic service, not far from here. The priest, Father John, impressed me even before I had had an opportunity to talk to him. He is what I would describe as young – maybe forty – and Irish. He is as fearless as a man can be, blessedly innocent and as shrewd as reality can teach. Below his Roman vestment he wore workman's trousers and ditto shoes. His is a not-rich parish, and he serves and serves. I have learnt to love that man.

> *Was my pathetic wish to 'look deeper' a prayer? If it was, it has been mysteriously answered*

And, finally, the Jehovah's Witnesses. They have knocked on my doors around the world: in Europe, Africa and India. I remember my astonishment at having two of the good souls rat-a-tat on my isolated door in the little town of Pigg's Peak in Swaziland. They only ask if they can help. Next Wednesday, at 7 pm (on the tick), Mr David Gibson and a colleague – both Jehovah's Witnesses – will be in my house, threading their way through their Bible, trying to persuade me that the supernatural passages about my Hero are a proven fact, and I will have to state painfully that I am not convinced. I have even wondered, uneasily, if I am a servant of Satan; I am a dangerous debater. The most formidable of the Plymouth Brethren, Edwin Cross and his truly delightful wife, expended so much time and good food upon me that I came to dread that their efforts to rescue my soul from scepticism would always be a lost cause. When I told Edwin he urged me to remember that, come what may, I would always be welcome among the Brethren. And that sentiment applies to all those Christian denominations that have suddenly entered my life.

Through this mass of experience I have made a startling discovery. I have had to consider them all – Plymouth Brothers and Sisters, Anglicans, Roman Catholics and Jehovah's Witnesses – and if you isolate the true Christians amongst them all, they are all identical; not a shred of difference between them. I have informed the true Christians, each denomination, that it works 'because every time I am in your company, I feel better'.

Was my pathetic wish 'to look deeper' a prayer? If it was, it has been mysteriously answered. My Egyptian friend, Ehab Nashed, is absolutely clear – 'It is the will of the Lord' – and as my health improves he quietly utters, 'Praise be the Lord!' All I can say is, 'Thank God for true Christians.' If you know what I mean...

ISSUE 198, SEPTEMBER 2005 BY AXEL SCHEFFLER

ISSUE 6, MAY 1992 BY JOHN RYAN

An Enemy of the People

*Oldie cartoonist **TONY HUSBAND** trusted Dr Shipman to treat his family.*
Then friends and neighbours died, and a different picture emerged...

The rumours began in Gee Cross, a village on the edge of Hyde, shortly after Kathleen Grundy had been buried. In the Queen Adelaide, a village pub, I was told that the police were investigating Mrs Grundy's death. A car had been seen outside her house. Suspicions were aroused. Had she died naturally after all? Some time later Sheila Mellor called round. She told us her mum, Win, had died suddenly. Their doctor, Dr Shipman, had told Sheila and her sisters that Win had died of a heart attack brought on by angina. Win, who was very close to her family, had never mentioned angina, though he said she had suffered from it for some time. Dr Shipman did not take kindly to the girls questioning him. He stormed out of the house, leaving the girls with their dead mother still sat in the chair where she had died. We stayed with Sheila for many hours in the garden, stunned by Win's death but not suspicious.

I had met Shipman on a number of occasions. He wasn't our doctor, but came out for emergencies or stood in for a doctor on holiday. He treated our son Paul when he was a baby, and later as a toddler. To be honest, we were always pleased when the doctor at the door was Shipman. You see, he had a reputation in the area for being a good, honest and reliable doctor. No frills, no charming bedside manner, just straight to the point and usually the correct point. He'd treated my mum as well, when she was dying of cancer, and my dad remembered Shipman as brusque and business-like but someone you could trust... and we did.

When the news about Shipman began to emerge, we, the people of Hyde, couldn't believe it. We heard about the bodies being exhumed, we saw his surgery close down, we saw his interview outside the back of the surgery as Primrose, his wife, drove away in the car. He looked assured, annoyed that all this coverage was stopping him getting on with his task of mending the people of Hyde. We didn't believe he'd done it.

Then I began to meet friends and acquaintances who were directly involved, those whose relatives had died under Shipman. A different picture began to emerge. They told of his coldness, how he seemed to toy with the relatives before telling them the bad news. One lady, still shaken by the incident, remembered Shipman telling her over the phone that her mum had died suddenly. She dashed to her mum's house, and entered to find her having a cup of tea with a

friend. Shocked, she rang Shipman. 'Oh, I got it wrong,' he said. 'I meant your mother-in-law.' Another friend from my golf club got a call from Shipman saying his gran had died in his surgery. He dashed down to the surgery to find Shipman with a patient. Shipman pointed to the examination room; my friend went in to find his gran uncovered on the table with her eyes still open. He closed his gran's eyes and covered her up. When he asked Shipman how he could be so callous, his reply was, 'I had living patients to see.'

I remember going in the middle of the night to see our next-door neighbour Frank. Frank had stomach cancer and his wife Marina had knocked us up because Frank was in a lot of pain. I went into the house to hear Frank crying out in pain. He was writhing in his bed, being held down by his nephew. Apparently, Shipman had not arrived that day to administer Frank's daily morphine injection. I was enraged. Frank was a dear old chap and no one these days, I thought, should ever have to suffer like that. When the emergency doctor came to give Frank his painkillers, I was adamant he pass on a message to Shipman that he must never leave Frank like that again. Looking back, I can't help but feel that Shipman was saving the morphine for other uses.

The list grew, and the list was endless. Shipman was tried for just fifteen of his victims, though we all know there were many more. Of course, the verdict was never in doubt. But as I listened to the names being read out in rapid succession, I broke down. All those people, many of whom I knew, murdered by this creature – it was all I could take. We were numb from what we were hearing and watching on TV and radio. We felt betrayed and raw. The world's media were poking about in Hyde's business, calling it 'an uninteresting little town', 'a town full of old people' and – with our connection to the Moors murders –'the centre of evil'.

Hyde is none of these things. It is a close little town, with its share of characters and rogues, of course, but it also has a deep sense of community. Neither is it a tired old folks' home – there's a healthy mix of young and old. Now that the press circus has left town Hyde's people are closing ranks, licking their wounds and looking after each other. We won't get over Shipman. He wheedled his way into the heart of Hyde and tried to destroy it. He didn't do that. He left wounds that may never heal, but he left a community that will come through – definitely.

'Champagne for one, what a saddo'

'Personally, I'd recommend a bit of
self-restraint, you fat bastard'

'Heinz or Campbell's?'

'My husband eats like a bird –
do you have any regurgitated insects?'

THE END OF
The End of the Affair

Artist and costume designer **JOCELYN RICKARDS** *remembers her affair with Graham Greene*

I knew Graham Greene from 1951 until his death in 1991. I have always thought that I knew him well – until quite recently, when he re-emerged as a child-hating Lothario, consumed by an obsessive and jealous passion for Catherine Walston. On television, in print and on the radio, we have been regaled by William Cash and the relics of the Walston family trotting out their recollections of a dour, ill-tempered manic depressive who insisted on having his newspaper ironed if it had been touched by any other hand. Even the BBC connived at the dishonesty inherent in all this reassessment by showing what purported to be the dedication at the front of *The End of the Affair*: 'To Catherine' was spelled out across the screen, yet in fact the dedication simply reads: 'To C.'

I have not read William Cash's *The Third Woman* ('The Secret Passion that Inspired *The End of the Affair*' is its unwieldy subtitle), and since I declined to be interviewed for it I have no right to quibble. But what secret passion is he writing about? Surely not the very open affair Graham and Mrs Walston conducted for a decade.

Graham and I met on the opening day of the Festival of Britain, at a party given at the Institute of Contemporary Arts by the National Book League. I arrived with Freddie Ayer. Graham was standing inside the first room and on the threshold of the second, an unenviable scrum of the great, the good and the mediocre. Freddie – one sniff of the elephant shit – was off to join the throng, having first introduced and abandoned me to Graham. We stood idly talking: I looked into Graham's empty glass, took it from him and said, 'If you promise not to move I shall get you a refill.' He promised, I returned with both our glasses generously topped up, and we continued our conversation. The evening continued at Wilton's restaurant in Jermyn Street. Before leaving the party Graham had scanned the inner room for someone else to ask to dinner. 'How about Rose Macaulay?' he asked. 'Oh yes, I like her,' I replied. Graham was then forty-six and I was twenty-six – it always seemed to me to be a mathematical conundrum that the twenty-year difference in our ages should have remained constant when it appeared so limitlessly inconstant.

After dinner Rose packed us all into her tiny car, more like a treadle sewing-machine than a car, and intrepidly set off to show us the Festival lights, driving the wrong way down a one-way street. Every other motorist honked and shouted at her as she continued imperturbably, no hint that she might possibly be wrong in her gothic features, no disturbance to the grey ruched velvet toque crammed onto her head. We went back to Graham's apartment in St James's Street for the life-giving support of whisky-and-soda. My memory of the rest of the evening is enfeebled by the passage of time, but I do recall remarking that I always confused *The Heart of the Matter* with *The Death of the Heart*. Freddie tut-tutted and frowned, but Graham just gave me a rueful smile.

> *Suddenly the gear changed and we became enthusiastic bedfellows. 'We could marry,' he said*

The following evening at the Coq d'Or Graham and I continued our conversation while Freddie and Solly Zuckerman wandered the groves of academe. During dinner my wandering hands were aching to steal into Graham's. We went on to the Festival, where I was overcome by hiccups. Graham and I arranged to meet for lunch the next day. I was suffused by guilt and had a hangover; I didn't have Graham's telephone number, so I rang directory enquiries and asked them to get on to his St James's Street flat and see if he would accept my call. By the time we were connected he was laughing and said, 'I tried to give you my telephone number last night but you scorned it.' We decided to meet the following week instead.

Astonishing as it now seems, it took us until 1953 to go to bed together – Graham was occupied by Catherine Walston, I by Freddie Ayer. I grew to love Graham before we became lovers and before I fell in love with him. We passed the next two years lunching and dining, going to the cinema and the theatre. He taught me about the traditions of the London music halls which were dying around us. We exchanged thrillers and detective stories, and he introduced me to Rider Haggard. I can still see the dark green bindings with gilt lettering, and *She* remains one of my favourite novels. Both afflicted by hay fever, we swapped anti-histamines to alleviate the symptoms of stuffed-up noses and inflamed, tear-drenched eyes. Then suddenly the gear changed, and we became enthusiastic bedfellows. 'We could marry,' he said. 'I could get a divorce and we'd have a civil wedding.' 'Oh, Graham, you don't have to go through all that rubbish for me.'

He flew off for a holiday with Catherine, writing a long letter from the plane and using the word 'like' instead of 'love' – 'The trouble is I like you and I like her too.' When he returned I asked him if he'd been serious about marriage: 'I was never more serious in my life.' In retrospect, I think he was beginning to try to escape from Catherine.

'Promise me you will never become a Catholic.' (He had no need to ask, I was never tempted.) 'Promise me you will never be analysed. You are all right now. You might never be again.' This time I promised.

Catherine and I only met twice. Graham brought her for a drink to Freddie's flat over a bootmaker and tailor in White Horse Street, Shepherd Market. Again the rueful smile as he followed her up the lino-covered stairs to the entrance. 'You are having an affair with that girl,' she said as they left, Graham told me later. The next time was Coronation Day, when she scrambled over the adjoining iron balcony from the Walstons' flat to Graham's in St James's Street to talk to Kitty and Malcolm Muggeridge. Graham was away. I liked her better that time – her bare feet and jeans suited her more than black silk and mink – but she was no beauty.

I loved the womb-like safety of St James's Street, the ever-expanding collection of books, the paintings I shall always associate with him: a large Jack Yeats of horses and their riders, predominantly cadmium orange and ultramarine; the only Lowry that ever really moved me, a seascape with not a cockroach-like figure in sight, the impasto uniformly heavy and beautifully painted. There was also a small Italian primitive of a procession of soutane-clad priests, their round-brimmed hats on their heads, walking in single file across the canvas, their rosaries swinging like beaded bags from their waists. I painted a companion piece of nuns on a beach – armed with telescopes and ropes going to the aid of a shipwrecked boat.

'I've got sand everywhere'

Alone of all the men I have ever known, Graham was never assailed by the 'What shall I wear today?' syndrome. His wardrobe was reduced to a spartan, well-tailored simplicity. Three identical grey suits, three identical dark red ties, one black for funerals and God knows how many cream silk, collar-attached shirts. He was able to get up, bath and dress while thinking of something else.

He infected me with a passion for Guerlain's geranium soap – large curving cakes of warm, pinky orange, wrapped in silver paper and thin pleated tissue paper.

When the lease for St James's Street was drawing to an end we set off to search for somewhere else. The first place, owned by the playwright Denis Cannan, was on the south bank of the Thames, a double bow-fronted Georgian house of very fine proportions. On the way there in a water taxi Graham grew excited by the idea of owning a speedboat and travelling backwards and forwards by river – this from a man who never learned to drive a car. However, neither of us felt adventurous enough. Ultimately 'C6 Albany' became available, a fiendish stone staircase leading to a generously proportioned set of rooms.

We continued to eat our way round London restaurants. I never much liked Rules, but the Café Royal Grill Room and Simpson's in Coventry Street – where, from the first floor, one could look at Piccadilly Circus and down the Haymarket while the oysters and Black Velvet effortlessly slid down – were my preferred haunts. Best of all I liked the Connaught, handy for Farm Street and Sunday lunch after Mass.

Our affair, so long in starting, gradually peaked, and then quietly diminished into an ever more loving friendship. After me he had an *amitié amoureuse* with Margot Fonteyn, and then came Anita Björk.

The night before he left England to take up residence in France we dined together at the Ritz, where we had so often met for drinks. His going left a huge gap. He had an apartment in the Boulevard Malesherbes in Paris and one on the seafront in Antibes. Gradually the sea withdrew and was replaced by a parking lot, with the Mediterranean beyond. We met briefly once more, downstairs in the Ritz Bar. He was looking sunburned and happy and talked for the first time of Yvonne Cloetta. 'I'd like to meet her,' I said. 'She doesn't want to meet you.' Yet again the rueful smile. I was profoundly shocked. We were joined by Clive Donner, with whom I was living and subsequently married. I introduced them, and the three of us dined together. Clive asked Graham if he was in a state of grace. He paused a long time before saying, 'No.' Graham stayed with Yvonne Cloetta until he died, and I, thank God, grew more attached to Clive by the hour.

Graham remained a most beloved friend – abidingly loyal and affectionate. One of the pleasures of going to the South of France was to meet him at La Résidence des Fleurs for a drink and then cross to Chez Félix in the port for steak and *pommes frites*. This stooped, gentle man was in no way recognisable as the ogre presented in the television programme featuring Catherine's sister, her son and desperately angry daughter. I could not make out what Graham had done to anger her so much: surely the sins were Catherine's, sins of maternal omission and absence. Perhaps the hero of the whole saga was Harry Walston.

I burned most of Graham's letters to me. The few that remained I recently gave to Nick Dennys, the son of his favourite sister, Elizabeth. Nick now occupies the role of friend once held by Graham. I still keep the copy of a letter Graham wrote to Freddie: '...Jocelyn has always behaved like a gentleman...' They are dead now, and I have no need to continue behaving like a gentleman, but it is the only compliment I was ever delighted to receive.

Delights of the deathbed

*The novelist **DAVID HUGHES** lies back and thinks of miseries*

Illustration by Peter Bailey

These short pieces belong to a bedside book of three-score-essays-and-ten designed to stop me going down without a fight or ending up terminally bored. My mind is freed from fag to engage in positive reflection on all the negatives in life which will never trouble me again or on the angst I evaded. Thus is a lifetime's ragbag of quotidian miseries (and strokes of luck) transformed into the delights of the deathbed...

A blessing to be counted is having for a lifetime eluded human violence in a century shattered by it. (Tempting fate? I have left it too late to tempt anything, thank goodness, especially women.) By the accident of age my father missed the trenches of the First War and was too old for active service in the Second. I succeeded to his luck by being too young by a couple of years for my body to be shot down over Germany or my conscience to be blown to bits over Hiroshima. The worst injury my father sustained in ninety years of life was dislocation of the shoulder

when on his unlit bike he careered into a Canadian soldier in Market Street, Alton, during the blackout. Also on a bike, my mother was pursued in broad daylight by an ME 109 that peppered her with bullets down a summer lane near Chichester in 1940. She flapped into the ditch, the bike zig-zagging on in panic; both survived without even a puncture. And both parents went on comfortably to bring me up and teach me to cycle.

So, with seven days in hand, I lie in bed thinking with gratitude that I have never been mugged, except arguably by brains superior to mine in argument. Only once have I had my face slapped, by a woman whose lower lip I had just bitten in temper; we made it up in bed. I remain to this day unstuck by human fist since a gang run by Peter Woolgar (how could I forget the name?) set upon me after school on the day before or after France fell (I have forgotten which). And, oh yes, now I remember, there was a trivial instance of road rage a quarter of a century ago when in the Brompton Road an ape of a driver smashed his knuckles into my teeth and ripped my shirt – and I not even at the wheel, but an innocent passenger in a car with left-hand drive. To the eternal relief of my eating habits I had to have my front teeth extracted soon afterwards. A shy plastic grin replaced them, making me look more like a television announcer than the gap-toothed man I knew from the bathroom mirror, but it no longer hurt to eat toast and my lip-biting days were over.

These, however, are the only scars I have to show for having survived the twentieth century. It may never be healthy, let alone at the last minute, to savour the luck one has enjoyed; the very fact of luck continuing seems to offer you a false entitlement to more of it. Perhaps, within the week, someone will have stumbled on a miracle cure for whatever is wrong with me. Perhaps my luck will hold out longer than my body is likely to. I trust not. My children are eagerly waiting. The idea of making room for somebody else is one to die for.

N obody in his right mind wants nausea added to disease, so I shall try not to think of the reek of chicken fat. But my mind, right or not, will be enjoying the prospect of never again having to confront this bird. From parson's nose to gizzard, from claw to coxcomb, I have always found it repellent. Even chicks as fluffy as lightly scrambled egg make little appeal. Brown hens strutting in farmyards visibly resemble the smell of their ordure. At times, lying in ozoniferous sunlight or walking in a pine forest, I have only had to breathe in for my nose to recall, against all likelihood, the smell of chicken roasting in a Provençal street on market days. It asphyxiated every other southern scent: herbs, fish, fruit, olives, garlic, all sickened by that sweaty visceral hum of fowl sizzling on a spit.

In no restaurant have I ever ordered chicken or knowingly consumed it. It is a proud record. There might have been soups in which I hardly detected its presence. But even when disguised by as strong a flavour as tomato the fatal taste gathered on my tongue in a thin irreducible patina of fat, and that blew my tastebuds. Now at last I can relax my lifelong fight against the ugly strut of this maltreated bird which, when plucked, resembles parts of the male body better clothed by a codpiece.

The source of my objection lay tangled in wartime. Instead of unobtainable turkey or scarce beef or black-market pork or a nice leg of lamb from the farmer, chicken was served on Christmas Day with a juicy ceremony beyond its due. We kids had to eat the rubbery brown bits. We made do with a minimum of breast. Fat lay in lagoons on the gravy. What a child once resisted sends a man back to childhood even on his deathbed. What's that, nurse? A chicken sandwich? Take it away, if it's the last thing you do.

W hen I think of public transport on which I shall never have to travel again, unless as ashes to a pauper's grave, I will snuggle down in bed to summon up an icy moment at the lowering of a November afternoon when I stood at the top end of Whitehall waiting for a 3 or a 159 bus to take me home. As was usual in a lifetime of London patience, three 12s, a couple of 24s, a 53 or two passed at speed to prove that other people going elsewhere were favoured by this unjust efficiency of the system. At our bus-stop, where a few of us shivered and peered into the dying light, a towering white lorry almost twice as long as a bus occupied the space at the pavement's edge, not only blocking our view of the buses we wanted, if they ever mate-

rialised, but belching enough fumes from several exhausts to pollute an entire bus garage. Past this refrigerated space, the size of an iceberg on wheels, funnelled an unfriendly wind from the north which made my eyes water and blurred the lamps across the equally hostile space of Trafalgar Square. I already had a phlegmy cough; these conditions were going to whip it into pneumonia.

With a sense of cold loss I thought of all the wonders I was missing within yards of where I stood. Behind me were inscribed on the twilight the clean lines of William Kent. Opposite his Horse Guards' Parade stood Inigo Jones's Banqueting Hall on whose ample ceilings swirled the even ampler shapes of levitating women born of Rubens's vivid and capacious fantasy; and not much further from my shuddering form, respected even by buses going to wrong destinations, reared Edwin Lutyens's Cenotaph, which commemorated millions who had died in far worse straits than mine had ever been and by the courtesy of whose sacrifice I now shuddered here freely waiting for a bus. Over my right shoulder loomed the remains of the old Scotland Yard whose inadequacies in detection Sherlock Holmes was never slow to point out, and opposite me and behind the fumes shimmered the façade of the Whitehall Theatre, long famed for farce and family merriment. A whole culture preserved within a stone's throw of me, and, by golly, here I was thinking only of the shape of things that did not come: buses! At which moment a 159 screeched round the corner and put me, so to speak, out of my misery.

But, warm in bed, I shall remember the particularly mortal impact of that misery, the chill biting into the spine and the nose gagged with gases, and how no lure of art or any gentle association in the world is strong enough to diminish them one iota, and how gladly I lie snug in a reminiscence that need never again become a reality.

As for the aforementioned ashes, I prefer the thought of them rattling on their last journey in the luggage area under the stairs protected by a conductress in shiny black trousers built on the scale of a Rubens goddess.

David Hughes died in 2005

'*Have you forgotten, Thompson, this is hair-shirt Thursday?*'

PARADISE for Sale

Novelist **JOHN BOWEN** *felt it might be time to put his house on the market – but is the grass always greener?*

We live on the border of Warwickshire and Oxfordshire, half a mile from the road down a metalled track, below woods and surrounded by fields in which sometimes cattle graze, sometimes sheep and always rabbits. We are just over a mile from the village as the crow flies, two miles by road, eight miles from the town. In snow or ice we need a four by four to get out, and heavy rain makes tunnels in the rockery. The seeds of nettle, dandelion and thistle blow in from all directions; bramble and ivy creep into and through the hedges; bindweed and ground elder were here already like a fifth column when we bought the place and have consolidated their network since. Cows, which are moved, as it seems on a whim, from one field to another, leave trails of slurry outside our front gate.

Three years ago we decided to sell. It was common sense; I was over seventy, could not expect to keep my driving licence forever and had already discovered that even half an hour of weeding is murder on the back. We should move somewhere smaller among neighbours and within easy reach of shops and a doctor. Years ago I had fallen into the septic tank while pruning the dogwood when a cement slab suddenly split. Though my wellies filled with sewage, I had managed to pull myself out; I should never be able to do that these days. It was

the clinching argument. We phoned a firm of rather swanky estate agents.

There were two of them, both well-spoken, one like everyone's favourite uncle, the other sharper, leaner, probably the product of a minor public school (we thought Lancing), with teeth like a freshly painted white picket fence. They were delighted with the house. 'What we're selling here – it's so neat – is something you don't actually own. It's the view. Basically we'll be selling the other fellow's land, that's the joy of it.' So they sent a photographer to take pictures of the view, and advertised it in the local papers and in *Country Life*.

People came by appointment, couples in BMWs (one in a Porsche); some brought children and one brought a cat in a basket. We made the discovery which, I suppose, all house sellers make, that at least half those who view have no interest at all in buying, but come for the chat and to see how other people live. Professionals came, driving up from London and making a wide sweep of the Cotswolds on behalf of rich clients who could not be bothered to do it themselves. One arrived on a cloud of Trumper's Curzon cologne. 'I'm looking for somewhere bijou for a couple of minor royals,' he said; then, after a cursory up-and-down, 'But perhaps this is just a tad *too* bijou, what do you think?' It had never seemed bijou to us but maybe the minor royals would not be doing their own gardening.

We had been told that the mingled aromas of baking bread and freshly

ground coffee would sell a house, but neither of us can bake bread and supermarket ciabatta heated in the oven does not have the same effect, so we put on a CD of Bach's *Well-Tempered Clavier* and hoped for the best. Even on sunny days we lit a fire to show off the ingle-nook. We grew sick of the patter ('and the Compton Wynyates windmill is just behind those trees') and began to take turns, one giving the conducted tour while the other scurried ahead from room to room doing last-minute tidying.

Our estate agents were wrong. The view, although spectacular, worried many of our clients; at least it worried the wives. They would stand unwillingly on the upper lawn, staring at a landscape which went on for miles, and they did not see the windmill, the tower of the village church in the valley, the play of light and shadow on the patchwork of fields in different shades of green with the browny-yellow of wheat or barley and the blue of linseed. What they saw was a vision of crazed rustics in dirty corduroys rushing towards them across those empty fields, intent on rape and murder. 'Have you been burgled very often?' they would ask, and we would reply, 'Never in thirty years,' and they would give a disbelieving sideways smile and nod, and we would never see them again. Well, it is true that local villagers did once flay the parson alive for insisting on the payment of tithes, but that was two hundred years ago.

Those who are serious come more than once. The family who made an offer came four times, bringing friends to advise them and all four children. We accepted their offer. Soon there would be an exchange of contracts. We had better start house-hunting ourselves.

For five weeks we saw houses every day, sometimes as many as three. Anything interesting had holes in the roof or a cellar liable to flooding or both – well, our own house, when first we came across it thirty years earlier as an uninhabited ruin, had holes in the roof and a dead ~~...~~ chimney. We heard ou~~...~~ the same inane conversation to cover up a total lack of interest as had been made by our viewers to us. We grew to understand estate agents' prose in which a house can be detached but is still overlooked, 'requiring some modernisation' means dry *and* wet rot, 'mature garden' that every shrub has become a tree and florindae have cross-pollinated with polyanthus, producing a hybrid from which strong men turn away, that 'with character' means that none of the doors or windows can be opened without a struggle or closed when once they have been opened.

We saw heart-rending houses. In one – where the owner's partner had recently died – rag dolls were propped in every corner, artificial flowers under glass set on every flat surface and over them all the dust lay thick. Another had next-door neighbours who kept geese which ate the antirrhinums.

Our friend, Valerie Wood, had told us to make and keep a check-list of criteria which must be satisfied if we were to buy. At the end of the five weeks we looked hard at that list. The house we were selling matched every one of those criteria and none of the houses at which we had so laboriously looked matched even half. So we decided to stay where we were. Our swanky estate agents were not pleased. The one became distinctly less avuncular and the teeth of the other glowed like those of a werewolf about to make a change. Our behaviour was irregular and irresponsible, they said, but luckily it was covered by their Terms of Agreement and we would have to pay them one per cent of the offer price.

Last November I was seventy-six. I suppose that soon we shall have to think of selling the house.

The world according to
Enfield Snr

In my opinion, there are too many opinions

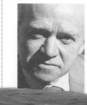

IN A RECENT *Oldie* my name appeared twice in that part of 'Readers Write' which is called Cancellation Corner. This sort of ~~...~~ had ~~...~~ of his subscribers. There is, though, one subject on which I can write with safety as I am sure that I have already been rumbled, and those who are inspired by my views to fly into a passion and wash their hands of *The Oldie* altogether have by now already departed.

The subject is the Royal Family, of which I am a staunch admirer, of all of them, in toto. Until recently, though, I had only a faint idea of Princess Michael of Kent; by now I realise that she is an excellent person, well up to standard. She gave an interview to the *Sunday Telegraph*, part of which goes like this: '"Newspapers today are full of comment," she says, settling into a garden chair and crossing her legs.' (That careful recording of the crossing of the royal legs strikes me, I must say, as a model of court reporting.) '"It's just people's opinions, it's not news any more. Everybody has an opinion. Who are these people who have opinions? Tell me! I mean, what right do they have to have an opinion?"'

What right indeed? I do so agree. There are far too many opinions flying about all over the place, and not just in newspapers. I am writing this in the quiet of my study, where all I can hear is a pigeon and a distant aeroplane, but as I look out of the window I know quite well that the seemingly tranquil air outside is actually alive with opinions – swarming with them, crawling with them, like maggots. If I put on the radio I could hear, on channel after channel, the ether being polluted with beastly opinions. I could, if I wanted, get the sound of awful people airing their horrid views on television. Out there millions of people with millions of mobile phones are bandying their opinions to and fro, and if they aren't doing that they are on the internet bouncing their opinions to heaven and back by satellite.

Then there are your Movers and Shakers. Exactly what they move and ~~...~~ ~~...~~ I have yet to learn, but ~~...~~ ey ought to ~~...~~ In pe~~...~~ Moved in ou~~...~~ ~~...~~ers, or having our principle~~...~~aken?

If I were a member of the House of Lords I should put down an amendment to the Countryside Bill to restrict the outpouring of opinions. Not that I am against private thoughts, you understand, merely against the wholesale visitation of them upon the public. But, being as I am a mere commoner, the best I can do is show you how to avoid having opinions on your own account, which will to some extent restrict the total number in circulation.

There is, I read, a proposal to have a television channel with a 'remit to foster experimental comedy and drama with a specific appeal to a younger, more uninhibited audience.' Belonging as I do to the older, more inhibited audience, I shan't watch it, and therefore will have no opinion about it whatever. I shall consign it to that limbo where Radio 1 and Radio 2 are lurking, to which I do not listen and am therefore free of any views about them either. There is, I read, a woman called Zoe Ball whose language is so vulgar that she causes people to switch off Radio 1 or Radio 2, whichever it is, but I have no opinion about her as I have never switched her off, never having gone to the trouble of switching her on in the first place.

You will find this kind of thing quite easy once you get the hang of it, and if we restrict the number of our opinions we shall be able to feel that we at least are helping to leave the rest of humanity in the undisturbed possession of a quiet mind.

THE GREAT
GAFFER

During his long association with John Gielgud, director **PATRICK GARLAND** *felt a little deprived not to have been the recipient of one of his celebrated gaffes. He needn't have worried...*

It must have been more than thirty years ago, and long before I was elected a member, that I spotted, one evening, in the upstairs bar of the Garrick Club, both Robert Atkins and Sir John Gielgud together; not actually among the same party – they had little in common – but astonishingly in the same room. I say astonishingly because it struck me that at the time they must have been unquestionably the two most imitated men in the English theatre. Every young actor could 'do' a Robert Atkins ('Now, listen here, old son') and a John Gielgud with facility. Bob Atkins disappeared years ago, and with him some splendidly foul-mouthed anecdotes, and I doubt many outside Regent's Park remember him now; but several journalists, after his death at the end of May, aged ninety-six, wrote stories and reminiscences about John

Gielgud, usually repeating the same old ones and in some cases misquoting them, so it struck me this might be the correct moment, and *The Oldie* the correct journal, to recall one or two which are less familiar.

I find it difficult to credit that the much-quoted gaffe Sir John made to Elizabeth Taylor – that Richard Burton 'married some terrible film star and went to live in Hollywood' – is genuine, simply because it seems to me direct, snobbish and rude, and none of these are characteristic of Gielgud's humour, conscious or otherwise. Although he did say, when somebody enquired of the career of Claude Rains, 'Oh, I think he failed, and went to live in America.' But, obviously, not to his face. He was hardly ever malicious, and never wilfully so, and if he was – as when he was discussing casting for *Much Ado About Nothing* with Michael Redgrave, and commented, 'Oh, Don Pedro is one of those tall, dull parts for tall, dull actors. You'd do it very well, Michael' – it was more absent-minded than insulting.

Most of his celebrated gaffes were involuntary and innocent, a quality which heightened his great flair for high comedy. There was never a Benedick to match him in spontaneity, wit and, perhaps unusually, virility. Almost everything he said seemed to be somehow by accident, as if he lacked what most of us are born with, a split-second safety mechanism, the warning signal between thought and declaration. When somebody said to Sir John, just as he turned away from speaking with a fellow-player, 'I never knew you knew so-and-so,' and Sir John said, 'How could I ever forget those terrible ears?' the young actor was in fact quite flattered. Nor was the designer offended who told John proudly that he was going to spend Christmas with the Oliviers, and he replied instantly: 'With the Oliviers? But they don't even like you!' Actors were frequently heard repeating happily the gaffes he had made, particularly their own, to amused colleagues.

Gielgud told me himself that a recording exists (I have a copy) of a truly dreadful radio production of him as Sherlock Holmes, with his old companion, Ralph Richardson, as Watson, in which he pretends to be a coalman in disguise and utters the memorable line: 'Good morning, matey, would you care for a bag of coal?' in his customary golden tenor tones, and Watson replies: 'My dear friend, Holmes, your voice, your face, are entirely unrecognisable!' 'It's terribly embarrassing,' said John, disparagingly. 'Actors put it on and play it to one another late at night. They even ring each other up and play it over the telephone.'

I think I hoped, during my long association with him over the rehearsals and production of *Forty Years On* (Alan Bennett's delicious comedy about an old-fashioned public school, which greatly contributed to John Gielgud's 'comeback' in the 1960s), that I would be the recipient of one of these memorable gaffes, assuming myself, and my role, to be an appropriate target, and even felt a little deprived not to receive one. It took some time, but I need not have worried. At the end of the year's run, he was appearing in *Caesar and Cleopatra* at the Chichester Festival Theatre. 'Who's directing?' I enquired suspiciously. 'Somebody called Robin Phillips, they tell me he's rather good.' 'Yes he's very good.' 'And quite young, isn't he?' 'Oh, yes, he's very young; we were both actors in our first jobs at the Bristol Old Vic.' 'Oh,' said Sir John, 'he's not so young then.'

There was occasionally to be found a curious element of surrealism, a gentle intrusion of fantasy, which gave his conversation a kind of sweetness entirely of his own, as when he gazed compassionately up at the barrage balloons over Piccadilly in the last war and murmured, almost to himself: 'Those poor dear boys up there, they must be terribly lonely.'

Jenny Agutter, tackling her first major Shakespearean role at the Old Vic, Miranda in *The Tempest*, in which Sir John was a memorable Prospero, told me he had turned to her in the wings on the opening night, seconds before their entrance, and almost as an afterthought said: 'By the way, Jenny, I keep meaning to tell you, don't worry about not being able to play Miranda; nobody ever could, not even Peggy.' His dear friend Ingrid Bergman, in a Somerset Maugham play he was directing, had the line: 'I was speaking to my mother on the telephone this morning.' After a few minutes' rehearsing on the first day, John interrupted: 'Ingrid, dear, could we change your line about the telephone, and say: "I was speaking to my Scandinavian mother..."?'

> ## Most of Gielgud's celebrated gaffes were involuntary and innocent

Perhaps, if forced into a corner to answer that tiresome question – which is the best evening ever spent in the theatre? – I would say any one of the four times I saw John Gielgud in the superb Shakespearean anthology, *The Ages of Man*. Not only, among the famous set pieces, did one see performed to perfection Prospero, Leontes, Lear, but excerpts from roles he was too old to play any more, like Hamlet, Romeo and a peerless Angelo, and even parts like Harry Hotspur, which he would never have played, not even in his prime. After one of these performances, invited by a mutual friend, I was nervous and tongue-tied in his dressing-room, when the distinguished Finnish director Caspar Wrede came round, with his actress wife, Dilys Hamlett, who not long before had played Perdita with him at Stratford-upon-Avon. After a few moments of casual gossip, Sir John suddenly asked: 'How's Dilys?' Pointing to his wife standing beside him, Caspar explained politely: 'But this is Dilys.' Without a moment's hesitation, John said: 'I meant Dilys Powell.'

I was a schoolboy in the early Fifties, and cycled all the way from Hampshire to queue most of the night for tickets to see his King Lear, with Alan Badel as a memorable Fool. Badel was renowned for being prodigal with criticisms of his fellow-actors, and as a young actor waiting in the wings for his cue, grew aware of Sir John as the mad King standing beside him, when he should have been entering from the other side of the stage. 'Excuse me, Mr Gielgud,' he whispered, 'but shouldn't you be coming on from the opposite side?' 'Yes, I know, but Alan Badel's over there, and he keeps giving me notes.'

It is well known that his relationship with Laurence Olivier had always been uneasy, compared, for example, with his relationship with Ralph Richardson. But I remember with what generosity he praised Olivier for his Romeo, when they alternated roles in his own direction of the play at the Old Vic in 1935. 'I probably had the edge as Mercutio,' he remembered. 'Larry was never very comfortable with all the swagger talk, and the poetry defeated him rather, but when it came to Romeo he was better by far than I was, because I did the verse, but he knew how to win the girl.' And later, joking, he said to me: 'Larry's a very great actor, but I'm the aristocrat of the English stage.'

But when Olivier ran the National Theatre in the Old Vic, he appeared to invite Gielgud to join him in a series of misfires. Seneca's *Oedipus* was hardly a success, and his brush with Molière failed entirely. Harold Pinter's *No Man's Land*, however, was an instant and self-evident triumph, with his great friend Ralph Richardson playing opposite. Gielgud modelled his characterisation of the poet, Spooner, on the dishevelled appearance of Wystan Auden, creating, for such a fastidious man, a shifty, seedy figure. The history behind the transfer to the Wyndham's Theatre in the Charing Cross Road is complicated, but due, in part, to the gravity of Sir Laurence's illness, which gave him no option but to revise drastically the Old Vic schedules, which had not been his original intention. When John Standing and Daniel Massey went together to the Wyndham's Theatre, saw *No Man's Land* and were knocked out by it, it was understandable that when they paid their respects backstage, they emphasised not only how marvellous it was for Sir John and Sir Ralph to appear together in a stunning new play, but how thrilling to have them both back in the West End!

'I know,' said Sir John, 'it is rather thrilling. But the whole thing wouldn't have happened at all if Larry wasn't dead – I mean, dying – I mean, much, much better!' Perhaps a rare example of the wish being father to the thought.

It is, after all, a genuine part of Sir John Gielgud's legacy to us all – not only the greatest lyric verse-speaker of his time, the outstanding classical actor of the century and writer of a handful of entertaining theatrical memoirs, but finally the inventor of a totally original kind of personal humour, a source of fun and irreverence for future generations, something to savour and remember. Whoever thought it would be a brilliant notion to invite Sir John to direct Laurence Olivier and Vivien Leigh, both at the height of their powers, as Malvolio and Viola in *Twelfth Night* was unlucky. When he was taxed by somebody for getting it all so wrong, Sir John replied disarmingly: 'Yes, I know – we all thought it was going to be good, and it wasn't.' It turned out to be a humourless catastrophe. Vexed by the failure of what she expected to be a personal triumph, the exquisite Vivien Leigh summoned the unhappy director into her dressing-room at the end of the Stratford run. 'Johnny,' she said, coolly and dispassionately, 'it is well known you are the best-loved man in the theatre, by the public and your fellow-actors, but you must understand, so far as your career as a director is concerned, nobody in the entire English theatre is ever going to work with you again.' There was a short pause. 'Edith might,' he said, 'at a pinch.'

'If you want to smirk, Roger, go outside'

FREEDOM TRAIN

KAROLA REGENT *and her sister were put aboard the train for England in 1939 to escape the Holocaust. They never saw their parents again...*

'Are you a *Kind*?' The question comes from a white-haired lady to a balding man of a certain age, who replies that yes, he is indeed a '*Kind*', or child. Variations on this bizarre exchange might be heard at any gathering of '*Kinder*' – all oldies now – who are linked by the single fact that they fled Germany, Austria or Czechoslovakia with the '*Kindertransport*' in the last weeks before the outbreak of the Second World War. Their ages ran from babes-in-arms to seventeen. For the most part they had not met each other since those few shared hours of travel in 1939 until the reunions of 1989 and 1999 to celebrate the fiftieth and sixtieth anniversaries of the *Kindertransport* year. Twelve thousand people came from all corners of the globe, with diverse histories and backgrounds but one common feature – a last-minute, near-miraculous escape from the most systematic and comprehensive policy of persecution and extermination of modern times.

We waved goodbye happily, still hearing their last assurances: 'We are coming soon'

It was after the *Kristallnacht* on 9th November 1938, when the Nazis broke into private Jewish homes in the middle of the night, destroying everything within, burning the synagogues and declaring many Jews to be outlaws, that my parents were at last forced to recognise that they must seize the opportunity offered by the *Kindertransport* of getting me and my sister out of Germany, in the fond hope that they could soon follow us. In answer to our anxious and repeated questioning, they assured us, 'Yes, we'll come soon, as soon as we can get all our papers through.' But they never came.

I remember the frantic preparations that took place once the tremendous decision to part with us had been taken. I was thirteen and my sister was nine. New clothes were bought, with room for growth and deep hems, to save expense for our relatives in London, who were refugees themselves. For us children there was an element of excitement and adventure in all these preparations, since we had assurances that our parents would be with us again.

At last everything was ready. We had received notification that our special train was to leave Düsseldorf station on 3rd May 1939. It was one of the last trains to pick up from Düsseldorf, and for those of my Jewish schoolfriends who were not on it, or had not already left, their next journey would be to one of the concentration camps.

Before we left the house that morning my father and mother laid their hands on our heads and blessed us for the last time. We found a very long train waiting at the station. It had come a long way, picking up children at different towns across Germany; Düsseldorf was the last picking-up point before the Dutch border.

I remember the moment of separation. We were all busy finding the right coach and compartment and stowing the luggage. Then the last clinging embrace – my face against the tweed of my father's coat, and the comforting feel of my mother's fur collar. Then we were on the train. We didn't cry then. We all knew we mustn't. I think we waved goodbye happily, still hearing their last firm assurances: 'We are coming soon. In a few weeks.' Then, as I saw their lonely figures receding as the train drew out, looking so forsaken, after all they had done for us – then I cried.

What I didn't know at the time, but learnt from a German friend after the war, was that my father had jumped on the train at the last moment as it curved around a corner. Anxious to see us safely over the Dutch border, he travelled all the way to the frontier. There, the frontier guards and some German officers came into each carriage and asked questions about our luggage – in particular, whether we were carrying any valuables. Some children had their cases opened and searched, but all passed off quietly in our carriage. My father left the train as unobtrusively as he had got on, and watched it snake its way across the frontier into Holland and safety.

We travelled by night boat from the Hook of Holland to Harwich and from

Family photographs from happier times: Father and daughters in 1933, and (above right) the author on her first day at school, 1932

there by train to Liverpool Street station, where we were to be checked and claimed by our sponsors or relatives. The whole journey had a somnambulist quality – train, boat, then train again – interspersed with endless standing in long, labelled files. The first clear picture that emerges is of our arrival at Liverpool Street station, a vast glass dome swirling with steam, and of filing through a door into a great grey hall. As we entered, our names were checked off a list and we were each given a packet of sandwiches, some chocolate and an orange. This orange, round and brightly glowing in the grey surroundings, suddenly cheered me and brought back a sort of excitement and anticipation.

Up to this point, all of us now assembled in the hall, though strangers to each other, had a shared experience of growing up in Germany, of gradual exclusion from society, of the growing threat of violence, and of a journey that had taken us from our homes and parents to a strange country and an uncertain future. From now on, our paths would diverge as chance decreed. But, for the moment, there we sat, bewildered and rather tired, waiting anxiously for our names to be called and to see who had come to claim us. For most of us, it would be strangers who led us away to a new life.

The negotiations that had led up to the *Kindertransport* had been hard, but had succeeded against all the odds. Voluntary associations in Britain – Jewish and non-Jewish – had banded together to press the British government to admit Jewish children. It was only after the excesses of *Kristallnacht* that the authorities at last agreed that unaccompanied Jewish and other threatened children up to the age of seventeen would be allowed into Britain so long as their maintenance could be guaranteed, either by individuals or by philanthropic organisations.

Time was short. Volunteers went to Germany and negotiated arrangements in the face of an obstructive bureaucracy. The efforts of the Jewish community and other bodies in fundraising and organising sponsors and guarantors, identifying sponsors and setting up reception centres and group accommodation for those without individual sponsors were, in retrospect, astonishing.

The precise terms of the arrangement had inevitably heartbreaking

consequences. Siblings separated by a few months in age became survivor and condemned. There were instances of babies (not officially admitted to the trains) being thrust by desperate mothers into the arms of those departing. A basket, ostensibly of belongings, was slid into a carriage at the last moment and was later found to contain, not provisions for the journey, but a living bundle. Between December 1938 and August 1939, ten thousand children were brought to Britain by the *Kindertransport* – and saved from almost certain death.

Once in Britain, experiences differed widely. Those without individual sponsors went to group accommodation in such places as a disused holiday camp at Dovercourt, near Harwich, where they at least had special language teaching and the companionship of each other. Some, like my sister and me, were fortunate enough to join relatives. Some went to grand houses, some to cottages; some were treated as family, others as skivvies. Some of the younger ones, who soon had no recollection of their background, quickly integrated into their new environment, while others suffered a lasting loss of

identity. The older boys joined up or went into other 'war work' – except for those who were deported to Australia as 'enemy aliens' on the *Dunera* (they became the '*Dunera* boys', and many returned to Europe in uniform).

Many of the original arrangements were upset by evacuation or by wartime calamity, or simply by reaching the school-leaving age of fourteen. When I arrived, I could only say 'Good morning', 'strawberry jam' and 'porridge' in the language of Shakespeare. But the Council School teachers were conscientious. They painstakingly corrected my stammering utterances and written absurdities until, after two years in a convent school, paid for by a generous friend of our then hosts – we had become evacuees since, and the aunt and uncle who first received us were dying – I went on to war work and then to university, to read English.

For many of the *Kinder* it took a long time to face up to their past, or to talk about it, even to spouses and children. For some of those, it was at the reunion of 1989 that they found release in the company of people with the same experience. Talking and listening finally opened the floodgates, and suddenly they couldn't stop the stream of mingled recall and questioning.

At the time of the 1999 reunion a plaque was unveiled at the Palace of Westminster by the Speaker of the Commons. It expressed gratitude to the people and Parliament of the United Kingdom for saving the lives of ten thousand Jewish and other children. The *Kinder* were always aware that, at a time of great misfortune, they had been plucked from a still worse fate. The plaque gives quiet expression to the gratitude they feel, alongside their awareness of having played a full and constructive part in the life of their adopted country.

'Bear with me'

The best of LARRY

Following Larry Adler's death in 2001, **RICHARD INGRAMS** *selected his favourite putdowns from Larry's video reviews…*

Witness for the Prosecution: Marlene Dietrich plays two parts, one a German, the other (and I'm not making this up) a Cockney whore. Oprah Winfrey could play a Cockney whore better than that.

Guess Who's Coming to Dinner: There is an anecdote – I hope it's true – that when Hepburn met Tracy, prior to their first film, she said to the producer, 'Isn't he kind of short?' Said Tracy, 'Don't worry, lady. I'll cut you down to size.'

Murder on the Orient Express: If Oscars were awarded for miscasting, a sure winner would be the genius who chose Albert Finney to play Hercule Poirot.

Tootsie: To me Hoffman was a man in drag, never more than that, and I kept wondering how come nobody else notices this. My hunch is that straight men can't successfully pass themselves off as women.

Silk Stockings: Fred Astaire had the sexuality of a take-away pizza. This unfortunately makes the love story difficult to accept.

Around the World in Eighty Days: David Niven takes just one bag on his voyage, but seems to have a different suit in each scene. That's some bag and I'd like to know where he got it.

Nicholas Nickleby (directed by Cavalcanti): The score is awful. Every odious act has its matching ominous chord and is about as subtle as the music for a Hanna/Barbera cartoon. It is by Lord Berners. Heroes are rewarded, villains come to no good. Total black, pure white, with no shade of grey in between.

That Adler sure can cavil, canti?

Strangers on a Train: Alfred Hitchcock, grand master of suspense, offers a story with no suspense at all – you know what's coming and you're always right.

David Copperfield: There are curious captions that come on to the screen as if it were a silent film, such as: 'Weeks pass amid old scenes.' Do they now!

Casablanca: This film started production with the script unfinished. Ingrid Bergman told me she had no idea whether she was to end up with Henreid or Bogart…

The Grapes of Wrath: All the characters are noble. They reek of nobility.

Henry V: A credible king has dignity and majesty. Olivier had it and Branagh hasn't.

The Band Wagon: I did a duet with Fred Astaire in a Ziegfeld production called *Smiles*, which gave a new meaning to the word 'flop'. How could a show with Astaire *and* me misfire? It's a puzzlement.

Mary Poppins: This picture is cute. I use the word in its toe-curling sense… I didn't watch it all. I couldn't.

The Dam Busters: There are almost no women in the film. The only romance is between Richard Todd and his dog, and I was sure that wouldn't last. I was right. The dog got run over.

Dr Zhivago: Mr Sharif coasts through the film with one facial expression – a semi-sardonic smile. He only scowls when he's in bed with Julie Christie, at which point, in his place, I'd have been grinning like a Halloween pumpkin.

Scott of the Antarctic: When everyone in the film grows a beard, excepting the dogs and penguins, it becomes hard to recognise individuals.

Kes: For most of the time I couldn't understand one goddam word.

Doctor in the House: Kay Kendall exemplifies Adler's Law that if a woman is both beautiful and funny she is bound to become a star.

Treasure Island: The billing is 'Walt Disney presents Robert Louis Stevenson's *Treasure Island*' and that whirring sound you hear is Stevenson spinning in his grave.

Death in Venice: Nothing saves this film from monotony, you can't hear the dialogue, and it never knows where to end. But oh boy, is it beautiful!

The Final Test: I'll bet no other *Oldie* staff member has played the mouth organ accompanied by Don Bradman on the piano.

The King and I: I have a feeling that if I were Siamese I wouldn't like this film at all.

West Side Story: This is the last of the great musical scores. Journalists use a weasel-word, 'arguably', when they're afraid to commit themselves. To hell with 'arguably' – these songs are terrific.

Camille: When she spoke her first line in *Anna Christie* in 1930, the ad headline was 'Garbo Talks!' For *Ninotchka* it was 'Garbo Laughs!' In *Camille* it could have been 'Garbo Acts!'

Larry at the Oldie of the Year Awards, 2000

The GOOD WHORE GUIDE

In his bachelor days, the **MARQUESS OF ABERDEEN** *knew all the best bordellos...*

Brothels, or bordellos, and their inmates are a contentious subject. Here, I am not concerned with any judgments but with my experience of the ones I knew as a bachelor.

First, Mme Jannette's in Beirut in 1942. Her establishment was a convenient two minutes' walk from the St Georges Hotel. She was a benevolent but strict madame. You entered a large room comfortably furnished with sofas and armchairs, in which she invited you to sit and have a drink or a cup of coffee. Strolling about or draped deliciously on sofas were attractive young girls wearing figure-hugging ankle-length silk dressing-gowns. You were invited to take your time in making your selection. I made mine quite quickly – a quiet, beautiful brunette.

You paid madame and the girl then led you to her own bedroom in which was a large double bed; leading off behind a screen was a bathroom complete with bidet. Over Olga's bed were colour photographs of her as the cover girl of Belgrade magazines. Poor Olga – she had fled Yugoslavia ahead of the German invasion, landed in Syria and perforce joined the only profession available. I tried to be as kind as possible to her then and on subsequent visits, and I believe she was grateful, regarding the urgent attention of a sex-starved subaltern as a necessary panacea.

Mrs Fetherstonhaugh's place in Elvaston Place, Knightsbridge, was listed in the telephone directory as 'Private Hotel'. My particular favourite was a Junoesque blonde with her own mews house. I shall not divulge her name – she may have made a good marriage: her enthusiastic and skilful performance would have made her a wonderful wife for the bed-work. Rumour had it that a Coldstream Guards officer was shown to a bedroom in the hotel and the girl assigned to him was his sister.

Mrs Fethers, as everyone called her, recruited secretaries and ritzy shop assistants. She was also known to try to recruit young wives whose husbands had a lengthy posting abroad. She was the soul of discretion, but nevertheless she was eventually driven out of business by the Home Office.

In 1945, when the militant feminists of Paris demanded, and got, the closure of all the bordellos, just one remained open (I dare say half the French Cabinet were clients). This was the Vicomtesse de Brissac's house in the fashionable XVI arrondissement. She herself – no doubt long disowned by that great family – was stout and heavily made up, but the girls were *soignée* and elegant.

My favourite, a chestnut-haired beauty, was fluent in several languages. She once lost her professional cool and called out in her extremity, *'Ach, mein Gott!'* Tactfully I didn't remind her that the Germans had left, defeated. But with her gift for languages (and my lack of them), she was excellent company to take out to dinner, followed by further romps in my hotel bedroom. Once again, no names, please. Rosa Lewis of the Cavendish Hotel used to say, 'No names, no lawyers, and kiss my baby's bottom.'

One particular night in Paris a friend of mine and I had a two-bedroom suite in the Georges Cinq Hotel: it was a very hot night, so at half-time we all got into a cold bath off one of the bedrooms with glasses of brandy: it was a very big bath and we all managed to get in amid shrieks of laughter. Having cooled off, we returned to our respective bedrooms to resume exertions. My linguist girlfriend said: 'You British are happily different to French men, who are played out by their mid-twenties.'

No. 72 rue Royale in Brussels was a posh establishment. I wonder what is there now?

The Trocadero bar in Copenhagen was full of glossy girls who were there to be picked up, and I was reminded of it when my wife and I were staying in Madrid with rich friends many years later. Knowing that they kept Spanish hours, and that the chef wouldn't have started cooking dinner, we set out for an evening stroll around the neighbourhood and came upon a very select-looking bar. We went in, sat down on a sofa and gave our drinks order to a waiter. When we looked round we saw that the customers were all glamorous girls and handsome young men. 'Ah,' we thought. 'This is where smart Madrid society gathers in the evening.'

When we got back to the house our friends said: 'We know where you have been.' Some friend had rung to say that an obviously British married couple had walked into the bar which was the one exclusive meeting-place for rich young Spaniards to pick up a girl for a weekend or even a Caribbean holiday.

My experiences of the oldest profession give me almost entirely pleasant memories. Perhaps I was fortunate.

'"Physick for the cure of thy Ague." When was the last time we cleared out this medicine cabinet?'

Torture *in triplicate*

Creator of Ivor the Engine **OLIVER POSTGATE** *endured a blizzard of Eurobilge*

Illustrated by PETER FIRMIN

I t is of course natural that anxieties should grow like weeds around the prospect of our integration into a Wider Community, but there is one insidious creeper that seems not to have received the attention it deserves, perhaps because although potentially poisonous it is not easy to spot.

Eurobilge grows spontaneously in places where there is no answerability, typically in institutions whose existence and level of funding is not dependent on the execution of its function. The first signs are a gradual thickening up of the ordinary processes of administration, which in time proliferates until it becomes an end in itself. By absorbing highly paid energy that could have been used productively, it can eventually develop to the point where nothing actually gets done and the institution becomes ornamental – a self-perpetuating, self-regarding orb of pure wastage, sailing serenely through the night sky...

That is quite enough of that but, believe me, I speak from the heart. Let me tell you what happened twenty years ago. I heard that an Institution had been formed to collect royalties from 'the simultaneous retransmission of television films by foreign stations', a procedure better known as piracy. I rang the nice lady who ran it, sent her a list of our films, and quite soon received a cheque for a small but welcome sum of money, amounting to approximately £1.24 per minute of the film. Very nice.

A few months passed and we suddenly received a parcel the size of a paving-stone from somewhere in Belgium. It contained extensive lists, all in duplicate, of Participating Rightholders and also a set of forms, in triplicate, which we were to fill in 'delineating the nature and character of output'.

I rang the nice lady, but her phone was dead. So I filled in the forms, sent them off and filed the rest of the material in a crate. Nothing happened for several months, but then another set of forms arrived. These were in landscape format rather than portrait but were otherwise identical in purpose. This time Rightholders were warned that if they failed to supply the information in the exact manner prescribed they would forfeit the right to receive any royalties from the retransmission of their films. I duly filled in the forms, but I also reminded the Institution that it had already had all the information it required, in triplicate, and that as far as I knew it had no authority to deprive people of rights that exist in law.

In reply there came, about a year later, another request for the details of our productions, in order to facilitate a revision of the computer programme. I pointed out once more – somewhat testily, I suspect – that they already had the information. I received no direct answer, only a general letter informing us of a Resolution of the General Council announcing the creation of a subcommittee of unclear purpose. I say 'unclear' because the language of the Resolution was not so much a translation into English as a transliteration: the words, syntax and grammar of the original language had been transferred verbatim into the recipient's language. This ensured that although the manner was sometimes inadvertently charming, the matter was wholly concealed. There was a good example of this in a document entitled 'Regulations Regarding the Procedures of Declaration of Works, of Claims and of Payments'. It went like this: 'No interpretation of one or the other of its rules could possibly replace the decisions taken by the Association's competent organs regarding its fields of activity regarding the matter or the place.'

As well as being opaque, this clause had godlike overtones in that it pronounced not only on what is, but also on what could possibly be – an area of conjecture usually reserved for the use of Providence, senior physicists and the Pope.

During the next decade I wrote to the Institution several times, inviting them to send us money, and received in return, from various departments, notifications of the appointment of Committees, Advisory Groups and Designated Organs. I got the impression that the Institution was growing in scope and scale to such an extent that it now resembled the civil service of some minor state or principality.

This impression was confirmed when we suddenly received a Special Delivery parcel addressed to all Rightholders, containing an impassioned letter commanding them as Loyal Members of the Institution to take no notice of the interferent utterances of some other body which I had never heard of, and instructing us to sign without delay an Instrument declaring irrevocably that the Institution was the sole body authorised to collect Royalties on our behalves.

As well as being opaque, this clause had godlike overtones in that it pronounced not only on what is, but also on what could possibly be

So, somewhere, war had been declared.

There followed an exciting period during which the administrative battle ebbed and flowed in a flurry of incomprehensible communications about unknown persons, interspersed with further requests for lists of our productions, in triplicate. Eventually the Institution seemed to have retreated to Switzerland, where, in the 1990s, it apparently regrouped and was able, after several applications, to send us some royalties. These were not clearly attributed because they had got the names of our films wrong – indeed, some of the payments appeared to be for films we had never heard of – but as, during the years, the royalty rate had inexplicably diminished from £1.24 per minute to £0.09 per minute, the sums involved were so small as to be derisory.

We resigned formally, but to no avail. Communications continued to arrive, and the crate of Eurobilge became too heavy to lift. Bearing in mind that the total amount of work done on our behalf by the Institution over two decades could have been completed by a competent secretary in something over ten minutes, I have begun to feel doubts about the advisability of having anything to do with the institutions of a 'Wider Community'.

What were you doing 40, 50, 60, 70 or 80 years ago?

50 years ago I was flying an RAF Shackleton from Cyprus to Malta. Near Crete we were intercepted by a cylindrical, metal-looking object with no visible means of support or propulsion but with a ghostly red light around the nose. It was early morning, but daylight. We flew westwards at 2,000 feet, 160 knots. Our friend formatted on our port side and, whatever we did, stayed there.

Twelve of us saw it clearly. I climbed to 10,000 feet, sent a sighting report and put my radar responder to NATO emergency.

Two hours later we were intercepted by two RAF Javelin fighters who said they could see the UFO. It immediately disappeared heavenward at colossal speed. Malta radar said they lost it at 60,000 feet, going too fast for them to measure.

After landing, we all, including the fighter pilots, reported what we had seen and it became an Official Secret. I was an experienced Squadron Leader pilot, had flown with the RAF since 1940 and survived the war and other operations. This thing was real and not a fantasy. I don't think anyone on this planet then or now could produce that sort of capability.

GORDON BURGESS

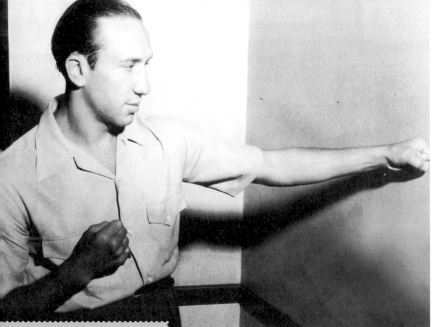

MAY 2001

RIP, *Maxie*

...and Daniel Mendoza, 'Dutch Sam' Elias, 'Ugly Baruk', Sammy Luftspring... **MORDECAI RICHLER** *celebrates the noble art of Jewish boxing*

As usual, early one morning in August, I climbed upstairs to my studio in our dacha on the shores of Lake Memphrémagog, in Quebec's Eastern Townships, and sat down at my long plank table, ready to settle into work on my book about snooker. I could no longer make out the cigarillo burns and tea stains on the table, because it was now buried end to end in snooker books by various hands, newspaper clippings, photocopies, stacks of *Snooker Scene* and tournament programmes and press releases. I had just had time to flick on the power on my electric typewriter when the phone rang. It was an old high school-cum-Laurier pool-room chum who was still driving a taxi at the age of seventy-three. Last time I had run into him, outside that singularly ugly warehouse where the Montreal Canadiens now play hockey of a sort, the Molson Centre, he had been trying to flog tickets for that evening's game. 'So,' Abe said, 'you became a writer and I became a scalper, and we're both old farts now.' We exchanged phone numbers. I promised to meet him for lunch one day, but I had never called. Now he was on the phone at 7.15 am. 'Have you seen this morning's *Gazette*?' he asked.

'Not yet.'

'Maxie Berger died.'

'How old was he?' I asked, because this information is of increasing interest to me.

'Eighty-three. I want you to write something nice about him. He was a good fighter. A *mensch* too.' A gentleman.

Back in the days when I used to hang out in pool rooms, boxers were greatly admired by me and my bunch of teenage hooligans, some of whom could rattle off the names of the top ten in each division, as listed in Nat Fleischer's *Ring* magazine. I had hoped to qualify for the Golden Gloves amateur tournament, but was taken out in a qualifying three-rounder; my ambition then was not a Booker Prize, or a perch on the *New York Times* bestseller list, but a Friday night main bout in Madison Square Garden in New York, sponsored on radio by Gillette razor blades ('Look sharp! Feel sharp! Be sharp!').

To this day, pride of place in my dacha's sports museum goes to a portrait of the great Daniel Mendoza. Mendoza was the first of a pride of Jewish boxers in England that included 'Dutch Sam' Elias, the Belasco brothers Aby and Issy, 'Star of the East' Barney Aaron, Ikey Pig, Bernard Levy and Moses Levy, aka 'Ugly Baruk'. George Borrow claimed that 'it is these that have planted rottenness in the core of pugilism, for they are Jews, and, true to their kind, have only base lucre in view...'

Much as it pains me, I am honour bound to admit that Borrow had a point. In *Prize-fighting: The Age of Regency Boximania*, John Ford quotes an account of an 1801 fight between the splendid Jew, Isaac Bitton, and Paddington Jones: '...while sitting on his second's knee, [Bitton] felt for the 1s 6d that he had put into his drawers, previous to the battle; not finding it, he refused to continue till he had searched for the same. Mendoza (his second) was quite enraged at this stupid conduct, and urged that the time was expired, but all his entreaties were in vain, till Bitton felt the money near one of his knees, when he resumed the fight and proved the conqueror.'

> **A down and dirty sport like boxing belonged to tough kids out of Italian, black, Irish and Jewish mean streets**

My trusty *Encyclopedia of Jews in Sport*, by Bernard Postal, Jesse Silver and Roy Silver, has it that Daniel Mendoza, born 5th July 1764 in Aldgate, was not only the first of his faith to become heavyweight champion (1792–95), but was also 'the father of scientific boxing and the man whose fists helped to stem a vicious tide of anti-Semitism in England'. Not universally, clearly, for when his arch-rival, 'Gentleman Dick' Humphries, defeated him before a large crowd in 1788 he proclaimed, 'I have done the Jew'. But, ho, ho, ho, when the done Jew met Humphries again in 1789 he thrashed him in fifty-two minutes. A year later Mendoza required only fifteen minutes to dispose of Humphries yet again.

Pierce Egan, that incomparable observer of the sweet science, wrote of Mendoza's triumph over Humphries in *Boxiana*: 'Mendoza in conquering so noble and distinguished a competitor added considerable fame to his pugilistic achievements; but the greatest merit was the manner in which it was obtained. Prejudice so frequently distorts the mind, that unfortunately good actions are passed over without even common respect; more especially when they appear in any person who may chance to be of a different country, persuasion, or colour; Mendoza, being a Jew, did not stand in so favourable a point of view, respecting the wishes of the multitude towards his success, as his brave opponent... But truth rises superior to all things, and the humanity of Mendoza was conspicuous throughout the fight – often was it witnessed that he threw up his arms when he might have put in a most tremendous blow upon his exhausted adversary...'

When I was a teenager I believed snooker to be a game played only by working-class delinquents like us. I was unaware that Montreal's most elite men's clubs boasted oak-panelled rooms with nifty antique tables. Okay, that was naïve of me. But I thought then, and still do, that no sport comes without its class or racial baggage.

Where I come from, hockey and baseball appealed to every class and faith, and our distinctions were limited only to where we could afford to sit. But in the Thirties and Forties we counted football, golf and tennis as strictly WASP as sliced white bread. We associated football with universities fastidious enough to have Jewish quotas, and golf and tennis with country clubs and resorts that wouldn't tolerate any Jews whatsoever. A down and dirty sport like boxing, on the other hand, belonged to tough kids out of Italian, black, Polish, Irish and Jewish mean streets. Jack Solomons, one of ours, was the promoter with heft in London, and Joe 'Yussel the Muscle' Jacobs called the shots in New York, where the great and near-great trained in Lou Stillman's gym. And welter-weight champ Barney Ross, the son of a Talmudic scholar, gave us bragging rights.

In those days boxing beat hacks in Toronto had not yet been muzzled by political correctness. Describing a 1934 fight, one of them wrote: 'For once, the Gentile barracking brigade will have to choose between the lesser of "two evils", when Sammy Luftspring and Dave Yack, a pair of Hebes, battle for supremacy in Frank Tenute's Elm Grove Show at the Mutual Street Arena on Monday night.' Not much later Lou Marsh, of the *Toronto Daily Star*, got to cover what was, as he put it, 'an honest-to-Henry grudge fight between a Celt and a Son of Moses', Sammy Luftspring *vs* Chick McCarthy. The good news was this promising 'slugfest' had attracted an all-Canada record attendance of six thousand, 'of which 5,795 talked turkey to the box office staff'. Luftspring won a unanimous decision, but not before, wrote Marsh, 'McCarthy opened the final round with a right-hander that made the aggressive little Jew boy lean like the Tower of Pisa.'

A couple of days after Maxie Berger died, both the *Toronto Globe and Mail* and the *National Post* ran obituaries, noting that Maxie had briefly been World Junior Welter-weight Champion. Lacking the earlier verve of the *Toronto Daily Star*, the tame *National Post* headline ran:

BOXER WAS LOVED
IN THE BRONX
A STAR IN QUEBEC
Fought Five World Champions
He Dressed Well
And Was Popular
With Women

In common with other newspapers, the *National Post* featured a silly photograph of Maxie, obviously retrieved from an ancient Canadian Press file. It harked back to the days when newspaper photographers in a hurry could be counted on to

Far left: 'a silly photograph' of Maxie Berger assuming his ring stance, leading with his left

Left: Daniel Mendoza, 'the most Scientific Boxer ever Known'. Engraving by H Kingsbury, 1789, after the painting by T Robineau

honour their own code of clichés, and it showed him assuming his ring stance, leading with his left. But he is standing in the corner of a room, wearing an open-necked sports shirt and trousers belted high, addressing a blank wall. His swept-back hair suggests that it was brilliantined or that he had just got out of a shower. 'Clean up good, Maxie, for Christ's sake. You know how long it is since they took your picture for the papers?'

Cauliflower ears. Soft dim eyes. Scarred eyebrows. Pulpy nose. Swollen knuckles. And no wonder. Over the wasting years the New York mob had fed Maxie to Fritzie Zivic, Beau Jack and the great Sugar Ray Robinson, among others. Maxie took on Sugar Ray in Madison Square Garden in 1942, and was knocked to the canvas twice before the referee stopped the fight. Maxie had wanted to continue, but the referee had shouted at him, 'Do you want to get killed?'

The son of immigrants out of a Polish *shtetl*, Maxie had an education limited to elementary school, after which he went to work as a grocery delivery boy. He learned to box at the Young Man's Hebrew Association (YMHA), which was then in the heart of the city's working-class Jewish quarter. He won a silver medal in the British Empire Games in the 1930s before turning pro, fighting out of the Bronx. Married four times, on his retirement he returned to Montreal and opened a custom-made shirt business where the smart guys could acquire those ghastly white-on-white shirts, inevitably worn with initialled cuff links, and what we used to call a one-button-roll sports jacket, with outsized padded shoulders.

I first encountered Maxie in the Forties in the Laurentians, our minor league Borscht Circuit, at the Castle des Monts Hotel in Ste Agathe. A seething Maxie came roaring out of the hotel pursued by a hollering wife. When we filmed my novel, *The Apprenticeship of Duddy Kravitz*, in 1974, I made sure there was a small part for Maxie. The *National Post* obituary writer noted that Maxie was 'like a character in a Studs Terkel novel', but Terkel never wrote a novel. The obviously nice man who had written Maxie's obit also had it that 'he became a stockbroker in the early Sixties, profiting from the Sixties stock market boom'. Actually, he served as a factotum for a brokerage house. In those days he would occasionally turn up in the Montreal Press Club, then in the Mount Royal Hotel, and I would chat with him there, an uncommonly gentle man who had taken too many punches to the head in close to a hundred fights. He was out of it for the last ten years of his life, a sufferer from dementia.

RIP, Maxie.

Alice Thomas Ellis

1932–2005

Alice Thomas Ellis on the cover of a collection of *Oldie* columns

ALICE THOMAS ELLIS, or Anna Haycraft to give her her real name, joined *The Oldie* as Religious Correspondent in June 1996 (Issue 87). She had previously written a column for the *Catholic Herald*, but was sacked at the insistence of the Catholic bishops following what were considered insufficiently respectful comments about the then Archbishop of Liverpool, Derek Worlock.

A Catholic convert, who had trained as a nun before ill-health intervened, Anna was at war not just with Derek Worlock, but with all the modernisers in the Christian churches, not to mention the charismatics, the happy-clappies and the feminists – all those who were trying to promote religion as sweetness and light.

She managed to annoy quite a lot of readers with her uncompromising views, but as someone who always agreed with Lord Beaverbrook that 'readers have got to be annoyed', I liked her style. What no one could do was dismiss her as some kind of latter-day hermit. She had lived a full life, writing a number of acclaimed novels and working alongside her husband, Colin Haycraft, at the publishers, Duckworth. A talent-spotter of genius, she encouraged and edited any number of novelists including her fellow *Oldie* columnist, Beryl Bainbridge. At the same time she was the mother of seven children and the author of the long-running 'Home Life' column in the *Spectator*.

Anna was also an inspired cook. Visitors like me to the Haycraft house in Gloucester Crescent, Camden Town, will retain an image of her standing by the stove, cigarette in hand, while her guests tucked into a delicious meal at the table – she herself abstaining. There was a melancholy serenity about her which was very reassuring.

Anna had her fair share of misfortune – the accidental death of a son, her husband Colin's death, the sale of Duckworth – but none of it dented her faith. She never sought to ignore the reality that religion involves difficulties and doubts – a far cry from the smiley face and the thought that Jesus Loves You.

RICHARD INGRAMS

Repentance

THE DEATH of Myra Hindley caused many people to express their opinions of her. Nothing new was said, as they repeated what they had always thought, that she was either damned or saved and no two ways about it. Some said, good, she's gone to hell and serve her right, while others explained that they'd met her and she was really awfully nice. One or two who had also met her said she wasn't, but that view does not sound so original or put the viewer in the position of sage and seer, able to discern, through the mire, the underlying worth of even the most reviled human being. One man suggested that she merely exemplified to an unfortunate degree the darkness inherent in all of us, to which one can only respond in the popular phrase – *Excuse me...* Humility is all very well but there is no virtue in pretending to a viciousness we do not possess. I'm sure most of us could kill if the need arose, but few of us would torture a child to death, and the hint that we all harbour perverse inclinations and are prevented from indulging them only by a hypocritical lack of honesty and the crippling constraints of society is, to say the least, impertinent.

It was said that Hindley was truly repentant, but one is inclined to agree with those who claim that if this had been the case, she would not have sought release from prison and would have revealed the whereabouts of the graves of her victims.

There appears to be a pervasive sense in the air around the *bien-pensant* that even the most deep-dyed villains improve with time, as though remorse were somehow inevitable and not dependent on the examination of conscience or the recognition of the error of their ways, and that they become fit for polite society after a given period of incarceration, having 'paid their debt' to the above. This is understandable in the purveyors of religion, since repentance is part of their stock-in-trade and if they doubted its existence they would lose their *raison d'être*, but in everyone else it seems irrational. Where is the evidence? I have a friend who drinks with a number of ex-bank robbers whom the starry-eyed might describe as 'reformed': that is, they no longer rob banks, though not because they have thought better of it. They have all retained a genteel sufficiency enabling them to live comfortably, and they are all, to be frank, past it – old and not very well. None of them evinces remorse. Robbing banks was what they did. They got locked up for it and now they're out. End of story. The two murderers I know (there may be others but these got caught) are what is known as 'in denial', refusing to entertain any thoughts of guilt or shame and insisting on seeing themselves as unlucky.

On the other hand, I know people who suffer agonies because they were inadvertently short with the girl at the check-out, or left the cat outside overnight. The greater the sin, the less the remorse.

ALICE THOMAS ELLIS, JANUARY 2003

Noël, Cole and me...

Namedrops keep falling from my lips, says **CHARLES OSBORNE**

I have often been accused of name-dropping, merely because I tend to repeat amusing or interesting anecdotes of people I have met over the years whose names are well-known. So I have decided to produce a series of articles in which I shall proceed to drop the names of the rich and famous – and, occasionally, infamous. I am strengthened in this resolve by having read, in a life of Noël Coward, that *Name-Dropping* was going to be the title of one of the last books he ever planned.

Noël Coward's name may as well be the first one for me to drop, for I knew Coward, though not at all intimately. Back in the mid-Fifties, when I was a recently arrived young actor from Australia, I lodged in Ebury Street, London, in the house of a retired actress of the Thirties, Oriel Ross. (I had been introduced to Oriel by Derek Patmore, whom I'll come back to in a moment.)

Oriel knew Noël Coward very well. His London flat was just around the corner in Gerald Road, and he often came to Oriel's parties. I can remember one occasion when Coward and Cole Porter played piano duets of each other's songs, and we sang along with them. Coward was always polite and charming to me, and when on one occasion I told him that I had played a character called Morris in one of his plays, *Present Laughter*, in Melbourne, he said, flatteringly, 'But you're far too young for Morris, dear boy. You should have played Roland.'

Coward never uttered any of his famous witticisms to me. I suppose he was careful about where to cast his pearls. Let me go back to Derek Patmore. He was the great-grandson of the Victorian poet, Coventry Patmore. His mother, Brigit Patmore, whom I knew only towards the end of her life, had been the inamorata of several famous literary figures. Ezra Pound described her 'as one of the most charming people on this planet', and she was the friend also of Hemingway,

Yeats, T S Eliot and D H Lawrence.

Derek introduced me to Stephen Spender – more of Stephen in the future – and also to Somerset Maugham, whose secretary Derek thought I might become. Maugham took me to lunch one day at the Savoy to discuss the possibility, but he and I took an almost instant dislike to each other, so nothing came of that. I had been, and still am, an admirer of Maugham as a novelist and playwright, but over lunch that day I found him an insufferably snide and unpleasant creature, and he clearly thought I was a dreadful little upstart because I did not wag my tail with delight at every nasty remark he made. I think now that my judgment of him was crass, and that beneath the sneering exterior he may have been a shy and vulnerable person. But I didn't wait around to find out. In any case, I got the impression that he was looking for something more than a secretary, and the thought of being chased around the office by the elderly Maugham did not appeal to me.

I wouldn't have minded being chased around a film set by Tyrone Power. When I was a twelve-year-old who went to 'the flicks' on Saturday mornings in Brisbane, I couldn't decide whether he or Hedy Lamarr was the most desirable. I didn't meet Tyrone Power, however, until I was in my late twenties and he,

'No, it's just a piece of plastic – but it lets me talk to myself without people thinking I'm crazy'

producing a film in London, was in his early forties. My agent put me forward for a role in the film *Seven Waves Away*, and this led to my being given tea by Mr Power somewhere in Park Lane. He looked older than when I had seen him in those movies fifteen years previously, but he was still very good-looking. Disconcertingly, almost his first words to me indicated that he thought I looked too old for the role he was trying to cast. (A cabin boy, I think it was.) So let's just forget it and talk, he suggested. We did. He was charming and friendly, and did not make me feel he was in a hurry to get rid of me. We talked about Bernard Shaw, whom he admired as much as I did. He said I would make a splendid Marchbanks in *Candida*, and I was able to tell him I had played the role twice in Australia.

Power was about to appear on stage in *The Devil's Disciple*, and invited me to come and see it at the Golders Green Hippodrome, and visit him backstage afterwards. I did go, and I thought he gave a fine performance as Dick Dudgeon, but I was too shy to go backstage. I've certainly changed a lot since then.

It was in Melbourne in 1946 that I had first played in *Candida*, at the age of nineteen. Some months prior to that, I had been Assistant Stage Manager for a theatre company. One day, an American star arrived to play the lead in our next show. She was Diana Barrymore, daughter of the famous John Barrymore, and although only in her twenties she was already an alcoholic. (She died in 1960 at the age of thirty-nine.) We sat in a circle for the first reading of the play. I was opposite Miss Barrymore, who fascinated me because she wore only a dress and shoes (no stockings), with absolutely no underwear whatsoever. She sprawled in her chair with her skirt hitched up, and I could see – well, more of the lady than I expected to see. I couldn't take my eyes off her, until she noticed my gaze and snapped at me, 'Don't worry, it's only a cunt. It won't bite you.'

THE MEN'S OUTING

WINIFRED FOLEY *grew up in the Forest of Dean, the basis for her 1974 autobiography,* A Child of the Forest. *Here she tells the story of a grand day out to London for the men of her pit village*

It was never actually established who was the bright spark that put forward the notion of a day trip to London – an extremely novel idea for a bunch of customers in a little mining village pub in the Forest of Dean in 1920. Once the idea was planted, it grew, fed on a rich atmosphere of pros and cons, excitement, arguments and nervousness at the grandeur of the proposition. Without giving offence to old Jarge, the simpleton, they simply explained to him: 'Thee 'asn't got the brains to appreciate the sights up there, old un.' Jarge amicably agreed, and they crossed him off the list.

Bodger was a different problem. Bodger's trouble was his love for cider. He was the only child of devout old chapel-goers. His father had some status in the village for the way he punctuated the minister's sermons with his powerful, sonorous Amens. His mother was as cosy, helpful and friendly as Little Grey Rabbit in the Alison Uttley books. They were both teetotallers. How they produced lanky, alcoholic Bodger was a mystery.

Bodger worked in the pit. He gave his mother a modest amount for board and lodgings and 'pissed the rest up the back wall of the pub', as one village male commented. Bodger was given the option and said yes.

Organising such a trip was quite beyond the participants' combined talents. They agreed to consult the village entrepreneur, Lewis Maton, who owned a quarry. He had built his own house and three cottages from his profits as a stonemason, and had been to such places as Bristol and London several times. 'If 'im do say yes we shall have to treat the mingy bugger,' it was unanimously agreed. ''Im can come free, we'll pay 'is share.' A consultation at the pub with two glasses of cider thrown in, and Lewis worked it all out. They would go on one of the Great Western Railway's cheap fare

It was an extremely novel idea for a bunch of customers in a little mining village pub in the Forest of Dean in 1920

days. He would book them a meal at the GWR's hotel at Paddington station, and be their guide around London. In the meantime they must put sixpence per week in the kitty while he worked out the cost.

It took a long time for the funds to be raised, but at last the great day came. Wives polished up their men's Sunday boots till you could see your face in them, made sure there were no marks on the navy serge suits used only for funerals, borrowed a tidy shirt if necessary, and were prepared to hide from the tradesmen so their men would not be without a bit to spend in their pockets. The emancipation of women was still a long way off. Men were superior creatures who could drive vehicles, understand mechanics, work down the pits and go to war; creatures to be waited on.

Maybe so. But their men were dumbstruck by the vastness of Paddington station and reduced to nervous, throat-clearing, awestruck creatures when they were ushered into the opulence of the GWR hotel's dining-room. Shy as cowed schoolboys, they took their seats at the tables

ILLUSTRATION BY PETER BAILEY

Lewis had booked for them. His sang-froid helped them to overcome their nerves – after all, he was a forester, same as them. They hid their rough, pit-scoured hands on their laps as the waiters put the food in front of them, and none dared to use the starched table napkins.

Bodger was the least impressed – he thought the food was very good, though grossly over-priced. He must have been out pissing his wages up the wall when Lewis had told them that the price of the meal was inclusive. When he had finished, Bodger handed the waiter clearing his pudding plate a half-crown and was flattered and taken aback by the effusive bowing and thank you sirs. As they trailed into Praed Street, one of the men asked Bodger what he had given the waiter. 'Only me 'alf a crown to pay for me meal. I didn't expect the bugger to kip bowing till 'is arse nearly touched the ceilin'.'

'You bloody fool, you'd already paid for your meal. That was included in the price.'

At the thought of all that cider money wasted Bodger nearly exploded, and had to be forcibly restrained from going back to demand the return of his half-crown. Comfort for him was soon at hand in a Praed Street pub called The Load of Hay. This time there was no hope of restraining him. For Bodger all the wonders of the world could not compare with a golden glass of cider. 'Let the bugger stop there,' they agreed after Lewis warned him to ask a policeman the way to Paddington station if he wandered about and got lost.

Led by Lewis, the sightseeing and gawping in the windows began – but young Stan Prentice, the only bachelor among them, soon found something more interesting to gawp at: tight skirt atop slim legs on very high heels, crowned with a head of yellow hair framing a face of scarlet lips and mascaraed eyes with a very seductive expression. Nineteen years old, Stan had arrived after a bevy of six sisters to a besotted welcome from his parents. They all spoiled him, and he had quite a jingle of money in his pocket. Stan followed the well-worn path of men and emerged from a shabby back street half an hour later minus every penny, taken from his pocket by an accomplice of his seductress. He was lost, hungry but not

unhappy when he found a policeman to tell him he'd been robbed.

When Lewis and his charges got back to Praed Street, Bodger was sitting up against the wall of the pub; the landlord had no room for customers when they ran out of money. Lewis hoped the missing Stan had found his way back to the station for the train that was nearly due. There was no Stan. Worried and distressed, they had no choice but to go without him – and there were no more trains that evening. When they alighted at Gloucester to change trains for the rest of the journey, the stationmaster was chatting to Lewis when an irate Bodger

intervened, wagging an admonishing finger in his face. Bodger told the stationmaster, 'You can take them bloody railway tracks up now, mister, for I shan't be spending money to see a dull old hole like London again.' Aided by a borrowed fare from the police station and a night in the waiting-room, Stan returned home the next day, a wiser but not a sadder man.

Wives and children were delighted with the gaudy trinkets their menfolk had bought them – with the exception of Lil, an early example of women's lib, who demanded, 'If the men could 'ave a day's outin', 'ow about one for the women?' Village life was beginning to stir.

★ Great Bores of Today ★ No.34

'...I don't bother with Google any more as a search engine it's really limited I've got Dogbag which is brilliant because it has links to all the others I keep my photos on Drumstick and I've got a separate file which I keep in Moon-house which is brilliant because it doesn't matter what computer you use it's available anywhere in the world and you can download 3 gigabites for free and if you want to find an old friend go to Boatrace it's brilliant...'

© Fant and Dick

To Joyce,
with love and scribbles

When Joyce Grenfell commissioned artist **JOHN WARD** *to paint her portrait, it was the start of an enduring friendship, and an unusual correspondence*

I first met Joyce Grenfell in 1950, when I was making drawings for a stunt that Stephen Potter (the Gamesmanship man) had thought up to illustrate accents and modes of speaking throughout the Kingdom, as part of the Festival of Britain. It took place in the Lion and Unicorn Pavilion. Joyce and Hermione Gingold did the voices – Cockney, Scottish, Irish, etc. – and I did the illustrations. My drawings impressed Stephen Potter: he sat for a portrait drawing, and through him I cadged a sitting from Joyce in her dressing-room at the St Martin's Theatre – a rather frantic effort, drawn directly in Indian ink and wash.

With typical informality, she appeared one day on the doorstep of our studio on Glebe Place. Would I make a small watercolour drawing of her sitting in her flat, just down the King's Road? She lived above a sweetshop, and she wanted to be drawn against a dresser full of china, some fine, some hideous. The hideous pieces were precious gifts, with great sentimental value. We were separated by a table, and she explained that she was in the dining-room and I was in the kitchen. The sink was behind me.

This commission came at a moment when I was scratching around for a foothold in the portrait world, and I had the notion that one might return to the custom of people being drawn or painted in their own rooms, surrounded by their own things. Joyce liked my idea, and when I had finished her portrait, over which immense care was taken by both of us, she sent me along to draw her friends: Virginia Graham; Victor Stiebel; the doorman at her favourite theatre; Mrs Agos, her 'help'; Dick Addinsell, who wrote many of her songs, and even her fearsome aunt, Nancy Astor. The fact that Joyce also dabbled in watercolours helped our friendship, and no one could have been an easier or more encouraging patron.

It was after we had moved out of London to Kent that our exchange of letters began. I had always been a prize bad speller, and I hit on the idea that this might not look so awful if accompanied by some scribbles. A painter and draughtsman is forever making studies – hands, heads, poses, etc., bits of drawing of no consequence – around which I could string my letter. Joyce was the best of correspondents:

her answers were prompt, and business was conducted efficiently but with a light, amused touch. Her efficiency was as formidable as her generosity, and both were demonstrated when I told her about the Stour Music Festival, which I was helping to organise with Alfred Deller, the great counter-tenor. Funds were urgently needed, for although distinguished foreign musicians would travel to Kent and play for peanuts for Alfred, more trumpets were always needed and pianos had to be hired.

'Oh,' Joyce said, 'I'll come to Canterbury and give an evening show.'

A hall was booked, and down she came. She examined the piano, for her splendid accompanist Bill Blezard was to be in attendance, asked all who were working there their names, and never got a name wrong thereafter.

The show was a sell-out. There was some dismay when the bouquet gathered from the extensive gardens of Wye Agricultural College was given to a nervous Alfred Deller to present – he left it on a radiator and the droop was all too clear. Joyce cottoned on to what had happened at once, and it probably became one of those incidents on which her repertoire was founded.

I had always been a prize bad speller, and hit on the idea that this might not look so awful if accompanied by some scribbles

I illustrated two books for her – *George, Don't Do That* and *Stately as a Galleon*. She insisted that the royalties should be shared, and I still get a nice dribble of money from the Public Lending Rights. Richard Garnett of Macmillan's watched over the publication, and he had to be drawn for the series.

Any contact with Joyce seemed to lead to odd wonders. She was a great fan and friend of Walter de la Mare, and I was sent to draw him. At some point in the sitting he nodded to a china cat ornamenting the fireplace. 'What name would you give that cat?'

I can't remember what I said, but later I discovered that the naming of cats was one of Edward Lear's tests of imagination.

Joyce opened windows to so much for me, and I remember her with great affection and love.

John Ward's letter, with its illustrated envelope, sent to Joyce Grenfell from Hereford at Christmas time, 1955. Opposite: his 1954 portrait of Joyce in her flat, 'against a dresser full of china, some fine, some hideous'

Max's MAN

*Oldie columnist **ALICE PITMAN** caught up with the curious career of Lord Beaverbrook's last private secretary, Colin Vines*

'If you want to know what Lord Beaverbrook was like as an old man,' A J P Taylor once wrote, 'then read *A Little Nut-Brown Man* by Colin Vines.'

Published over thirty years ago, the book is an account of the last three years of Beaverbrook's life from the perspective of the young author, then a gauche twenty-eight-year-old, dispatched in 1962 to the newspaper proprietor's villa in the South of France to work as his private secretary. Written in an unpretentious, unwittingly Pooterish style, and generally considered by many oldie journalists to be an underrated comic classic, Colin Vines described the agonies of working for a man for whom ritual humiliation of his young employee became a daily sport. It seemed that no matter how hard Colin tried, he seldom managed to keep ahead of Beaverbrook's wicked teasing. 'Every day was like picking my way through a minefield and with every move finding myself blown up,' wrote Colin Vines. 'His features, when I was near, were fixed in an angry, or disapproving, or disappointed, or disconcerting, frown; for my part there had to be extreme wariness, suspicion, the fear of being caught out.'

While the book succeeds in making us suffer with Colin Vines, its great achievement is to make us laugh at the same time. 'Colin Vines was so stupid,' A J P Taylor said, 'that he entertained Beaverbrook through his stupidity.'

In hindsight, this is something Colin does not disagree with. 'For example, we would be sitting by the swimming-pool and Beaverbrook would say, "Read the leader in the *Times*," and he'd go and turn the pool on to bring water up from the sea. It would make a hell of a row and he'd have me reading over this dreadful noise. He was an absolute devil!'

Beaverbrook, however, does not always come across as a complete ogre. He appeared genuinely fond of his nervous, chain-smoking secretary, referring to him by a variety of affectionate nicknames, from Destry (after Beaverbrook's favourite film, *Destry Rides Again*) and Young Lochinvar to Boy, General and Mister. 'You're a nice boy,' he once told Colin, 'It's only your memory, and smelling of smoke, that's against you.' 'I could never really understand why,' says Colin, 'but Beaverbrook was the only man who ever liked me. Extraordinary!'

Although Colin was never able to like Beaverbrook in return, he admired him greatly. 'He could do all the things I couldn't. He was rich, powerful, he employed two thousand people, he lived in marvellous accommodation, had an endless supply of money and he knew everybody on equal terms, mixing with the most distinguished people in the world. I thought, fancy being able to do all that, how amazing!'

Perhaps the most distinguished of all Beaverbrook's friends was Sir Winston Churchill, who came to dinner just two days after Colin arrived in the South of France. 'Churchill was very old, he was really past it by the time I saw him, and wasn't quite all there, though he had flashes. You see, Beaverbrook died from the legs upwards, while Churchill died from the head downwards.' In *A Little Nut-Brown Man* Colin movingly describes hearing Churchill and Beaverbrook singing old songs together after dinner on the patio: 'An amazing and rather sad sound.'

Although he did not realise it at the time, he now believes he was hired by Beaverbrook's then fiancée Lady Dunn as a way of supplanting the young female secretaries. 'He always had girls, attractive young women. When Lady Dunn got her claws into him, the first thing she did was to subtly get rid of the girl secretaries. She certainly didn't want pretty young girls around the place when she herself was fifty.'

Following Beaverbrook's death, Colin Vines worked briefly for his son Max Aitken (who clearly did not know what to do with him) before getting a transfer to the Manchester *Daily Express*. 'They sent me out to be a reporter, but I was no good at it. This news editor chap said, "Right, Vines, go down to Bellevue Zoo where there's a couple of deer, the first deer to be produced by artificial insemination!"' He dutifully dashed off to the zoo and when he got back to the office found he couldn't think of anything to write. 'I couldn't even write a caption to accompany the piece!' he laughs. When the news editor eventually asked for the copy, Vines told him: 'I'm awfully sorry, I can't think of anything to say.' He was sacked a day later.

Colin then went to work as a news typist for BBC External Services, where he stayed for twenty-two years, retiring prematurely due to the introduction of television into the newsroom in the late 1970s, which he says eventually drove him insane. 'My personnel officer referred me to the BBC doctor to see if he would diagnose me as mad, and thus suitable for early retirement. After five minutes' chat, the BBC doctor said firmly, "Well, I'll tell you this, you're perfectly sane. If you're mad it's only when you're in the newsroom."'

Top left, the young Colin Vines with Lord Beaverbrook in the South of France; and, above, in retirement with Alice Pitman's children

It was during the early years at the BBC that he wrote *A Little Nut-Brown Man*. 'I had to send it to Lady Beaverbrook to make sure that I wasn't going to be sued for libel. There's no libel in it, but people do sue, look at Robert Maxwell!' Lady Beaverbrook, who disliked the book intensely, sent it on to Max Aitken. 'He said, "What the hell are we going to do with this dreadful book?"' Trembling with fear, Vines was then summoned to the *Express* offices, where they offered to buy the manuscript from him for a derisory £500. 'Thank God the figure was so low, because then I could go ahead and publish it, thanks to Robert Pitman [Alice Pitman's father],

who recommended the book to the publishers. He thought it was good when nobody else did.' In fact some were most contemptuous of *A Little Nut-Brown Man*. Tom Driberg referred to it as 'a pathetic book' and its author as 'a miserable servant and craven rabbit'.

Colin Vines is a self-confessed maverick who at sixty-eight appears to have reached a state of oldie-induced contentment, despite suffering quite badly from emphysema. Yet he still feels very much an outsider. 'I have always felt detached from the world; I am someone who prefers to observe, rather than participate in life.' Spending time with Colin is like witnessing a man who has recently popped out of a pre-war time capsule into a modern world that he does not comprehend. Scantily-dressed models in the *Daily Telegraph*, smutty American TV imports and ubiquitous Muzak – particularly in his GP's waiting room – are just a few of the subjects which leave him chronically bewildered and furious. Certainly his voice, a cross between astronomer Patrick Moore's and Rex Harrison's Professor Higgins, seems to belong to a different era.

Before emphysema became a problem, he could often be seen zooming around the Home Counties on his motorbike, like Toad of Toad Hall, complete with monocle. When the mood took him, he would occasionally drop in on famous or distinguished people regardless of whether he knew them or not.

Why? 'I am an observer and I simply wanted to see what would happen.'

Once, he dropped in on Malcolm Muggeridge. His wife Kitty answered the door and when Vines, in full biker's regalia, introduced himself, she exclaimed, 'Oh, goodness gracious me! Malcolm! Lord Beaverbrook's secretary is here to see you!' Colin's memory of that occasion is forever clouded by the fact that Muggeridge had not read *A Little Nut-Brown Man*. 'I thought, bloody hell, how could you, one of the most distinguished journalists of the twentieth century, not have read my book? I was outraged! Absolutely outraged!' Later, he sent Muggeridge a copy and was so cross when Muggeridge failed to praise it in his thank-you letter that he wrote and asked for the book to be sent back.

Now retired, he lives with his wife Joy, a writer, in 'a rabbit hutch' in the Oxfordshire countryside. They have three children – Lucy, Edward and Luke

– all now in their thirties. When he is not tending to his garden, penning the odd obituary for the nationals ('the only form of journalism I'm any good at') or writing his journal (which he has loyally kept up since 1947), he pops down to the Tesco superstore in Bicester. Sometimes he visits his daughter Lucy and her three young children in Market Drayton, parking his caravan in her garden and staying for a few days. Colin also enjoys going to memorial services and often complains about them afterwards, either because the readings were boring or the acoustics were dreadful, or both.

> **When the mood took him, he would drop in on famous people regardless of whether he knew them**

Those far off days of 'absolute hell' spent running around like a headless chicken after the little nut-brown man still cast a shadow over Colin Vines. He frequently talks about Beaverbrook, and although he is adamant that he never liked him, I wonder if, with the passing of the years, he hasn't begun to feel a creeping affection for the old boy. Recently, he wrote to *Express* proprietor Richard Desmond asking if he could buy the Epstein bust of Beaverbrook.

'Oh, no!' Desmond replied, 'You can't have that! It's outside my door. It inspires me. If ever you want to come and have a look at it though, just let me know.' So Colin took him up on his offer. 'How do you do?' said Desmond, cheerfully emerging from his office, hand outstretched in greeting. 'Who are you?' asked Colin. 'This is Richard Desmond!' exclaimed Desmond's secretary, aghast. Desmond offered Colin lemon tea and a cigar. 'I can't have one of those!' Colin exclaimed, 'I'm dying of emphysema.'

Whenever he is asked about his time with Beaverbrook, Colin says: 'I knew Beaverbrook only at the end of his life and so as far as I have been able to make out, the person who said "All the best things and all the worst things you hear about Max Beaverbrook are probably true" got it about right. As for me, I think of echoing Prime Minister Bonar Law, who on his deathbed told Beaverbrook: "You are a very curious fellow."'

The same could well be said about his last secretary.

Modern life

What is... *chickenability?*

WALTER PATER wrote that 'all art constantly aspires to the condition of music'. In the food industry, it would seem that all groceries constantly aspire to the condition of chicken. All food manufacturers know that chicken is the touchstone of foodstuffs. So much so that in 2001 the marketing team charged with relaunching a popular British brand came up with the notion of 'chickenability'. The idea was that non-poultry food products could be marketed to represent the convenience and familiarity of chicken.

After a company merger, Young's Bluecrest, the largest producer of seafood in the UK, decided to focus their relaunch campaign on giving their fish products 'chickenability'. They realised that although consumers liked eating fish, they were put off by the attendant skin and bones. They therefore set about developing fish products which offered the accessibility and convenience of a cellophane-wrapped chicken breast, taking away all the 'nasties'.

The desirability of chicken rests on its familiarity and affordability. It is also a meat acceptable to most religions and cultures. As a white meat, chicken is the meat of choice for the health-conscious, and it accounts for nearly half of all fresh meat eaten in the UK. According to research by the European Commission, chicken is the 'meat of the future', and consumption is predicted to rise from the 21 kg consumed per capita in 2000 to 24.8 kg in 2008. Not good news if you're a battery chicken.

The rise of chicken poses a huge challenge to those products that aspire to chickenability. Can other foodstuffs ever win the accolade of 'the new chicken'? Or, as the *Grocer* magazine put it last year, 'Can salmon become the new poultry?' Will brainwashed consumers one day find themselves slipping microwaveable sushi-flavoured potato fingers into their shopping baskets with the easy familiarity of a pack of chicken drumsticks? And what about the vegetarians? According to the Vegetarian Society, five per cent of the UK's adult population is vegetarian and their numbers swell by an average of two thousand people a week.

Perhaps the world is ready for the next stage: courgettability.

The drive to supply the consumer's insatiable appetite for chicken is neatly satirised in Margaret Atwood's novel, *Oryx and Crake*, set in the near future of genetic engineering. Her fictional food scientists have developed an organism which they have affectionately dubbed 'chickienobs'. These are genetically altered chickens that have no feathers and no brains and produce only the most useful chicken parts, such as legs and breasts. This endlessly replenishing flesh can be sliced off in the manner of a doner kebab. Perhaps this is the ultimate in 'chickenability' – the boneless, skinless convenience meal.

The very inoffensiveness of chicken (inoffensive, that is, if you're not a vegetarian or a Buddhist) has a lot to answer for. Have you noticed that whenever someone tries to persuade you to sample something ostensibly unappetising – be it frogs' legs or pigs' testicles – they always use the line that 'it tastes just like chicken'? A recent edition of *Private Eye* referred to a story in which a pregnant woman from Brighton placed an advertisement for her placenta in the window of a vegetarian food shop. Her reasoning was that it would be a pity for such a nutritious piece of meat to go to waste. 'Fried with a little garlic and some oregano, it's delicious,' the woman claimed. 'A bit like chicken, actually.'

E E HARDING

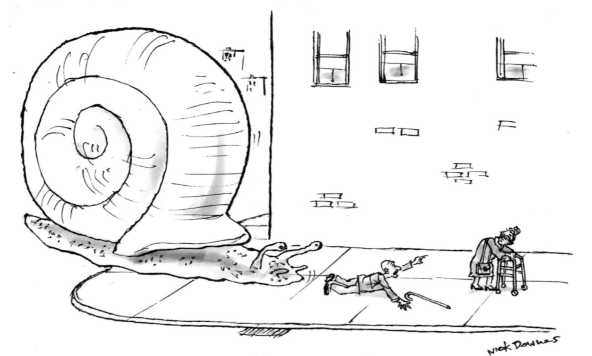

'Go on without me – save yourself!'

Olden life

What were... *spats?*

WHO WAS the last man in Britain to wear spats? Was it perhaps Lord David Cecil, that gauche-seeming Oxford don who spoke in shrill Edwardian cadences, and – if memory serves – displayed an anachronistically spatted foot on television? If so, how right that the last spats-wearer should have been a lord. Once a status symbol, spats have for long been little more than a running joke in the works of P G Wodehouse. His *Young Men in Spats* was published in 1936, when spats were already as rare as the collapsible top hat.

In Oxford Dictionary terms, spats were 'a form of short gaiter worn over the instep and reaching only a little way above the ankle, usually fastened under the foot by means of a strap'. They had four buttons down the side. Webster's Dictionary says they were worn 'for protection or appearance'. They were a supremely useless garment, but that did not prevent Lord Reith of the BBC wearing them. There is a glorious photograph of a white-spatted, top-hatted Reith towering above a scruffy-shifty Prime Minister (Ramsay MacDonald).

Spats were descended from spatter-dashes, a kind of long leggings to keep trousers or stockings from being mud-spattered. As such, well pipe-clayed, they formed part of military uniform. In mid-Victorian times, with trousers as we know them well established, and with less mud on fashionable streets, leggings became redundant, other than for sporting wear. However, sarto-rial taste ruled that, as shirts needed cuffs, so did trousers, the legs of which ought not to break directly on the shoe.

The only 'protection' they afforded was against puppy bites, but the flash of white, pearl, grey or lavender at the ankle lent, as it were, a polite footnote to the figure.

Vanity Fair's gallery of late Victorian and Edwardian swells shows Winston Churchill, Arthur Balfour and Thomas Hardy all wearing spats in formal attire, and the caricaturist 'Ape' is himself portrayed as a portly spatted figure who must have had trouble in reaching those eight buttons unaided.

That proper gent, Babar the Elephant, gets kitted out in spats

In a preface to *Joy in the Morning* (1947), P G Wodehouse reminisces about the spats he wore as a young man about town, *c.*1905. They lent 'a sort of gay *diablerie* to the wearer's appearance', causing cadgers in the street to address him as 'Captain' or even 'M'Lord', and it did much to win over otherwise suspicious butlers. The wearing of spats, Wodehouse says, went out with the moneyed, monocled, valet-employing 'knut', a breed killed off in Flanders. In the Jeeves annals we find Bertie Wooster led astray by a sighting of Old Etonian spats in a window in Burlington Arcade. Jeeves dislikes this purchase as intensely as he abhorred a scarlet cummerbund or a white mess jacket. When the young master says, 'All right, then... you may burn them,' Jeeves replies, 'I have already done so. Before breakfast this morning. A quiet grey is more suitable, sir.'

In *After Hours With P G Wodehouse* Richard Usborne recalls the strange story of the German spy who in 1942 was reputedly dropped near Dartmoor and was denounced as a suspicious character because he was wearing spats, having been kitted out by German intelligence in what was thought to be the correct attire for an upper-class Englishman. Usborne suggests that Hitler's interpreter, Dr Paul Schmidt, a devotee of Wodehouse, was possibly the brains behind this howler. Whatever the truth, it is a pretty story and makes a change from those tales of parachuted nuns wearing German field boots.

During World War Two British soldiers were issued with a little-loved form of spats known as 'anklets, web', into which the legs of battle-dress trousers were tucked. Failure to wear 'anklets, web' could result in a spell of cookhouse fatigues, or worse.

E S TURNER

Life', said Reg, 'doesn't bear much looking into.' I nodded. Later I discovered he was quoting from Joseph Conrad. Reg was keen on Conrad and used to bring brown paper-wrapped copies of *The Secret Agent* and *Lord Jim* down the freshly swabbed steps of the Ladies' Toilet. Here he would share his lunch and literary conversation in my little green attendant's booth amid the smell of disinfectant, packets of toilet rolls and the occasional swirl of water.

It was 1960. After ten years on the *Birmingham Post* I'd come south to seek fame and fortune and, not immediately finding either, accepted the 'position' of Temporary Supervisor, The Ladies' Toilet, Trafalgar Square, West End Division, London WC2. A large woman in violet overalls had handed me a bucket, mop, several slabs of soap, a pair of pink rubber gloves, my own set of overalls and a large key.

ILLUSTRATION BY PETER BAILEY

FIRE DOWN BELOW

There was absolutely no training – 'You'll learn on the job, dear' – and the hours were 9 am to 5 pm. Sharp.

Reg had the Gents' adjoining, and we used to swap notes, although I never quite plucked up the courage to descend the steps to his cubby-hole. From what he told me, we had a far better class of graffiti: things like 'Women have nothing to lose but their [lavatory] chains' and 'Edna O'Brien for Pope'. I once saw, and copied down immediately, the following lines:

Though death is always itching at our backs
And hopes and fears in equal strength we have,
There's nothing keeps a girl from high collapse
As sitting peacefully in London's Lavs.

I never knew who wrote it, and Reg was impressed. Being so close to such centres of excellence as the National Gallery, the Garrick Club and the crypt of St Martin-in-the-Fields, we naturally inherited a fairly high standard of scholarship and reference. Reg was fond of telling the story of a certain eminent Middle European art historian who apparently spent long hours in his

It was another peaceful day in the Ladies' Toilet for supervisor **PAULA KELLY** *when, suddenly, BOOM!!!*

favourite cubicle in the winter writing his magnum opus on the work of the brothers van Eyck. One day – and this was a little before the Wolfenden Report made life so much easier for some of our brothers – a tightly folded piece of paper was pushed through a tiny hole in the cubicle wall towards the perspiring sage. Unfolding it, he read, in clumsy capitals: 'WHAT DO YOU LIKE?' By the time he had composed, in reply, a reasoned account of the early life in Ghent of Hubert and Jan and their monumental commission of 1432 for the altarpiece known as 'The Mystic Lamb', the door of the next-door cubicle swung idly open and the questioner was long gone.

Reg was very keen on brasswork, and the smell of Duraglit hung about his person as he unwrapped his corned beef and tomato sandwiches during our shared lunch breaks. My forte was the floors, which were washed down

twice a day and once brought a Russian lady in patent-leather boots very close to a sticky end. Her language, I'm told, was unprintable. On the whole, though, my little realm was remarkably polite and ordered. I certainly never had a case of what you might call hanky-panky – apart, that is, from the strange events known ever after as the mystery of the exploding call-girl. It went something like this.

Early one afternoon – Reg had returned to his own kingdom and I was tidying up the crumbs and the grease-proof paper – there was a loud tapping on the glass window of my den. I peered out. A young woman was standing there, with red velvet dress and matching hair, swinging a handbag. I recognised her as one of the lady cruisers who used to pop in for a quick wash and brush-up between clients. Mostly rather easy-going and excellent company, and I'd made friends with several of them. Not this one, though. 'Yes?' I said.

'Change,' she said, waving a half-crown in my face.

With a roar not unlike the beginning of a Royal Salute, the cubicle rose up

'It's not my job to give change,' I said. (It's amazing how quickly one adopts the tone of officialdom, and anyway it wasn't my job and I didn't like her tone.)

'Well, 'ow am I s'posed to geddit, then?'

'If,' I said, with the icy tones of Joyce Carey's station refreshments supervisor in *Brief Encounter*, 'you'd be so good as to re-ascend the stairs and make some small purchase at Lyons Corner House or a similar establishment, I think you'd find that the cashier would furnish you with the necessary.'

She gave me a look, turned on her heel and disappeared up the curved tiled stairs. Whether or not she took the rest of my advice I don't know, but she didn't come back. At least, not immediately.

About two hours later, when the kettle was just boiling for my last tea break, there was a clatter of high heels and mascara and a woman in the identical red dress came almost tumbling down the stairs, shoved a penny into the slot, pushed through the rolling metal bar, dashed into a cubicle and shot the bolt. She didn't give me much time but I could see who it was. No sooner had she shut herself in than a second pair of feet came clattering down, much bigger and heavier, and round the corner came a large and panting man, wearing a hat and a look of profound hostility. I barred his way. Well, I drew the line at men – except Reg, and he didn't count.

'This is a ladies' convenience,' I said. 'I think you'll find the gents' adjacent.'

'I don't want the effin' convenience,' he said. 'Did a girl just come in 'ere? Red 'air, red clobber?'

'I am not at liberty,' I Careyed, 'to discuss my clients with strangers, and I'll thank you to withdraw from an area in which you are neither normal nor welcome.'

'I'll give you effin' normal,' he said and moved menacingly forward.

A whistle was not part of the equipment issued to an acting Temporary Ladies' Toilet Supervisor, but I might have improvised had not a far more interesting sound occurred.

With a roar not unlike the beginning of a Royal Salute, the cubicle in which La Pasionaria had taken refuge rose solemnly from its marble base, hovered for a moment in the dust-strewn air and then disappeared through the ceiling, disintegrating as it did into clusters of wood splinters and fiery tongues and leaving a clear view of London sky and one blackened and clearly bewildered pigeon.

'Christmas, Doris!' said the bloke. 'Wotcher want ter do that for?' And legged it back up the stairs.

I couldn't have put it better myself. Of Doris herself there was not a trace. And never was. The combined efforts of Reg, a police sergeant, Mrs Kenny from the newspaper kiosk and yours truly revealed nothing, not even a bit of handbag or a single singed red hair. Reg said it was like something out of Conrad or Dickens. Part of a Cold War plot or spontaneous combustion. It was certainly the most exciting thing that happened to me during my six months at Her Majesty's Convenience and probably the loudest thing to happen in a public toilet ever. The Sixties were off to a roaring start.

RANT

ONE OF the minor hazards of Olden Life was treading in dogs' messes. In those days the streets of our towns and suburbs were littered with dogs' messes in various stages of freshness, and they were usually trodden on by children who didn't look where they were going or adults making their way home in the dark. Bringing a dog's mess home on one's shoe was greeted with a terrible cry of revulsion and despair: suspects were told to stay exactly where they were and advance no further into the house, after which they were expected to stand, stork-like, on one foot and then another so that the soles of their shoes could be inspected. Removing the mess was a repulsive business, still more so if tractor-soled shoes were involved, and the shoes were eventually propped up to dry after being thoroughly scrubbed with Jeyes Fluid.

Persuading dog owners to clear up behind them is, needless to say, an American innovation, but it has come at a price. Modern dog-owners are expected to grab hold of the mess in a poly-thene bag which they then turn inside-out and knot at one end before dropping it into a bin marked 'Dog Waste', many of which carry a comical silhouette of an Airedale standing over a steaming mess scored out with a large red cross. The trouble is that many dog-owners are too lazy or too stupid to carry the exercise through to its conclusion: they pick up the mess and put it in the bag but then hurl the thing on the ground. The result is the indestructible dog's mess. Richmond Park, the towpath of the Thames and even the South Downs are now peppered with polythene-wrapped dogs' messes, some of which have been there, to my certain knowledge, for three or four years at least. Left to its own devices, excrement will dry out in the sun or be washed away by the rain in a matter of days: these new horrors seem set to outlive us all. It makes me quite nostalgic for the bad old days.

JEREMY LEWIS

Larry
1927–2003

L arry, whose real name was Terence Parkes, died in 2003 at the age of seventy-five. He had been a regular contributor to *The Oldie* since the launch in 1992, both as a cartoonist and as an illustrator.

Some cartoonists 'go off' as they get older. Larry never did. When he sent in half a dozen 'singles', at least one or even two of them would be accepted. I don't think any other artist had such a good hit rate.

Larry was equally good in colour, and illustrated Wilfred De'Ath's column for five years

[*see page 79*]. He was a convivial and modest man who once said, 'A cartoonist should have a hack's temperament and not be too precious.'

RICHARD INGRAMS

How's your father?

ANTHONY PERRY's *father left home in a newly purchased Lagonda car with a blonde lady when he was still a baby. Years later their paths crossed in a peculiar way...*

In 1963 or thereabouts, while still a youngish man hoping for elusive fame or at least fortune, I found myself attending the consulting rooms of one Dr Wilfred Bion at 135 Harley Street. I went each day for fifty minutes of beneficial psychoanalysis and an opportunity to whinge about how unfair life had been to me. I lay each day on his leatherette slab delving into my past, muttering imprecations against all those who had failed to love me and in particular, of course, my mother, who had clearly not wanted me and barely cared whether I lived or died. It was an expensive way of getting one's own back.

My father, Raymond, whom I had hardly known, came in for his share of abuse. He had left home in a newly purchased Lagonda car with a blonde lady while I was still a baby – on the advice of a psychiatrist, so my mother claimed, who had told him that a little of what he fancied would do him good. Such advice we should all get, and I never saw him again or heard from him until I was nineteen.

I phoned him up when I came out of the army. 'Hello, old boy,' he said, as if we had parted the week before, and suggested we meet for dinner at the Café Royal. 'You'll recognise me, I'm as bald as a coot.'

We were friends for a couple of years and then we had a serious row over the ownership of my grandfather's ivory-topped swagger stick (dig that, Dr Freud!), after which he moved away to the country and I lost track of him again.

So each day I lay, consorting with my new father, pouring out my woes and trying to shift the blame for my delinquent and unfulfilled life onto my unloving parents.

But something rather surprising was to happen. After one particularly satisfying session I came bounding down the stairs, full of useful 'insights', stumbled, picked myself up and leant against the hall table for a moment.

There, on the table, was a letter addressed to me. 'A R Perry', it said.

I am Richard Anthony, so sometimes people put 'A R', but something rumbled in my head. I went down to the receptionist. 'Is this letter for me?' I asked.

Was it really possible that, as I lay on Dr Bion's couch, just above me had been the soles of my father's shoes, with his feet inside them?

'No, it's for the gentleman in the flat upstairs.'

I hadn't seen my father for years but my brother had once given me a HUNter telephone number for him – the relief exchange then covering Baker Street and Harley Street. My mind spun. Could it possibly be...?

Then, 'Would Mr Perry perhaps be a bald-headed man, about sixty?' I asked. 'A Mr Arthur Raymond Perry?'

'Yes,' she said brightly. 'Do you know him? He's just moved. I've promised to send on his letters.'

Was it really possible that, as I lay recumbent on Père Bion's couch, staring up at the ceiling, just above me had been the soles of my father's shoes, with his feet inside them? If you don't believe me or fail to regard this as wholly extraordinary, stop reading now and get on with your miserable, unanalysed and entirely predictable lives.

And it really was true, and I remember hugging the news to me – barely able to wait to report to the stern and impenetrable Dr Bion. He would be surprised. Perhaps he would begin future lectures: 'I once had an interesting patient [me] whose uncaring father...' And the psychoanalytical world would come to a numbed halt at the amazing situation when it was written up in the medical journals.

Alas, it was not to be. The moment I arrived at the next day's session I blurted out my story. There was a long silence. Bion seldom rushed into print but there was a longer silence than usual.

'What,' he eventually asked, 'what significance do you attach to this coincidence?'

And there was none. It was just that, a coincidence, albeit an extraordinary one. Maybe he knew, or had wondered as I talked about my parents, whether the Perry upstairs was my father. He was incredibly smart and knew almost everything so he probably knew that too.

I learnt later that he was quite a big name in the analysis business, but I developed feelings of gratitude and affection for him as a human being. When he died in 1979 I was upset and felt that I had lost a father – far more so than when my own father died a few years later.

115

HAMMING IT UP

STANLEY PRICE *once followed Jacques Tati around New York in pursuit of an elastic sandwich*

Between 1949 and 1959 Jacques Tati made three films of comic genius, *Jour de Fête, Les vacances de Monsieur Hulot* and *Mon Oncle.* It took him another thirteen years to make the next two, which were not as successful, and that was that. Tati, as I learned to my cost, was a perfectionist.

Tati came to New York to publicise *Mon Oncle,* and *Life* decided he was worthy of a 'picture essay'. I was chosen as the reporter, presumably on the grounds that I had the best English with a French accent. The photographer was the unusually genial, for a *Life* photographer anyway, Yale Joel. In my mind Tati was forever Monsieur Hulot, thin, stooping, hesitantly bird-like in movement. In person he turned out very well built, straight and un-avian. In advance Yale and I had decided that our story would

'That is it,' Tati said. 'Only in America are there such sandwiches. I do that for you. It makes funny pictures, yes?'

be Tati's reactions to Manhattan. Given his visual genius it seemed impertinent to tell him what pictures we wanted. We would leave it to him. Tati liked the idea of going round New York responding to whatever took his fancy. We suggested it might be fun to photograph him in the raincoat, hat and umbrella of Monsieur Hulot. His face fell. 'But I have not brought them with me.'

I said we could buy something similar here. He looked at me piteously. The reporter was clearly a moron. It had taken him two years to find the right raincoat and get the hat into the right shape. At our expense we cabled Paris to have the items expressed to us. Meanwhile we went off in search of Tati-friendly locations and situations.

He was fascinated by how passengers got into the low-slung New York taxis, the sculptures at the Museum of Modern Art – his body language reacting intuitively to them all – and by Katz's famous delicatessen on the Lower East Side. There Tati watched an elderly rabbi eating a pastrami sandwich on rye with coleslaw. The rabbi held the immense

sandwich with both hands to contain the mountainous filling. The stringy pastrami was as hard to bite free from the sandwich as spaghetti, and in his exertions the coleslaw kept spilling up the rabbi's sleeve.

'That is it,' Tati said. 'Only in America are there such sandwiches. I do that for you. It makes funny pictures, yes?'

Next day the Hulot costume arrived. Tati put it on and was transformed. The short, bedraggled raincoat and battered hat made him taller and ganglier. He paced the hotel room for us like a short-sighted ostrich in search of a lost egg.

Meanwhile, for a considerable sum – money, in those palmy days, was never a problem for Time-Life – I arranged to borrow the lunch counter of a local delicatessen. Tati arrived and inspected the pastrami. It wasn't elastic enough for him, so he ordered the ham. It was a jumbo sandwich with mayonnaise and coleslaw. Tati took a bite. A long piece of ham disengaged itself and hung down his chin. Joel was photographing happily.

'It's no good,' Tati said. 'The ham should stretch from the sandwich into my mouth. We need some elastic under the ham so I can really pull it.'

'Elastic?' we said.

'We put the elastic under the ham. Broad elastic or rubber. It won't show in the picture.'

The deli owner wanted us out by lunchtime. Time was flying. Maybe a garage would sell me an inner tube I could cut into strips. I rushed out onto Fifth Avenue. The nearest garage was probably three miles away in the Bronx. Opposite was the elegant Saks department store. I raced in and asked the nearest salesgirl if she had any broad, thin rubber. 'What for?' she asked.

'Just need it in a hurry.'

'How about elastic?' She produced a reel of thin elastic.

A brainwave struck. I got the elevator up to the lingerie department. I found a salesgirl in a quiet corner.

'Could I see the cheapest corset you've got?'

Here, I could see her thinking, is a cheapskate with a fat wife. 'What size foundation garment, sir?'

'It doesn't matter, but it must be pink.'

She produced a $20 pink foundation garment. I put down a $20 note.

'Have you got any scissors?' I said. 'And don't ask me to explain.'

She handed me a pair of scissors. She clearly had no intention of asking a crazed pervert to explain anything. I cut the elastic side panels from the foundation garment, took them and ran.

Back at the deli, time was running out. Joel said, 'Jeezuz, where have you been?'

'It's a long story,' I said, handing Tati the hard-won elastic panel. He reassembled the sandwich with the ham laid on top of the panel. He bit and pulled and Joel clicked away.

'It's no good,' Tati said.

'It's fine,' Joel said.

'No,' said Tati. 'The elastic is not stretchy enough. I have idea. We need surgical gloves. We cut the fingers off.'

I was out of the door, sprinting for the corner drugstore. I bought a pair of pink surgical rubber gloves, raced back and handed them to Tati. He couldn't cut the fingers off with a knife. The deli owner, by now convinced a story would appear in *Life* sending up his sandwiches, reluctantly brought Tati some scissors. He watched him remove the pink fingers, slit the glove and remake the sandwich again. Tati bit, Joel clicked, the stretch was wonderful, but the ham fell off.

'Still no good,' Tati said.

'Time's up,' the deli owner said.

'I know how to fix it,' Tati said. 'We do it perfect tomorrow.'

Out of Tati's earshot, Joel said, 'We don't do it perfect tomorrow. Somehow it ain't that funny any more.'

'I know,' I said, and for the first time I cursed a rabbi.

That evening I went over to Tati's hotel to talk to him about the art of comedy. I went up to his suite. He was sitting in a chair with a large ham sandwich in front of him, busy with a needle and thread sewing a piece of ham onto the doctored surgical glove.

Next day we went all over town taking pictures. Somehow the delicatessen and the ham sandwich got forgotten, but I couldn't help wondering what the chambermaid was telling the others: 'You'll never guess what I found in that crazy Frenchman's room!'

ISSUE 63, JULY 1994 BY QUENTIN BLAKE

ISSUE 193, APRIL 2005 BY ROBERT GEARY

Some facts about Nina Bawden, CBE. She was born in London in 1925, educated at Ilford County High School for Girls, and then at Somerville College, Oxford. She has written twenty adult novels, seventeen for children and her 'almost an autobiography', *In My Own Time*. She has served as a magistrate, also on councils for various literary bodies, such as PEN. She was married to Austen Kark, formerly Managing Director of External Services for the BBC, who was killed in the Potter's Bar rail crash of 10th May 2002, in which she herself was seriously injured.

We starting talking as if we had known each other for years.

I'm going to quote from *Carrie's War*, one of your children's books: 'Things are seldom as bad as you think they are going to be. Not when you come to them. So it is a waste of time being afraid.' Do you remember writing that?
I do. It was very important to me. Because when this dreadful thing happened at Potter's Bar...

The train crash?
Yes, when my dear husband was killed – murdered by the railway – and I was badly injured. I was surprised that I was able to bear it better than I would ever have imagined. I don't know why. We were always taught, I suppose, to endure things. And it seems reasonable. Everyone's life isn't happy. When things go wrong you have to accept them and work them into your life somehow.

That's what you hope you can do, but the crash was such a huge catastrophe to have to endure.
I suppose you decide you are going to go on living. You do just have to accept it. You are not special. You have to live with things.

They say some survivors of a disaster feel guilty...
I don't feel guilty. I just feel sad. In some ways I feel all our life together was a dream. I feel angry that Austen didn't survive as well. No, I don't feel guilty I survived – astonished, and in some ways sorry. Crushed up in the carriage, I said, apparently, that I did not want to stay. But the squadron leader who saved my life insisted I stayed, so I did. Sometimes I wish

Nina Bawden

The acclaimed novelist and children's writer talked to Oldie agony aunt **MAVIS NICHOLSON** *about her life and work, and about the pain of widowhood*

I hadn't, but on the other hand the children were glad that I had. And my husband was such a brave chap that he wouldn't have wanted me to give up. I nearly died and people thought I was going to die and, because I didn't, you feel that you have a duty to keep going.

While you were so badly hurt, you didn't know your husband had died.
No, I didn't understand anything. I didn't know how ill I was, how hurt I had been, and for a long time I didn't know why I was ill. People said I had

been in a train crash and I knew that was rubbish because that was a bad dream. And then they said Austen was dead and I didn't believe that either.

Slowly I began to, though I don't quite believe it even now. I am trying to work it into what I am going to write next. They showed me a film of it and I watched with interest, as if it was happening to someone else.

Do you think you were protecting yourself?
That's what they all say – that I am self-protective and very lucky. I have

been given some pills, which help you to bear things a bit better.

What else helps you survive this amputation, as I call it, the death of a spouse? Religion? A belief in life after death?
No. It's my children and my grandchildren. And I accept all invitations; for when I am not doing anything I feel very ... [*long pause*] ... low. And a bit scared of being alone.

I'm scared, and I panic as to whether I can see the next week through...
Yes, that's it. But I don't know about grief. I don't know what it means quite. I can't believe he's not there. If the phone rings I think it might be him. I never saw him dead or dying – I think that's what it is. I shall probably write a children's book about a crash. Not a terribly sad book, for I can think of some funny scenarios to put in.

Do you think writing is a therapy?
Not for me. Nor was my participation in the protest about the crash. I did it because if I could get some notice taken of me perhaps it would help those who were in a dreadful way. That sounds a bit pious. I don't mean it to be.

It doesn't sound it. What has been a huge comfort for me was my husband telling me when he knew he was dying how he had loved his life with me, loved his children and friends, and how he had succeeded more than he'd hoped. I remember you writing in your autobiography that your son, a schizophrenic, left a letter like that when he committed suicide.
Indeed. Nicholas left a message saying that he had done it to save us from more grief; to please forgive and be happy. It would have been awful of us to blame him after that. He was a lovely chap.

My husband left me a letter too. He had to have a terrible operation and thought he was going to die, so he wrote it then and sealed it up. He came out of the hospital fit as a flea, of course. He wanted to throw it away but I wanted to keep it.

I would have preferred a letter, so I could have Geoff's real words in front of me. But it is a good idea, isn't it?
It is very consoling. I keep the letter and I read it from time to time. It doesn't change anything, of course. But it is nice.

Will you write one?
You have to be in a particular position to write one. Like you are just about to go and have an operation. It wouldn't be valid if you did it out of the blue.

To go back to the first quotation about things not being as bad as you'd thought they were going to be. Did you think evacuation in the War was like that?
Yes, I did. When I was evacuated at the age of thirteen, my friend Jean and I were looking forward to it enormously. We were escaping from our parents and we thought the new home would be more interesting. We were transferred to Aberdare in South Wales and we thoroughly enjoyed it.

So you don't have the sharp criticisms that others have expressed about evacuation – how badly organised it was, etc?
No, I was astonished when a few years ago I went to a meeting about evacuation and everybody said how badly they had been treated and what a trauma it had been. I banged my glass of wine down and said: 'Would you rather have been bombed to bits?' It was the most amazing thing the Government did, removing all those children from centres of population.

Were you aware of watching people as a child?
I liked to be an observer, but not at that time with a view to writing. Though I hoped I'd be one day. In my elementary school I was asked what I'd like to be. I said I'd like to write stories, and my teacher said why not.

That was a very good teacher.
She was, and I did write some short stories, but they were not at all good.

I wrote adult books first. Then I wrote for children because my own children were reading novels which they didn't find interesting and they said, why don't you write a story for us? I said: No, I can't do that. I'm grown-up. They said, don't be so silly, so I wrote a book for them about the house next door. They enjoyed it, but my agent said it's no good, you know, you've got a madwoman in it, and the children are poor, hungry and cold.

Anyway, it did get published and it did very well. And I have never looked back.

Do you think you have to have a different approach towards children's novels?
No. I can remember what it was like to be eleven and twelve. Children are the same as they always were. They know a bit more, like how to fix the video, but that's all.

Beryl Bainbridge was talking on the radio about how she didn't have to make up her characters because actual people were enough to go on.
I disagree. I think you actually start off with somebody you've met, maybe, but then you develop that character. They are all part of you really. You can't define it, nor understand how it happens. A magic process really...

Is there a patch of your life that was idyllic?
A lot of it was. I have had a good life on the whole. But I am always a bit surprised when things go right.

Are you? Then you are a bit like Carrie in your book.
Yes. Always pleased when things happen nicely.

Did you expect to be as successful as you are?
No [*laughs*], of course not. I never expected to be successful. I am astonished. But I am always delighted that people like my work. I feel it is a very fortunate thing. I am a naturally modest person.

You don't mean you have an inferiority complex?
No. I haven't at all. I am probably confident that I always do my best. I don't think I have ever let myself down particularly. I do my best and I am modest about what I achieve, but I know I cannot do any better.

Confessions of an anorak

Twenty years after he'd hung up his binoculars for good, **CHRIS DONALD** *– founding editor of Viz – was forced to confront the shameful truth: once a trainspotter always a trainspotter...*

The other day I spotted my first train in over twenty years. I've seen a lot of trains during that time, but not spotted them as such. There is, of course, a huge difference.

The train in question was a little red steam engine which bore the famous initials 'LNER' on its cab side. I made a note of its number, which was 54007. Anoraks among you will already be waving indignant fingers in the air. Quite apart from the fact that the London & North Eastern Railway's locomotive livery was green (or black, or occasionally blue or grey), never red, LNER locomotives should, of course, have four-digit numbers, not five. Even after nationalisation in 1948, the five-digit series '5XXXX' was allocated to engines of the former London, Midland & Scottish railway, not the LNER.

'For goodness sake! Can you believe that?' I said to my wife.

'What?' she asked. Her interest in trains is fairly limited, so I explained these laughable inconsistencies in layman's terms. She didn't seem greatly concerned. 'If it bothers you, why not complain to the girl on the checkout?'

We were in a supermarket at the time, and the train I had spotted was one of those coin-operated children's rides that clutter the exits. I tutted and shook my head. If a supermarket can manage to get the fifteen-digit bar code right on every one of the tens of thousands of items they have on sale, surely they can manage to come up with one historically accurate train number. But years of experience have taught me that pointing this out to a dim sixteen-year-old on a supermarket checkout would be a frustrating exercise at best, so I decided to let it go.

I stopped being a trainspotter – technically speaking – way back in 1978. I didn't like the technological changes that were taking place. Not in railway technology, but in trainspotting technology. Long before the arrival of mobile phones the Dictaphone was making platform ends noisy and unsociable places to be. Instead of intensely scribbling numbers down in a notebook, people were shouting them into the palms of their hands.

Chris Donald – self-portrait

I stopped being a trainspotter back in 1978. I didn't like the technological changes taking place

And early camcorders were being used to film passing trains which could then be spotted later on a TV screen.

The natural time to give up trainspotting would be once you have spotted every train. In the late Fifties that was nigh on impossible, with a tangled railway network and over fifteen thousand engines to look for. But fifteen years later, thanks to the efforts of Dr Beeching and a newly installed computer system, life was a lot easier for the anorak. There were fewer than three thousand engines at large on a much slimmer system, and anyone with access to a BR computer terminal could pinpoint the precise location of any one of them at the push of a button. (Well, five or six buttons, perhaps.)

Thus, by the age of eighteen, my much-travelled friend and mentor Justin had collected the number of almost every engine in Britain.

But would he stop there? Not likely. The next step is to start collecting the numbers of carriages, then coal trucks. It was at that point – when I realised that I would never find closure, and that trainspotting would be a perpetual occupation – that I decided to walk away, to rinse out my flask and hang up my binoculars for good.

Twenty-four years later I still don't feel entirely cured, and I'm sure my wife would agree. What, she will ask, is the difference between the Class 25 model railway engine she got me for Christmas, and the Class 25/3 model railway engine I now want for my birthday? And why, she will continue, must I insist on numbering all our holiday photographs on the reverse with a seven-digit number before anyone is allowed to look at them? (There is an entirely logical reason for that which I could explain here, but perhaps it would be best if I didn't.)

I believe that trainspotting was just one symptom of an underlying problem which, I fear, is with me to stay. Anoraxia, you might call it. Or a degree of Asperger's perhaps. At the end of the day, you can take an anorak out of his anorak, but you'll never take the anorak out of an anorak. If you see what I mean.

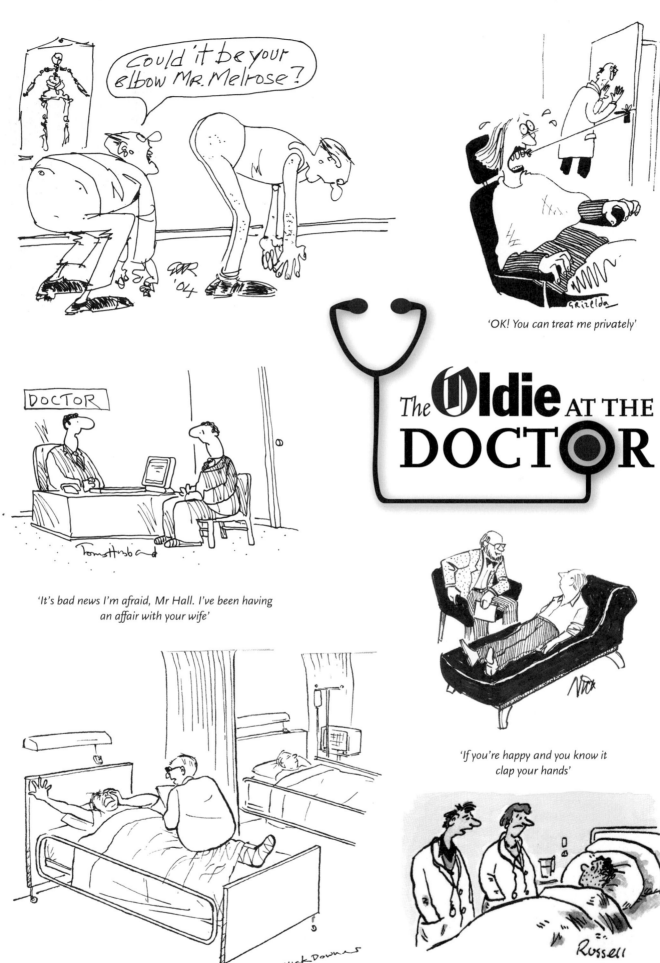

'Could it be your elbow Mr. Melrose?'

'OK! You can treat me privately'

The **Oldie** AT THE DOCTOR

'It's bad news I'm afraid, Mr Hall. I've been having an affair with your wife'

'If you're happy and you know it clap your hands'

'We'll see if there is something we can get you for the pain'

'This adverse reaction to the treatment is just nature's way of telling us we don't know what's wrong with you'

Anatomy Lesson

Forty years after **ANTHONY SAMPSON** *first famously analysed Britain's power structure, he was at it again. But who had changed the most, the country or him?* **Illustration by TROG**

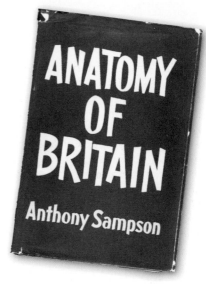

I was thirty-three when I first decided to write a book about Britain's power structure, when Macmillan was Prime Minister, and people were first becoming fascinated by 'the Establishment'. I was in full rebellion against the chorus of old fogeys lamenting the good old days when politicians were giants and Britain was the world's greatest power.

My *Anatomy of Britain* became unexpectedly popular when it was published in 1962; and I kept rewriting it under later Prime Ministers. Power-watching turned into a kind of hobby, like bird-watching or gardening. But I had to face up to the fact that I was ageing as well as my country. Would my views seem as irrelevant to the young as the old fogeys had once seemed to me?

Eighteen months ago, and forty years later, I began a final *Anatomy*, which is just being published as *Who Runs This Place?* (John Murray). I could not forget that I was now much older than most of my subjects or my readers. Not only policemen but cabinet ministers, ambassadors or company chairmen looked younger and younger. My contemporaries, who had once been cheeky critics of their own professions, had reached the top, become pompous and self-important, and had retired into nostalgia and mutual admiration.

There was no escaping the generation gap, and the change of manners. When I wrote a formal letter asking for an interview, I would get a reply from a chatty secretary by email, or a phone call to 'Anthony' with references to 'bear with me' – which (I was warned) was best translated as 'you silly old fool'.

The interviews themselves, I realised, were expected to conform to an art form which was quite distinct from the normal conversations I had once enjoyed. The tape recorder had hardly appeared on the scene when I had begun my anatomising: now it had transformed the relationship. Going through my old files, I discovered a tape which I had made in 1961 on a bulky old Grundig machine, labelled 'Gaitskell'. When I eventually managed to replay it, I heard the voice of Hugh Gaitskell, then the Leader of the Opposition, saying: 'What a remarkable machine – how does it work?'

The whole machinery of government and business has been geared to topicality and instant reaction

Now politicians and businessmen assume that everything is recorded: the sound-bites trip off their tongues so glibly that they sound like hand-outs; and it is hard to persuade anybody that they are off the record. All information has been prepackaged, gift-wrapped and neatly labelled, to avoid any personal interpretation. Secretive old institutions like the Treasury and the Palace all have their websites, with bland statements of policy and purpose designed to be lifted straight into an article or book. And the whole machinery of government and business has been geared to topicality and instant reaction, to ensure that all news is fresh, with a sell-by date, like supermarket lettuce. Tony Blair prefers not to talk about history, and New Labour does not want to hear about Old Labour. Michael Howard is successfully obliterating the memory of IDS and Hague. But is it really so new? When I wrote my first *Anatomy* I reckoned that Britain's institutions were more deeply rooted in their history – at least in Victorian history – than they appeared. And Blair's Britain today, for all the talk about New Labour, is much less new than it is presented. History keeps on reasserting itself, in awkward ways. All ageing commentators have moments of *déjà vu* as they hear about reforms, modernising, restructuring or rationalising. Wasn't that what Harold Wilson, Ted Heath or Margaret Thatcher had promised – only to find the old British habits once again reasserting themselves? And when Blair and Bush resolved to go to war in Iraq, they evoked all kinds of memories of rash imperial adventures in the history books, above all of the Suez War of 1956 which provided my own experience of post-imperial hubris: a lesson that I thought the British had finally learnt.

Was I sounding like one of the old chorus I had mocked forty years ago? I was going on about Macmillan and Suez as they had gone on about Lloyd George and the Boer War, boring their children to distraction. Not for nothing they sang: 'Lloyd George knew my father. My father knew Lloyd George.'

And yes, I knew Macmillan: I talked with him about the Suez War, and the mistakes he made. But I still think that his mistakes are relevant today. The Empire may have disappeared, the old Establishment may have crumbled; but Prime Ministers' ambitions and self-deceptions have not changed much.

As I wrote my new *Anatomy* last year, I tried to trace in detail how No 10 had rashly committed itself to the Iraq war; and I was reminded of the same hothouse atmosphere which led to the Suez debacle in 1956. If Blair had taken more note of the oldies who had warned him about the dangers of occupying Iraq, he would have avoided many of the disasters which followed. Britain's anatomy may look quite different today, but the backbone is still crooked.

Anthony Sampson died in December 2004

BRAVE NEW WORLD

The eyes have it

JANE THYNNE *has been writing the Brave New World column since 2010. She's also The Oldie's resident Mrs Thrifty, writing the Tips for Meanies each month*

THE EYE IS the window of the soul and all that, but in future it might well be your PIN number and your passport too. Iris recognition is the very hottest topic in the world of biometric identification, making fingerprints look hopelessly old hat. Unlike a DNA swab, iris recognition is non-invasive, quick, convenient, and pretty much ideal for airports and security controls. It's precise too. Iris patterns are thought to be unique – the arrangement of iris tissue has been compared to throwing a plate of spaghetti on the ground – and what's more, irises can't be forged, stolen or used after death. All of which points to a future where your iris is your ID, scanners will be found everywhere from computers to door security, and a mere glance at a machine will suffice at the checkout, dispensing with the need for purses and credit cards.

But there are spookier aspects to iris recognition. The Pentagon is currently funding the development of street cameras which can covertly photograph your iris even when you are walking along with your head down. Called Smart-Iris, the 'versatile non-co-operative security cameras' can zoom in on a face, no matter the angle or speed of movement, and focus right on the iris. Stuck anonymously on a wall or traffic light, the camera could scan all passers-by without them knowing. What are the privacy implications in all this? And what happens when this foolproof new technology inevitably goes wrong? Already it has been mooted that contact lenses can cause problems by having a different reflectivity of light, and coloured lenses can also cause a glitch. Despite what is said about irises remaining the same through life, the ageing iris can show evidence of change. All these concerns are currently unresolved, but this is a subject, undoubtedly, worth keeping an eye on.

Tips for Meanies No.33

A Meanie of my acquaintance spent a fortune on expensive anti-dandruff shampoos until discovering the thrifty properties of Listerine mouthwash. Listerine contains the essential oils thymol, eucalyptol, menthol and methyl salicylate which are thought to be effective against the fungus *pityrosporum ovale*, which is the main cause of dandruff. Sloosh a capful onto the scalp and leave for five minutes before rinsing off. Try it for a week – not on broken skin – and wear your black polo neck with abandon.

JANE THYNNE

The Oldie's theatre critic **BERYL BAINBRIDGE** *was told to give up the ciggies, or she might not have a leg to stand on. But kicking the habit of a lifetime had some surprising side-effects...*

FAGS FOR THE MEMORY

On Christmas Eve last year I spent two hours in the casualty department of the Whittingham Hospital. This was due to confiding in my eldest daughter that my big toe had become frozen stiff and that I had a pain in the calf of my left leg. She, being medical, instantly thought of vascular difficulties, a diagnosis later confirmed by the doctor on duty. Days later, owing to the intervention of good friends, I was seen by a private consultant and learnt that the condition is known as claudication, from the Latin *claudicare*, meaning to limp, a distinctive style of perambulation caused by the veins in the leg, or legs, becoming blocked up. Why this should happen is mostly down to us living too long. It may also have something to do with smoking.

My father, once a consumptive boy who, at the age of ten, was employed as a cabin boy on a sailing ship to New York, was never without his pipe. During the Second World War, when tobacco was rationed, he smoked Kardomah tea leaves. Every five years or so my mother bought a packet of Craven A

and transferred the contents to a silver cigarette case which was only brought out on Boxing Day. My Auntie Margo had a hacking cough and was never without a Woodbine, and my uncle, who had money, smoked very fat cigars. I had a cough too, from tuberculosis, though I never knew that until fifty years later when I underwent an X-ray for persistent bronchitis.

I became a smoker at the comparatively late age of seventeen while understudying the Duchess of York in *Richard III*. The actress playing the part smoked like a chimney – though not, of course, in her Shakespearean role – and had endured a difficult love life, the details of which confused me. There was someone called Hilary who had hit her, and a chap called George M Burton who had proposed marriage and then disappeared. 'Men,' she said, blowing smoke-rings at me, 'are to be avoided, my child. They encircle nothing but misery.'

I gave up smoking, without the aid of pills, hypnotism or patches, seventeen days ago, having been told that if I didn't I mightn't have a leg to stand on. Well-meaning friends hastened to assure me that within forty-eight hours I would see an improvement in my complexion, my eyes, my hair.

Needless to say, I'm still looking. What I have noticed, and deplore, is a return of my sense of smell. I had no idea that the odour of leftover food could pervade a house. Nor had I realised that I would regrow hairs in my nose, causing prolonged fits of sneezing.

I have no urge to take up the habit again, but I now talk to myself – mostly about Winston Churchill – sing hymns out loud while in the queue at the bank, and find it extremely difficult to construct a worthwhile sentence. I also have two recurring dreams which I remember on waking, one a rerun of that scene in the film *The Young Lions* in which Montgomery Clift lights two cigarettes, and the other of myself standing in the middle of some huge railway station listening to a voice on the loudspeaker urging me not to board the 9.45 train to Warrington.

The Churchill obsession is quite interesting. Did you know that by the time he'd turned eighty he had coronary thrombosis, three attacks of pneumonia, a hernia, two strokes and something known as a senile itch? All the same, though often setting fire to himself, he still managed to enjoy a cigar.

Whether we are in a pleasant or a painful state depends upon the kind of things that pervade and engross our consciousness. Intellectual occupations will go a long way towards one's peace of mind, always supposing one can look forward to a cigarette during or when the task is done. That I no longer can is now a serious problem, and one that seems unlikely to go away for some time, for I don't believe it has much to do with nicotine withdrawal. That's a factor, of course, but so is age and the length of time one has persisted in a habit. I simply don't feel like me without a packet of cigarettes to hand, and I have become a stranger to myself. If I was more interesting I might want to get to know me, which is an odd thought and one that swirls through my head like dissolving smoke.

Beryl Bainbridge died in 2010

'Common sense has prevailed'

ISSUE 95, FEBRUARY 1997 BY DEREK RAINS

ISSUE 97, APRIL 1997 BY ALAN DE LA NOUGEREDE

Power behind the crone

FLORA HINTON *remembers a time when the real movers and shakers in business were not the high-powered executives, but the old biddies with the tea trollies*

Where are the crones? There was at least one in every office before the new technology and obsession with youth took hold. In the late Sixties and early Seventies I was assistant story editor in a film company in Soho, and by far the most powerful people in the building, populated though it was by famous old has-beens and streetwise young hustlers (now venerated auteurs), were the three middle-aged biddies who operated the tea-urn and the mailroom. (And Mr Stoddart, more of whom later.) Despite the fact that secretaries wore hot-pants, where in more conventional organisations women were forbidden even to wear trousers, and young men wore floppy hair, jeans and an air of jaded knowingness, Ivy, Mary and Mrs Holder were the people to know. In fact, if you didn't know them, your time there was never going to amount to anything very much.

Mrs Holder, who ruled the mailroom, was never known by her first name, unlike her sister, Ivy (half of the tea-urn team), or her husband, Alf, who was senior messenger and occasional chauffeur to the mighty. Between them, the family had most angles covered. Mrs Holder had deep-dyed black hair, impermeable make-up and pretentions to gentility, and pronounced her husband's name as 'Elf', which at first I took to be his nickname – he was tiny and shy,

whereas Mrs Holder was neither. She sat like a spider in her airless room, spinning tales outwards and reeling in tasty morsels captured by her spies, and left her centre of operations only once a week, on payday, when she processed round the building collecting premiums for her notorious Christmas Club. £1 a week (plus an extra 6*d* for her trouble) meant that when divvying-up time came round you had £52 to spend on presents, a moderately princely sum in those days, and Mrs Holder was entitled to everyone's accumulated sixpences plus the interest on the principal. The more that went in, the greater the profit for Mrs Holder, so refusal to enlist in the Club was a personal insult to her. It was a protection racket in all but name, and you opted out at your peril. Takings were banked weekly, and the force of her insistence on showing bank statements to prove that everything was above-board was such that it gave rise to an unvoiced suspicion that she was up to no good. Unfounded, of course, I must make that clear. Very clear. Even so, more than thirty years on, I am writing under a *nom de plume*.

Ivy and Mary were, by the nature of their duties, more peripatetic. The trolley came round daily at 11 am and 3.15 pm, and you welcomed their stewed tea and flaccid biscuits with a show of real enthusiasm if you had any sense. They went everywhere and saw everything, soaking up, embellishing and redistributing stories of

feuds, liaisons, takeovers, makeovers, secrets and lies. Their coarse jokes and irreverent banter made them fearfully popular, and you trembled as they passed, well aware that your craven camaraderie was nothing but grist to their mill once they got back to base.

I include Mr Stoddart the stationery-cupboard manager because he was, effectively, an honorary crone. He wore a starched white coat like a first-year medical student and lived with his unmarried daughter in Billericay. His sphere of influence, although narrow, was intensely focused, as he was able on petty grounds to refuse supplies of almost anything he pleased. 'Correction fluid?' he would sneer. 'Planning to make a few mistakes, are we?' His bitterness originated,

apparently, in blighted attempts to win prizes for his pelargoniums at the Essex County Show, but flannelling offers of sympathy were firmly rebuffed. (He was sometimes referred to as 'the ink monitor', a reference meaningful only to a genuine oldie.)

I miss them. What has taken their place? More importantly, where are those jobs? Just when I am ripe for turning into Mrs Holder myself, the ideal employment for my declining years has vanished beyond my grasp.

Down with email, Starbucks and the water-cooler. Send in the crones!

R S Thomas

ARTHUR ARNOLD *recalls his encounter with the poet*

DECISIONS, in retrospect, are often impossible to explain. For instance, why did my normally sensible friend, John Bolton, Head of English at Coalbrookedale High School, decide to hold a poetry speaking competition in the spring of 1957? And why did the already distinguished poet (and reclusive vicar of a remote mid-Wales parish), R S Thomas, consent to adjudicate the event? But these events did occur – although, in the context, 'collided' might be a more apposite verb.

The great man arrived in good time to enjoy a dinner with the Headmaster served in the privacy of his study. The Head was a good-natured, sociable man who had gladly entered into the spirit of the occasion so it was surprising, to say the least, when, a mere fifteen minutes later, his worried face came round the door of the men's staff room, saying, 'Take him off my hands, John, for God's sake, I don't know what to do with him!'

R S Thomas: poet, priest and disapprover of poetry read aloud

Even the spring sunshine coming through the window could do nothing to lighten the leaden gloom of Thomas's aura

There was still half an hour before afternoon school. What could be done but show the honoured guest into the staff room, which was quickly vacated by all those who thought the event was a waste of time anyway. The art teacher, also an affable man and himself a published poet, was introduced but fared no better than the Head in getting more than minimal response to any conversational endeavour. Even the spring sunshine coming through the window could do nothing to lighten the leaden gloom of Thomas's aura.

In desperation, the afternoon bell was rung early and the school filed into the assembly hall. Girls far outnumbered boys in entering the competition – sensitive, imaginative girls almost by definition, and something of Thomas's reputation already filled them with awe and apprehension. One entrant withdrew, physically sick, though fortunately not publicly so. The programme made its nervous progress and finally Thomas was asked to nominate the winners. I don't think anyone disagreed with his choices but many were amazed when he began his overall adjudication by saying, 'I don't know why I have come here today, because I think poetry should never be read aloud.'

The Head invited the sixth form and any other staff or pupils who wished to take advantage of our distinguished guest to join a discussion in the library. Thomas said he had nothing to add to his previous homily but consented to answer questions. A mischievous member of staff asked, 'If, despite your disapproval of reading poetry aloud, you were nevertheless placed in a situation where you had to do so, could you please show us how it should be done?' Everyone held their breath. Thomas sighed, 'Have you a copy of Hopkins?'

John Bolton whisked a volume of Gerard Manley Hopkins's works from a shelf and Thomas began –

'Margaret, are you grieving
Over Goldengrove unleaving?'
as if reading the funeral litany over a dearly loved parishioner. Stifled sniffling began among several sixth-form girls and by the time he reached *'And yet you will weep and know why'*, audible sobbing had half the audience in its grasp.

The ritual parting cup of tea was foregone. We watched his departure from the staff-room window as his little Austin A30 van rolled down the long ramp to the school gate. Before turning into the road he paused, looked back, raised his hand and, for the first time, smiled.

I t was the only summer holiday we had as a family. The acceptance of my novel for publication had unsettled my husband, perhaps to the degree of needing to restore his self-esteem. The same day that, puzzled, I consulted the kitchen calendar and realised that I must be pregnant was also the day I realised he was serious about a woman he worked with.

However, I was confident that the week away would make everything come right. Admittedly, it had been a mistake opening my own bank account in my pen-name without telling him (he would have stopped me, that's for sure), but I so longed to surprise him with a dressing-gown for his birthday. We didn't have a joint account and I had to save out of the housekeeping money for presents. Any money I was given by relatives at Christmas or on birthdays was whisked away – of course, orchestral musicians were abysmally paid at this time, 1959, so I understood the necessity – for the quarterly bills and so forth.

Suddenly, from firm footing we stepped into soft, yielding sand. Now both children were wailing

We had two planned children already, one of each kind. Left to arrange details for the holiday, I chose the most reasonable lodgings at the nearest coastal resort, a tiny place I'd never heard of. The landlady was round and pleasant, we were her only self-catering guests and it was a nice house with a small garden. But the nearby beach was a disappointment – sandy enough but huge, with the sea a long way off. The children got tired just walking to it, though they forgot when actually in the water. An empty silent expanse, we were always the only people on the beach.

The worst part was after the bathe, faced with the long trudge back. On this particular day, our little boy started grizzling and asking to be carried. My husband, preoccupied with his thoughts, was irritated and strode on ahead. I picked up the child, then the little girl was jealous and dragged on my hand so I was virtually pulling her weight along.

THAT SINKING FEELING...

Trapped with her two children in quicksand,
MARY CECIL POOK *caught a strange look in her husband's eyes...* **Illustration by PETER BAILEY**

Suddenly, from firm footing we stepped into soft, yielding sand. It was an effort to lift one foot, then move the other up. Now both children were wailing. We were sinking down into the sand, every step more of a struggle until... we were standing still, unable to move forward.

Calling out to my husband, my stomach became a black hollow. When a child, I had been horrified by a story about a pony named Heather who sank in a quicksand while her best horse friend looked on helplessly. They said goodbye to each other. The end was described in graphic

lingering detail. All the feelings which had traumatised me then were now engulfing and gripping me like a claw.

My husband turned and stood watching us. Away in his deeply-in-love dream world, he was seeing this miracle happening before his eyes: the ground opening to swallow the obstacle of us. Equally unbelieving, we watched him watching us.

One minute there was nobody on the beach. The next, as if from nowhere, a man came swiftly running. He reached us, pulled us onto firm sand, then led us back to my husband

– who was laughing it off as if only joking. But the man ignored him, walked away without a word or smile, and I was too shaken to thank him. There was no sign of him when we continued back to the house, the children reassured and comforted.

While I was putting them to bed that evening, my husband slipped away and had a long conversation with Mrs Pearce, our landlady – well, more of a monologue really, as the murmur I could hear was mainly his voice. Back upstairs he gave me a strange look, a sort of satisfied small smile behind it, but not half as strange as Mrs Pearce's expression at breakfast next morning. For the rest of the week she avoided speaking to me, and all the pleasantness was snuffed out. I guessed my husband had told her some tale or other just in case, getting his version in first. He needn't have bothered: my early conditioning inhibited any such disloyalty.

It was all so indigestible. I persuaded myself I'd been mistaken: the Heather story had caused me to panic and I was imagining things. I never told anyone until long after my divorce the following year, when there was a second daughter, born on St Valentine's Day, would you believe. There was a woman with whom I felt a rapport. It was at a house-party holiday for one-parent families, and we were unlikely to meet again. Sitting together on another beach, she listened in silence, then after a longish pause said she'd had a similar experience, standing at the end of a pier with her disenchanted husband. She had become aware – intuitively or telepathically – that he wanted to throw her over the rail into the sea. She had turned and walked quickly back to the shore, saying it was getting a bit chilly.

In both cases an unforeseen opportunity had presented itself, provoking an overwhelming temptation. There is a great difference between such an impulse and a planned murder, we agreed. All the same, we stared at one another uncomfortably. We had survived. How many others hadn't?

In my eighties now, the vivid memory still erupts occasionally, pounding on my mind as if it was only yesterday. Then I have to rub it out all over again. I've often wondered about our rescuer and wish I'd made some attempt to find him and say thank you. Then again, as he'd vanished as mysteriously as he had appeared, was he a man at all? Or was it an angel assuming human form for a matter of minutes? You do hear about such things.

'Well, you'll think they'll taste like mackerel, but they won't'

Voices from the grave

Every month Oldie readers send in extracts and quotes from long-ago published books which still have a quite uncanny relevance today...

'It is true that every new premier and every new Government, coming in because they upheld a certain thing as necessary to be done, were no sooner come in than they applied their utmost faculties in discovering How Not To Do It.'
From *Little Dorrit* by Charles Dickens (1855). Spotted by B K Bunker

'No repose, thought Poirot, no feminine grace! His elderly soul revolted from the stress and hurry of the modern world. All these young women who surrounded him – so alike, so devoid of charm, so lacking in rich, alluring femininity!... a woman with ample curves, a woman ridiculously and extravagantly dressed! Once there had been such women. But now – now –'
From *The Capture of Cerberus* by Agatha Christie (1947).
Spotted by Jack Critchlow

'The ordinary method of replenishing the Party Funds is by the sale of peerages, baronetcies, knighthoods and other honours in return for subscriptions. The traffic is notorious. Everyone acquainted in the smallest degree with the inside of politics knows that there is a market for peerages in Downing Street, as he knows that there is a market for cabbages in Covent Garden; he could put his finger upon the very names of the men who have bought their "honours".'
From *The Party System* by Hilaire Belloc and Cecil Chesterton (1911).
Spotted by The Ed

(nearly)
I once met...

Big Bill Campbell

WILLIS HALL *made eye contact with his great hero – well, nearly*

I AM DEEPLY grateful to Jack Maddox, whose recent piece about Big Bill Broonzy (*Oldie* 179) evoked memories of the time when, as a short-trousered schoolboy, I once nearly met Big Bill Campbell. Big Bill C was another icon of the musical scene: a guitar-strumming, rootin' tootin' cowboy vocalist (long before the term 'Country and Western' had been dreamed of) who first appeared on this side of the Atlantic in the late 1930s, when he and his singing cowpoke pardners broadcast regularly on Radio Luxembourg.

When war broke out Big Bill Campbell and his pardners hightailed it to England's shores and laid down their bed-rolls in a brand new bunk-house, which the BBC kindly provided for them.

Every Sunday afternoon, Big Bill Campbell and his Rocky Mountain Rhythm gathered around a micro-phone, strummed their guitars, slapped their double-bass and sang for us, the British listening public, and in return we trilled with them along the 'Red River Valley', yodelled down the 'Santa Fe Trail', toe-tapped to 'Ragtime Cowboy Joe', became 'Old Cowhands From the Rio Grande' or, in sentimental mood, drifted in chorus 'Along With the Tumbling Tumbleweeds'.

Big Bill Campbell had more than one string to his bow. He and his trail buddies became so popular that their illus-trated adventures appeared every week in cartoon-strip form in my favourite comic, *Radio Fun*. I was Big Bill Campbell's number one fan.

Imagine my joy when *Radio Fun* announced the founding of its Big Bill Campbell Fan Club. Membership was all too easy: after filling in the coupon included on the page and despatching it to the editor together with a *6d* postal order or the same amount in postage stamps, the lucky applicant would receive a fully authenticated Certifi-cate of Membership (suitable for framing); a copy of the *Big Bill Campbell Song-Book*; and (most desirable of all) an official Big Bill Campbell Fan Club lapel badge, to be worn with pride at all times.

Having posted off my membership application, I pelted home after school each weekday afternoon for about a fortnight, anticipating the arrival of my Fan Club member-

Every Sunday afternoon, Big Bill Campbell and his Rocky Mountain Rhythm gathered round a micro-phone and sang for us

ship. When it finally dropped through the letter-flap, the pack had much to commend it – but the lapel badge proved something of a disappoint-ment. Instead of the snazzy chrome-and-enamelled job I had anticipated, it turned out to be a circular piece of cardboard, about three inches in diameter. It did contain my printed personalised membership number, but I was invited to inscribe my name myself, in ink, on the dotted line across its middle. There was a small hole at the top into which the owner should insert a loop of fine string, or wool, through which a safety pin might be passed, and thus the badge could be attached to the jacket lapel. A note inside the pack explained that, because we were in mortal conflict with Adolf and his gang, the metal that had been intended for the badges had gone instead towards the manufacture of fighter planes and guns on battle-ships. I was gosh darned all in favour of anything that helped the war effort, but even so, while both my Membership Certificate and my Song-Book were often displayed to jealous schoolmates or admiring visiting aunts and uncles, my card-board badge of membership lay hidden in a cupboard.

I remained a fully paid-up but inactive member of the fan club, but having been admitted into my local church's Wolf Cub pack, my loyalty was beginning to shift from Big Bill Campbell to Lord Baden-Powell. An important announcement in the Fan Club's weekly newsletter enticed my allegiance back to Big Bill C. Big Bill and his Rocky Mountain Rhythm's weekly radio shows had been such a success that a nationwide tour of variety theatres was about to take place. 'And just lookee here, fan club members, if Big Bill and the Boys are coming to your local theatre, be sure to go along and say "Howdy-do",' the newsletter urged.

An announcement in the *Yorkshire Evening News* revealed that Big Bill Campbell and his Rocky Mountain Rhythm would be appearing at the Empire Theatre in Briggate, Leeds – ten minutes' tram-ride from the top of our street. And so, on a summer's evening in the early 1940s, accompanied by my mother, I strode up the marble steps of the Leeds Empire, dressed in my school blazer, woollen tie, polished shoes, stockings held neatly in place below the knee by elastic garters – and with a three-inch circle of white cardboard dangling from my jacket lapel on a loop of darning-wool attached to a small gold safety-pin. Without it, how could I expect to benefit from the 'downright, doggone hot-diggedy cowhands' welcome' that Big Bill had in store for me? How else would my hero recognise me as one of his own?

In any event, I would not be the only member of the audience displaying a personal pasteboard badge of identification. But when we made our way to our front row seats in the upper circle and I glanced down over the edge of the balcony, there was no other badge to be seen. Perhaps they had all got their dates wrong?

At last the curtain rose on Big Bill Campbell and his Rocky Mountain Rhythm. I recognised each of them from their *Radio Fun* cartoon images – but would they recognise me? As they went into their opening number, the entire audience hummed or sang along with them. I gave Big Bill a hesitant wave but got nothing back. As the show continued, I undid the safety-pin, removed the badge from my lapel and, holding it by its darning wool loop, leaned over the balcony and waved it furiously in my idol's direction – but not once did Big Bill's eyes focus on mine. I managed to hide my disappointment on the tram-ride home, but after we got there, I put my badge back in its cupboard.

After Big Bill and his Rocky Mountaineers had moseyed on to faraway theatres in faraway towns, I gave my allegiance back to Lord Baden-Powell. Formally initiated into my Wolf Cub pack, I received my official Wolf Cub badge – not a three-inch circle of paste-board, but a snazzy gleaming metal item designed to fit neatly and securely in the lapel buttonhole.

With hindsight, things might have been different. If only my mother had booked two seats in the front row of the stalls, instead of in the upper circle, Big Bill Campbell would have spotted my cardboard badge straight off, invited me up onto the stage, the Rocky Mountain Rhythm would have hoisted me shoulder-high and, in front of the Empire's Friday night open-mouthed packed house, afforded me that downright, doggone, hot-diggedy gen-yew-ine cowhands' welcome...

Well, anyway, that's what I like to think might have happened.

'Your ideas are outstanding, Beresford,
I'm glad I thought of them'

ISSUE 224, NOVEMBER 2007 BY BOB WILSON

ISSUE 225, DECEMBER 2007 BY POSY SIMMONDS

STUCK IN ★★★ IRAQ

When foreign correspondent **PATRICK COCKBURN** *went to Iraq in 2005,
he found Baghdad a town under siege, where foreigners were forced to stay
in concrete fortresses – a fact little reported at the time*

The symbol of post-Saddam Iraq turned out to be grey concrete blocks that look like gigantic tombstones. Measuring nine feet by four feet and thick enough to deflect the blast from a car bomb, they have sprouted everywhere. Walls of them protect every US post, government ministry, police station and hotel in Baghdad.

Month by month my own hotel looks more like a medieval fortress. I live in the al-Hamra, housed in two large functional white buildings in the Jadriyah district of south Baghdad. We do not depend on the concrete tombstones alone. Cars trying to reach the hotel have to approach it via a side street defended by guards armed with submachine guns. There are movable metal spikes on the road to puncture the tyres of suicide bombers. A guard

searches under the car with a mirror on the end of a pole in his right hand and a pistol in his left. If he does find a bomb, he plans to shoot the driver in the head before he can detonate the explosives.

It was not always this bad. Immediately after the fall of Saddam Hussein, hopeful Iraqi translators looking for jobs used to pin letters to the hotel advertising board. By the summer of 2004 these stopped appearing – too many Iraqis had been threatened or killed. My translator tells his neighbours that he is the manager of an internet company. These days the only notices on the hotel board are from foreign companies offering armoured vehicles for sale.

For the first year after the fall of Hussein the security around the Hamra was limited. The guards were relaxed and waved through drivers they knew. The suicide bombings started in August 2003 but at first they did not seem to be targeting hotels. Iraqi friends still wandered in to sit by the swimming pool. The main danger seemed to be from drunken South African mercenaries who had taken over several floors of the hotel.

The turning point was in April 2004. The first American attack on Fallujah led to a general uprising of the Sunni Muslims west and north of Baghdad. I was caught in an ambush of American oil tankers trying to follow an Arab aid convoy to Fallujah. We drove off the road and lay on the ground with other Iraqi drivers while the American troops and the resistance shot it out just over our heads.

A week later I tried to go to the Shi'ite holy city of Najaf which had been taken over by the Mehdi Army militiamen of Muqtada al-Sadr. I sat in the back of a car wearing a red-and-white check keffiyeh (Arab head dress) to hide my brown hair and white skin. The disguise turned out to be a bad idea when the militiamen peered closely at my face. Some of them seemed to think that the quickest way to deal with the problem we presented was to shoot us immediately. Others, fortunately the majority, wanted to bring us back to their headquarters in a mosque. After a few hours we were released.

After the twin Sunni and Shia uprisings it was impossible to move safely outside Baghdad, and even inside the city it was dangerous. In the past I always used to enter Iraq by the long road from Jordan through the western desert. It took ten or twelve hours, but I liked watching the early dawn as we drove towards Baghdad. There were a few bandits on the road but they mostly seemed to be interested in transporting loot in their elderly white pick-ups. But as

the Americans began to lose control, the bandits and the resistance started to put up checkpoints on the roads looking for foreigners to kidnap or kill.

I used to drive around Baghdad in a modern Mercedes. These days I sit in the back of an elderly Toyota which looks the same as any car driven by an Iraqi. We don't wash it very often so the dirt on the windows makes it difficult to look inside the car. Bassil the driver turns off the main road whenever he thinks that another car might just possibly be following us and weaves through the side streets.

Sometimes I think this may be a little unnecessary. But then something happens which leads to a resurgence of paranoia. Not far from the Hamra is a pretty light-blue mosque called the Mustafa, close to the Tigris river in the grounds of what used to be called Saddam University. When the US Ma-

> **Who would have understood, watching the triumphant coverage of the election, that all roads out of Bagdhad are cut by insurgents?**

rines stormed Fallujah last November refugees from the city set up a camp around the mosque. I went to see them just before Christmas, but they seemed suspicious and hostile. I did not stay long. A few weeks later a correspondent from *Il Manifesto* went to the same mosque. She had been promised an interview with a sheikh from Fallujah. Instead, two car-loads of gunmen arrived as she was leaving and kidnapped her.

I try not to stay in one place for very long. It is easy enough to meet ordinary Iraqis by stopping beside the enormous lines of cars – sometimes

several miles long – waiting outside petrol stations. Sometimes they sleep in their cars two nights running. This is relatively safe because I do not have to leave the car.

The real worry is commercial kidnappers who prey mainly on Iraqis. They know they can get more money if they kidnap a foreigner. The problem is that there are now so few foreigners left in Baghdad, the pool of available kidnap victims is small. Those remaining stay in the Green Zone or fortified hotels like the Hamra. The BBC and Reuters live in a heavily guarded street close to the Palestine and Sheraton hotels. At the time of the election at the end of January, my colleague Robert Fisk and I were meant to have lunch with a BBC correspondent at the Hamra. Just before he was supposed to arrive there was an apologetic telephone call. He said he had been forbidden to go

out by the BBC head of security who said the lunch 'was not an operational necessity'.

There is nothing wrong with television correspondents not leaving their buildings except under armed guard. The fault is more that they do not admit on air that their movements are so limited. Who would have understood, watching the triumphant coverage of the election, that all the roads out of Baghdad are cut by the insurgents or by bandits? If any of the 275 members of the newly-elected National Assembly tried to leave the capital without an armed guard their throats would be cut.

Ironically the more dangerous Iraq becomes the easier it is for Bush and Blair to claim that much of the country is peaceful and blame the media for exaggerating the insurgency. Before the US election the interim Iraqi Prime Minister stood beside Bush at a White House press conference and said that fourteen or fifteen out of the eighteen Iraqi provinces were 'completely safe'. In fact the exact opposite is true. The only safe provinces are the three Kurdish provinces in the north. But it is impossible to prove how dangerous the rest are without getting killed.

It was one of those winter nights that the Fifties specialised in. The fog had come down like some oily blanket while we were in the cinema in Hampstead. Now it appeared to be oozing up from the dank pavements as well. It swirled and crept around us as we stood debating where to go next. It was foul with a yellow reek to it that got in the back of the throat and stayed there, so it didn't take much persuading to get me into the pub with my friends.

Frances, another nurse, was there and she lived near Ladbroke Grove – which was on my way home to Shepherd's Bush, so we could travel back together.

I wasn't eager to get home to my digs, where the landlady had a tendency to open her flat door as I went past. She seemed to see checking me in and out as part of her duty as an ex-ward sister. She would say nothing, but it was a very loud nothing. Her expression spoke volumes.

We told ourselves that the fog might lift by the time we went home. I think we knew this was unlikely, but the call of a warm bar, drink, and good company overcame any common sense. At closing time we gave up on the idea of the walk to the tube. We ruminated about staying over on somebody's floor but we were both working early so we went to look for a taxi. Several wouldn't attempt the trip to Shepherd's Bush via Ladbroke Grove. Finally, we found a driver who was reluctant but would take us, and we set off south. The nearer we got to the Grove, the worse the fog got and, finally, the driver said he wouldn't go any further. He left us standing and made off towards Kilburn.

'Don't worry; you can sleep on my sofa,' said Frances, which seemed like a good idea to me, and we walked the last half mile happily enough, making idiot jokes about getting lost in the fog. We left the broad Grove and it was all change to narrow streets, where the street lights were barely visible as we made our way towards Notting Dale. We came to a corner and turned into a nasty mean cul-de-sac.

The houses pressed into one another as if seeking protection from the world – or perhaps that's my hindsight imagination talking. The house was certainly thoroughly unprepossessing the night I was there. It was narrow and hard against a wall at the end of the cul-de-

At death's door...

MO FOSTER *spent a night at her friend's flat just off Ladbroke Grove in the late Fifties. But there was something chilling about the place that didn't feel quite right*

sac; it appeared to be melting into the ground. As we opened the front door, the smell of mould and damp came out and joined the fog to wrap round us so that we were thoroughly chilled.

I shuddered as we went into the front room, and my friend laughed and hurried to put pennies in the meter. They crashed noisily to the bottom. When she lit the fire it popped and burped out pallid heat in the way of gas fires in those days.

'Anything's better than living in the nurses' home, believe me,' she said, and I agreed.

We were still merry from the pub and smoked and talked for a while. She

worked at St Giles's Hospital and we regaled each other with increasingly raucous tales from the wards. She dug out some whisky and boiled a kettle on the ring by the fire and we sat drinking sweet toddies. It must have been after one in the morning when we put blankets on the sofa and she gave me a pillow. I was asleep immediately.

I woke, not knowing where I was, with a feeling of pressure in my throat and of not being alone. I could hardly

I woke, not knowing where I was, with a feeling of pressure in my throat and of not being alone. I could hardly breathe and was rigid with fear

breathe and was rigid with fear. The gas fire had gone out and the darkness was nearly palpable. It was as if it had a life of its own; I felt with my feet for my shoes and found the light by feeling round the wall. I made for the outside lavatory along the passageway and past a scullery and washhouse on my left.

Finally, I sat, and while I felt for paper, the door shut firmly as if it had been pushed. Now it was pitch-black and though it was winter, it felt as if there was warmth rising up from the ground. A scuttling nearly had me in fits, and it was a relief to realise it was only a rat or a mouse. I shoved the door hard and it came open. I scurried back to bed and waited, rigid, for daylight.

Left: 10 Rillington Place, guarded by policemen in 1953. Above: John Christie, previous tenant – and murderer

In the morning, both scratchy with hangovers, Frances and I hardly talked. I grabbed a cup of tea and we went our separate ways. As I rushed towards Du Cane Road, I noticed the name plate: Ruston Close. It seemed familiar to me but I couldn't think why, and the thought disappeared among the maelstrom of morning bed baths. At lunchtime I asked a nurse who was local about the address and she told me that was the name they had given to Rillington Place. I remembered the details I had read at the time, how the washhouse had bodies in the walls, and the feeling I had last night, and I went cold again. But I wasn't sure it was the same house. When I next saw Frances, I asked her and she was both insouciant and cool, which is some trick. 'Yes, that's the house, how else could I afford two rooms?'

I never felt the same about Frances, and certainly never went back to her house. I knew I wasn't being logical, but I gave her a wide berth from then on. The house was torn down along with the whole area when the Westway was built.

Are you an Oldie? tell-tale signs

WE FIRST PRINTED *this simple self-diagnosis in 1993. In 2005 we revised it for newer readers, for those who were still unsure – or simply for those who had forgotten...*

1. When you hear of 'Big Brother', do you still think of George Orwell?
2. Do you not only talk to yourself, but see nothing odd about it?
3. Do you know quite a lot of poems by heart?
4. Do you spend more than an average amount of time in stationery shops?
5. Do you refer to 'the wireless'?
6. Do you remember who was 'Awfully worried about Jim'?
7. Are you obsessively concerned about the size and shape of spoons?
8. Do you mend clothes rather than throw them away?
9. Do you write letters?
10. Do you still wind your watch up?
11. Do you know what a pronoun is?
12. Are there at least ten people in your address book who are dead?
13. Do you know any prayers apart from the Lord's Prayer?
14. Do you save string?
15. Are you frightened of going to the Barbican?

16. Can you waltz?
17. Do you go around turning lights off?
18. Do you clean your shoes with a brush and proper shoe polish?
19. Have you ever been to a Japanese restaurant?

20. Do you own an iPod?
21. Do you shout at the television or radio?
22. Did you watch *Grumpy Old Men* and think: 'They're not old!'
23. Have you come to hate Christmas?
24. Have you now forgotten where you were when Kennedy was shot?
25. Have you taken out a subscription to *The Oldie*?

If you answered 'Yes' to more than ten questions (and 'No' to questions 19 and 20), then congratulations! You are most definitely an Oldie. If you haven't yet answered 'Yes' to number 25, then subscribe NOW!

ILLUSTRATIONS BY ARTHUR ROBBINS

To China with the
SUNSHINER

In 1974 starry-eyed **DAVID ERDAL** *went to Mao Tse Tung's China full of idealism*

I arrived in Peking in 1974, two years before Mao died. At twenty-six I was a full-blown 'sunshiner', a starry-eyed foreigner believing that the sun shone from Mao's backside. His moral leadership had forged the peasants into a powerful guerrilla army, expelling foreign imperialists and corrupt Chinese alike.

I was there to teach English but my purpose was to learn revolution, to improve the world. And I felt well-qualified: in the UK I had spent two years as a Trotskyist, a shop steward, a flying picket and a roving party organiser. I also had a degree in Chinese, although at Peking airport, after the long flight on an empty China Airways Boeing 707, I had difficulty understanding the language.

I stayed for a few days with two minders at the Friendship Hotel, a walled ghetto built for Russian experts in the Fifties, now housing all 'foreign experts'. Exquisitely polite treatment of 'foreign friends' served to keep us isolated. Politics seemed hardly to count: Americans breakfasted with Albanians, and shared across their ideological gulf their frustration with

Chinese xenophobia. We were shown round monuments, factories, schools and communes, and were fed the party line, which I later learned ruled regardless of facts. For foreign friends there was tea, but for the locals only hot water. I took reams of sunshiner notes, and gradually my ears became attuned to the spoken language.

In Tientsin, the old port of Peking where I was to teach, I was lodged for my first ten months in what had been the Astor House Hotel, built around 1900 when Britain held one of twenty-two forcibly taken concessions. I was usually the only resident – the Chinese needed a special pass to get in.

I was keen to get close to the people – to travel by bike, to wear Mao clothes, to live on campus and eat with the students, joining in their political study sessions. This was not what the authorities had in mind. They provided a limousine – the equivalent of a private helicopter in a developed economy. I had to live and eat alone in the hotel. This was how it should be for foreign friends, they explained. So I bought a shapeless Mao uniform and a bicycle, and threatened to strike if I was not allowed to eat with the

students and go to political study. After a few weeks of battling I was closer to being integrated than most foreigners. The only overt barrier was the fact that I still lived in the hotel.

My fervent revolutionary mind began to face puzzles immediately. A new constitution for China was passed by the people's congress – but it had been held in secret. Answering my questions, a party member admitted that there had been no choice of candidate and no discussion. Pressed on 'no discussion', he came out with: 'People who have opinions are class enemies.' How did this fit with Mao's writings on revolutionary democracy?

To criticise the leaders, who claimed to welcome criticism from the masses, the constitution guaranteed the right to put up 'big-character posters' (posters written in large characters and stuck on walls in public places). Soon I saw this tested in practice. An elected student leader wrote a poster criticising his head of department for dictatorial behaviour. In response, all classes were cancelled for a week and every day the poster-writer was dragged, bound, on stage while the students yelled abuse at him for hours on end. I knew that

Left: 'Glorious leader, righteous people', propaganda poster from the Chinese Cultural Revolution, 1966–76. Below: David Erdal standing with a peasant and his daughter

most students agreed with him, but no one stood up for him. At the end of the week this confident, friendly young man was a wreck. He could no longer walk across open spaces, could only look at his feet, spoke to no one.

Later, two dissidents – people of astounding bravery lightly worn – explained why no one had supported him. If you expressed mistaken views but recanted, then you could remain a student. But if anyone supported you, you became conspirators and would all be sent to a camp for 'thought reform through labour'. So his best friends had to abuse him the most.

This Maoist refinement meant that it was rarely necessary for secret police to come calling. Everyone was at risk, and so everyone would join in to 'explain your mistakes'. Otherwise it was a conspiracy.

The only people I saw who really didn't give a damn were peasants – they alone were prepared to laugh at party pretensions. As stinking intellectuals, we teachers had to do periods of 'open door schooling' – physical labour with workers or peasants – to learn good attitudes from them. Twice I lived with peasants on a commune for a few weeks, working in the fields during the day and sleeping five to a kang brick-bed at night. I loved it. And I certainly did learn from them.

One method used by the party to maintain control was to launch campaigns. When a new campaign started everyone had to memorise and repeat at political study the *People's Daily* editorials. One day an official from a distant provincial town arrived at the commune to launch a new campaign, 'Criticising Water Margin'. Why the peasants should listen to a fourteenth-century novel being attacked as 'capitulationist' was beyond me. That evening, sitting in the open on little stools listening to the incomprehensible editorial being read monotonously by the official, the old peasants started keeling over into the dust, exhausted after their long day of labours in the fields. Their co-ordination was balletic. But the reason they could get away with it was chilling: for them things

could not get any worse. They worked seven days a week, virtually never got any cash, and although they produced large quantities of wheat and maize there was never any decent food. I remember Granny Sung, wheeled out for a 'speak bitterness' meeting. She finished lambasting the landlords of the old days by saying 'and all we ever had to eat was sorghum'. Then off we went to eat our daily ration of sorghum. It wasn't writing big-character posters, but the message was clear.

Eventually the sunshine failed. The people were living in fear, the system was undeniably evil and everyone was trapped. If the leader of my college had not punished the poster writer so viciously, then he too would have been reported and he could have ended up in a labour camp. In my now demoralised evenings I took to drinking a great deal of rather fine Tangshan beer, and singing revolutionary songs from the

hotel balcony. The masses, bored stiff with their diet of propaganda films, responded. A large crowd started to collect every evening. So I got moved onto campus, to live with the masses at last.

The whole Mao era has been magnificently illuminated by Jung Chang and Jon Halliday in their biography: *Mao – The Unknown Story* (Jonathan Cape, 2005). Contrary to the myth, Mao did not inspire the peasants – there were no uprisings to support the Communists. Nor did he care about them. Some seventy million Chinese civilians died as a result of his lifelong lust for power, an endless campaign to become and stay the leader, and then to build China into a superpower to lead the world. From the first he had no compunction about torturing and killing his own people, driving whole armies to their deaths in the civil and Korean wars to help him secure his leadership goals. He prevented the Communists from fighting the Japanese occupation. He knowingly starved the peasants in their millions, taking their grain to pay for arms for the superpower project. That is why Granny Sung was still eating sorghum – and she was one of the lucky ones. Mao's greatest skill was intimidating those around him, and the Water Margin campaign, it turns out, was a disguised attack on premier Chou En-lai. All of this is told with wonderful, horrifying lucidity and colour, the fruits of ten years of rich research. A really significant book, and not just for ex-Maoists.

'We are gathered here today more in celebration of his life than in sadness at his death'

A KNIGHT to remember

LUCY LETHBRIDGE's *first experience of a naked man was in the unliklely setting of a talk by Shakespearean scholar Sir George Wilson Knight...*

Illustration by ROBERT GEARY

Apart from a tantalising glimpse of a streaker in the woods, the first time I saw a naked man he was standing on a stage in front of an amazed audience of teenage schoolchildren. It was the early 1980s, I was a convent schoolgirl, and the naked figure was Sir George Wilson Knight, author of *The Wheel of Fire*, and many other seminal works of Shakespearean criticism. He was then in his mid-eighties.

My boarding school was stuck away down a very long drive in rural Surrey, and there wasn't much to do in the evenings except crowd round one small television with 150 other girls, so when six of us were offered the chance by our inspiring English teacher, Miss Jenkins, to go and see Sir George give a talk on Shakespeare, it offered a tempting diversion. Most exciting of all was the fact that the event was to take place in a boys' school – Dulwich College.

We travelled by minibus, all six of us glistening with freshly-applied passion-fruit lip potion, Miss Jenkins at the wheel. On arrival, we took our places in the school hall among a sea of adolescent boys to whom we feigned indifference. This talk was obviously a grand occasion, and stops had been pulled out: in honour of Old Alleynian Sir George, there was a mountainous flower arrangement at the front of the stage; the headmaster was looking nervous. When everyone was seated in respectful hush, a frail, snowy-haired figure in a grey suit appeared on the stage, leaning on a stick, and the Head leapt to his feet and made a speech of welcome, with a great deal of jocular murmurs: 'So proud, so honoured'; 'All the way from Canada' (the great man had taught at the University of Toronto for many years). Then the lights dimmed, the

Head reverently took his seat and the frail figure began to speak.

Sir George seemed distracted from the very beginning. It was difficult to make out what he was saying as his voice was light and quavery, and a flustered master in the wings hastily adjusted the microphone which then

Sir George returned to the stage stark naked except for a tiny leather loincloth and a moth-eaten woman's wig

emitted ear-splitting howls. Sir George looked rather bored, muttered a few general words about wheels of fire and flies to wanton boys, then leaned on his stick and, looking straight at the audience, told us that he had always wanted to be an actor and now, in his last years, no longer had any desire to talk about Shakespeare but instead wished to act out his favourite tragic roles. With that he walked off the stage.

The headmaster craned his neck into the wings anxiously, the microphone squawked and the audience shuffled their feet. When Sir George returned he was stark naked except for a tiny leather loincloth and a moth-eaten woman's wig. We were stunned into amazed silence, but Wilson Knight appeared to have forgotten our existence: his voice was now an actorly boom, and without bothering with preambles, he launched straight into mad King Lear, hurling his spindly body about and berating nature, gods and man with his walking stick. He went through Hamlet, Othello, Coriolanus and Julius Caesar, clenching his fists, rolling his eyes, beating his breast and obviously enjoying himself enormously. An hour went by. The headmaster looked stricken, the audience was glued to their seats. Looking back it seems curious that nobody sniggered, but perhaps it was because even we callous adolescents were struck by the poignancy, the tragic pathos, of this aged titan and his hour upon the stage.

Wilson Knight had exhausted all the major roles by the time he reached Timon of Athens, but he went out with a spectacular finale. 'Lower the lights,' he boomed, pointing his walking stick into the wings; the flustered master trained a single spotlight into the darkness. Wilson Knight gazed out at us from beneath his acrylic beehive hairdo: 'This is the moment,' he cried, 'when Timon of Athens abandons civilisation and flees to the woods'; and with that, and a theatrical flourish, the old man pulled at the leather ties of his loincloth; it dropped to the floor and he stood before us – naked completely.

I can't remember exactly what happened next, except that the headmaster clambered onto the stage and, bright red, shook Sir George's hand vigorously, 'Thank you, thank you... I'm sure everyone here will agree... absolutely fascinating...' while gesturing to the audience to start applauding immediately – which we did. Apparently quite unabashed, Wilson Knight took a deep bow, then came forward to accept a bouquet of flowers from the dazed head boy. Smiling happily, waving graciously, he walked off the stage with all the dignity of Irving or Olivier.

In the minibus on the way back to school, we were almost completely silent. There seemed nothing to say, but an awful lot to think about. Navigating the rainy night-time road back to Surrey, Miss Jenkins gripped the steering wheel, looked straight ahead, and said only that she was 'Very, very sorry' that we girls should have had to be witnesses to such a thing. She hoped our parents wouldn't mind.

Years later someone told me that in the last years of his life Wilson Knight quite often took his clothes off: it was a party piece of his. And as to whether I was forever scarred by the experience... Well, only time will tell.

'Your son has head lice. Unfortunately, they belong to a protected species'

As a hiding place from the wind and a covert from the tempest

by Kit Wright
Illustrated by Peter Bailey

Rain is falling, time out of mind,
On this sad park, in this same city,
And running forever down the regulations
On a wooden notice,
Undersigned:

BY ORDER OF THE BOWLING CLUB COMMITTEE.

High ash trees in their lamentation
Career and weep in the riding rain
Over the roof of the Bowls Club Pavilion;
Likewise the streaming, bobble-hung plane
Guards the toy picket fence, sitting so pretty
By the formal and hopeless official ditty
With its stout refrain:

BY ORDER OF THE BOWLING CLUB COMMITTEE.

And I believe in the Committee's powers
As the rain keeps falling for unfathomable hours...
And none hereabouts may be stabbed or shot,
For the members of the Bowling Club Committee say not.
As the waters fountain down their holy mountain,
Cruelty and Treachery and Hate shall be demolished,
And Death shall be abolished
And replaced by Universal
Tenderness and Pity:

BY ORDER OF THE BOWLING CLUB,
HEAVEN'S HIGH-ROLLING CLUB,
BY ORDER OF THE BOWLING CLUB COMMITTEE.

Enoch Powell

On a dark, rainy evening in Wolverhampton
DAVID THOMAS *had an unexpected customer*

Robert Geary

Enoch Powell wasn't much of a customer. His wife was the one who spent the money, regularly buying kitchen utensils and garden tools from my father's ironmonger's shop in Wolverhampton's Chapel Ash.

During its final years the shop's trade had declined and my father ran the place alone. From time to time he'd ask me to take over so that he could enjoy a much needed weekend break. It was towards the end of a dismal November day and I was looking forward to closing up and heading homewards. There had been no customers since half past five and, as I began to cash up at ten to six, rain was falling steadily in the darkness outside. There were rarely any customers during the last half-hour of the day and I often wondered why my father never chose to close the shop that much earlier. It was only years after that I realised the shop's closing time coincided with the opening of The Clarendon, the congenial pub only a step away, where Dad invariably put a full stop to the day's business.

I was locking the back door when the phone rang. I picked up the receiver and heard the unmistakable tones of Enoch Powell. He had a curious accent – what I can only describe as 'posh Wolverhampton'.

'Don't close yet,' he ordered me. 'I'll be there in five minutes.'

I was very young and he was a distinguished statesman, so I did as I was told. All the same, by five past six I decided he wasn't coming after all, so I switched off the lights and made for the front door, which I'd locked while counting the day's takings. As I reached it there was a loud tapping on the glass. The prominent eyes of Enoch Powell peered from his pale face into the gloom within. His moustache quivered with urgency and water streamed from the broad rim of his black Homburg hat. Reluctantly I let him in and locked the door behind

Enoch Powell's pale face peered into the shop. 'It needs a new washer,' he said, holding a brass tap up

him, wondering what problem was so urgent it was worth braving such foul weather. He marched up to the counter, pulled a green-stained brass garden tap from the pocket of his heavy overcoat and placed it in front of me. 'It needs a new washer,' he said, flatly.

I turned on the lights again and asked him what sort of washer it needed. He didn't know; he couldn't get the thing apart. Great, I thought. After several minutes of futile struggle, engaged in a sort of arm-wrestling match with Mr Powell, who held the tap in the grip of a large wrench while I heaved on an equally large spanner, I gave up. 'It's not going to shift,' I said. 'You'd be better off with a new tap.' Enoch Powell, however, gave up less easily.

'We need a vice,' he said. 'You must have one in here somewhere.'

I should have replied with a categorical 'No'. Unfortunately, I hesitated. 'Not really… There's a very old thing upstairs, but…'

He jumped on this eagerly. I explained that there was no light on the top floor; electricity had never been installed beyond the first flight of stairs. In fact, the upper storey of the house was now used only for the storage of unwanted clutter; piles of dusty hessian sacks in which lawn seed had been delivered, broken tools long forgotten and unclaimed by their owners, and several life-sized cardboard figures bearing cheerful smiles as they demonstrated some new product or other. Many years ago, the front room of the top floor had been a simple workshop. The bench my grandfather once used was still there, but it now leaned awkwardly at a sharp angle since one of its legs had become detached. The vice was completely rusted over but eventually I managed to open its jaws and, while Enoch held the torch, I tightened them on the resisting tap. Slowly I prised it apart. I picked up the pieces and, taking the torch from Enoch's hand, led the return to the ground floor, periodically shedding the light behind me. It wasn't so much courtesy as a desire not to be crushed to death by a falling Enoch Powell.

Behind the counter, on a high shelf reached only by the small wooden ladder kept for the purpose, was a box of leather washers. I climbed up and brought it down. Inside, the box was partitioned by interlocking cardboard dividers into twenty-four small compartments, each containing a different size or shape of washer. On the underside of the lid was a diagram replicating its contents with a brief description of each item – three-quarter-inch cup, half-inch heavy duty, etc. Unfortunately, the compartment that should have contained washers of the sort needed was empty. Somehow, I wasn't surprised.

Mr Powell reached into the box and picked out one of the three-quarter-inch cup washers. 'This should do it,' he said. 'It just needs trimming to shape.'

So, naturally, that's what I did. I took up a Stanley knife and trimmed the cup-shaped flange until I'd achieved a three-quarter-inch flat washer – more or less.

I squeezed it into the tap, reassembled the various bits and handed the product of half an hour's labour to what I assumed to be a highly satisfied customer.

'How much do I owe you?' he asked.

I peered at the lid of the box where prices had been written in pencil, probably by my grandfather twenty-five years earlier.

It read '6d' – six pence in old money.

I should have said six shillings but I was anticipating a handsome tip.

'Sixpence,' I replied.

And that's what he gave me – sixpence – not a penny more.

By the time Enoch Powell had departed into the night, it was turned half past six. I switched off the lights once more, stepped into the still pouring rain, locked the shop door and walked, very briskly, to the pub.

Not so grim Up North
Life in the Pennines

by Geoffrey Moorhouse, June 2009. Illustrated by Peter Brook

SO LAMBING is over for another year. The firstborns were dropped in one of our pastures on March 2nd, which is regarded as a bit early at this altitude, though not by those who farm three or four hundred feet below us. Lambs were to be seen round Skipton towards the end of February, but no one would dream of starting them up here, where the temperatures are crucially lower, and the weather is more likely to be dangerous.

The day I saw twins trotting behind their mother across Nigel's field also brought steady rain, with low cloud sagging down Ten End, and two days later this had turned to snow; not like the heavy falls we had in the previous month, but enough to blanket the hills and dump a couple of inches on my lawn. Of the two, if we have to make a choice, we'd rather have the white stuff at lambing than torrential wetness. Newborn lambs can survive snow if the ewe puts them between her fleece and the lee of a drystone wall; but cold drenching rain knocks them over and out at any time in their first week or so.

The timing can be controlled to some extent, because our Swaledale ewes come to season in September and October, and it is up to the farmer to decide when he will put them to the mostly Blue-faced Leicester tups. Each male is given a chestful of distinctive raddle (sometimes green or blue instead of red) so that it will mark the female in mounting her, the surest way of establishing parentage. Five months later the lambs appear amid the timeless rituals of shepherding.

Lambing is imminent when the pregnant ewes are brought down from the tops to the home pastures, where they will be more accessible if problems arise. Throughout April, when scores of births happen every day, the nights are punctuated by the sound of tractors rumbling up and down the lanes, as Nigel and John, Dennis and Bill and the others invigilate their flocks to see if any mother is struggling, if any infant has strayed in the dark; for it will be unwelcome to any other ewe and will starve if it is not reintroduced to Mum. Most ewes drop twins but some have triplets, a nuisance if one is rejected because its mother cannot cope with more than two. A solution is to skin a stillborn lamb and cover the reject with the pelt; and usually, after the bereft parent has sniffed about a bit and been deceived, she accepts the waif as her own and starts feeding it.

It's a marvellous time, which lifts the spirit as does no other moment of the year. For new lambs *are* the most adorable creatures in the world, as they hop, skip and jump about the parish, absolutely delighted to be here. I giggle like a child when they do vertical takeoffs, or go helter-skeltering in a mob round a field, then suddenly stop, wondering how they got from there to here, before rushing back whence they came, scrambling to be first.

This annual nativity has been going on without interruption ever since the Brigantes were here three centuries before Christ, long before French Cistercians brought commercial sheep-farming to the dale. It means spring has come at last. So, this year, did the arrival of the lapwing which was wheeling and plunging below the cloud on the flank of Ten End the day our lambing began, the first of its kind to return from wintering where tides and rivers meet around Morecambe Bay.

ILLUSTRATION BY PETER BAILEY

*When **JERUSHA McCORMACK'S** husband died suddenly, she found the traditional platitudes about grieving to be useless – until she was shown a ball in a jar...*

Enduring Grief

Ten years ago my husband died, suddenly, without warning, after a complicated, if routine, operation. That day a world opened which I had never imagined before.

In the world of the day before, we were safe. My husband was reasonably well. The boys, eleven and seventeen, were growing up fine. We had two secure, professional jobs. Our mortgage was under control. Our anxieties – centred upon ageing parents, the boys at school or office politics – now seem so predictable.

From the moment the hospital rang asking me urgently to come in, I knew my husband was dead. But at the same time I did not know what was going to happen from moment to moment. I did not know what to do.

Yet I knew certain things had to be done in a certain order, even though they were contradictory. I had to go in to the hospital to be told my husband had died, although every instinct told me he was dead. I had to see him to say goodbye, even though I knew he had left. Somehow I had to involve the boys in this, but at the same time I had to protect them.

I remember looking over at them as I put the phone down, thinking: 'I don't have to tell them this. I can just pretend nothing has happened.' Because once I told them, their childhood would be over. It was then that I made a resolution: however bad this would be, we were going to meet it head-on. That meant, first of all, not being afraid. It was as if I understood, instinctively, that my worst enemy would not be pain, but fear.

Still, when the shock wore off, the pain was intense; so bad at times I could not even find a physical position that was comfortable – much less eat or sleep. But I learned to say to myself, it is only pain. It is not good or bad, but a sign we have been wounded. If we pay attention to the wound, if we do not ignore it, we will heal. But how? Some months before, a Buddhist friend had told me, 'Life is suffering'.

Now his words came back, along with their corollary: 'Everything changes. And everything is interconnected.' Over the first weeks, this became my mantra, my first clue to the way ahead. If everything changes, death is just another change among many. We have been changed and will in turn be changed by what we change.

But the world did not want to accept change. Something had gone missing. So it should be replaced – immediately – to get back to where we were before. Thus, within the year, people started to ask, 'Have you recovered yet?' Recovered what? I would ask myself. My world had disappeared with my husband. I had not only lost a husband and a father to our children, but also income and status. Invitations had started to dry up. The phone calls fell off. My husband's friends, with notable exceptions, avoided me. Evidently, I was a social embarrassment, a wet blanket, the *memento mori* at the birthday party.

Then someone was sure to ask me whether I had begun dating again. What? How do you begin dating when you haven't dated for over thirty years? When you are trying to hold down a full-time job, raise two now vulnerable boys and hold on to your sanity when almost everyone else seems to think you have become another person? All this too on little sleep, poor appetite and scattered concentration. For my mind was no longer my own. It was entirely preoccupied by the question: what do I do now? As I am clearly not going to recover – in the sense that things are never going to be the same again – what direction is open to me? Why, when everyone at some time or another is going to go through this experience, has someone not plotted out some routes for the journey?

Instead of routes, what society offered me were deflections: a whole catechism of clichés as threadbare as they were useless. It was a conspiracy: I would act the poor, mousey, perhaps pious, widow and allow them to inflict these aphorisms on me in the interests of my well-being.

Then someone told me there was a map; it was a book called *On Death and Dying* by Elisabeth Kübler-Ross. She told me I would go through different emotional reactions in a predictable order, beginning with denial and ending with acceptance: 'the five stages of grief.' Very tidy. Now I could get on with it – suffering by schedule. Except when I tried to pay attention to them, the stages got all mixed up – if I could identify them at all. As far as I could see, denial would veer suddenly into acceptance and then back again into anger. I dared not believe in hope.

Then one day I saw a notice for a talk on helping children through bereavement by Barbara Monroe, the Chief Executive of St Christopher's Hospice in London. When I arrived, what I saw resembled a physics lesson. On the table before her was a very large glass jar. Beside were three balls: one large, one medium-sized, one small. Without a word, she began to stuff the

large ball into the jar. With a great deal of effort, she wedged it in.

'There!' she said. 'That's how grieving feels at first. If grief is the ball and the jar is your world, you can see how the grief fills everything. There is no air to breathe, no space to move around. Every thought, every action reminds you of your loss.'

Then she pulled the large ball out of the jar and put in the medium-sized ball. She held it up again, tipping it so the ball rolled around a bit. 'Maybe you think that's how it will feel after a time – say, after the first year. Grieving will no longer fill every bit of space in your life.' Then she rolled the ball out and plopped in the small ball.

'Now, say, by the second or third year, that's how grieving is supposed to feel. Like the ball, it has shrunk. So now you can think of grief as taking up a very small part of your world – it could almost be ignored if you wish to ignore it.'

For a moment, considering my own crammed jar, I thought of leaving. 'That's what everyone thinks grieving is like,' the voice continued. 'And it's all rubbish.'

I settled back into my seat. Two other glass jars were produced from under the table: one larger, one very large.

'Now,' she said, imperiously. 'Regard.' Silently, she took the largest ball and squeezed it slowly into the least of the three jars. It would barely fit.

Then she pulled the ball out and placed it in the next-larger jar. There was room for it to roll around. Finally, she took it out and dropped it into the largest glass jar. 'There,' she said, in triumph. 'That's what grieving is really like. If your grieving is the ball, like the ball here it doesn't get any bigger or any smaller. It is always the same. But the jar is bigger. If your world is this glass jar, your task is to make your world bigger.'

'You see,' she continued, 'no one wants their grief to shrink. It is all they have left of the person who died. But if your world gets larger, then you can keep your grief as it is but work around it.'

Then she turned to us. 'Older people coping with grief often try to keep their world the same. It is a mistake. If I have one thing to say to all of you it is this: make your world larger. Then there will be room in it for your grieving, but your grieving will not take up all the room. This way you can find space to make a new life for yourselves.'

'This is it!' I said. 'A way out – a way to remake my life.'

That was eight years ago. For what the balls and jars gave was a new way to imagine grieving – and how it might be turned around. Having emigrated in my head to a place where I am neither married nor unmarried, neither desolate nor jubilant, I am now, literally, in a new country – China – and enlarging my life.

'The Mitchells' fancy dress party – I suppose you will be going as a pirate again?'

Who's this guy FAWKES?

TROG – *aka Wally Fawkes – was a regular Oldie illustrator, drawing a caricature for the books pages every month between 2001 and 2005 before failing eyesight forced him to retire. In 2007* **MARGARET CRICK** *met the veteran political cartoonist*

Wally Fawkes, the political cartoonist Trog, had an oldie moment recently when he was at the doctor's surgery for his flu jab. 'I was in the waiting room with a lot of slightly apprehensive elderly people in various stages of decay when over the speakers came a faint sound of music. Suddenly the Nelson Riddle strings filled the room and the next thing we heard was Sinatra singing "And Now the End is Near". We all looked at each other and exploded with mirth.'

Fawkes will be eighty-three in June, having retired after sixty years as a cartoonist because failing eyesight meant he could no longer see well enough to draw. He is sad there are politicians coming onto the stage whom he's never cartooned, like David Cameron. His compensation is being able to draw on his other prodigious talent, that of being a jazz musician. 'I think I would be a bit sadder about the whole business if I didn't have the clarinet playing, but it's a very good outlet to have.' He is self-taught, saying the instrument took him up when he was eighteen, in the Benny Goodman era. When Fawkes heard the clarinettist Sidney Bechet he was 'swept away'. He says all he knew about the clarinet was that you blew down the narrow end; but it wasn't long before Bechet was describing him as one of the world's best.

His first band was the George Webb Dixielanders, to which he recruited the trumpeter Humphrey Lyttelton, then an art student. Lyttelton returned the favour in 1948 when he formed his own band and Fawkes was a founder member.

The two played together for years; but eventually Fawkes found there was a conflict between the pressure of touring every weekend and his Fleet Street day job. 'I was getting further and further behind, and I had to make a decision to keep the music for pleasure and the cartoon drawing as a livelihood, because unless you're a band leader you don't make much money out of music.' He still plays today.

Many musicians have begun their careers at art school and Fawkes thinks there's a empathy between cartooning and jazz. 'You're drawing in the air really. With jazz, you've got to keep to the same chords and get them right, but you start improvising, as with a caricature. The clarinet and the pen are similar: with the clarinet you depend on the reed at the end, and with a pen it's the nib. You dip the nib into ink and you dip the reed into your head. The artist whose drawings most look to me like music is Quentin Blake – he's one of my favourites.'

Art was his first talent and he knew he loved drawing from childhood. At fourteen he won a scholarship to Sidcup Art School. His promising art student years were cut short by the War, and he was forced to leave and earn some money for his family who had sailed to Britain from Vancouver during the depression years, 'unaware there was a depression here too'. His first job was to camouflage a factory in Woolwich. 'I spent all summer doing it and then it was bombed; I got a rejection slip from Hitler – the severest criticism I ever got.' From the remains of the bombed-out factory, Fawkes rose again by winning a competition sponsored by the Coal Commission (who employed him to trace maps of coal seams). The

Tony Benn December 2002

Max Beerbohm April 2003

Janet Street-Porter August 2004

Queen Victoria October 2002

ISSUE 104, NOVEMBER 1997 BY TROG

competition entry had depicted a boxer apprehensively approaching the ring. 'I was into boxing then; I was very aggressive in those days.'

Luckily for Fawkes, the art competition judge was Leslie Illingworth, the *Daily Mail*'s political cartoonist, who became his 'fairy godmother', giving him his first newspaper job. 'I started on the *Mail* on my twenty-first birthday doing little column breakers. Leslie was the great man in my cartoon life.' Fawkes took the pen-name Trog from his band's nickname, the Troglodytes, and returned one day a week to art school, this time Camberwell, where he was taught by John Minton. Three years later, the *Mail* asked him to draw a strip cartoon, for which he created a small woolly creature called Flook, who became a household name. Originally meant for children, the strip evolved into a gentle satire and political commentary and was written by colleagues including Lyttelton, George Melly and Barry Took. It lasted thirty-five years, by which time Fawkes had become disillusioned with the paper's politics and was contributing cartoons to the *Spectator*, *New Statesman*, *Punch* and – in the Seventies – to the *Observer*, for which he drew two cartoons a week, one for the leader page and a 'Mini-Trog' for the front page.

His friendship with Lyttelton – whom he recruited to the *Mail* – has lasted a lifetime. Lyttelton describes him as 'tall, placid and easy-going, with a deep-rooted aversion to anything which threatened to make life complicated... and a Groucho Marxian sense of humour... He doesn't believe in speaking one word when none would do.'

Fawkes thinks good cartoonists need highly trained graphic skills and political awareness, but he doesn't believe in taking work too seriously. 'It's just part of the paper which is fish and chips the next day.' Nevertheless, his originals are sought after by many politicians, including the jazz-loving Ken Clarke, who says Trog is his favourite political cartoonist. 'When I was a small boy I was a fan of Flook... Probably my favourite Trog – although it's not terribly flattering – is of John Major and myself as a couple of beached whales.' Trog returns the compliment by saying the Tories should have put Clarke in control after Thatcher, although his own leanings are to the left. 'I'm all for the left being sensible, or at least regaining its senses. I like New Labour but not the present leader. I've done lots of cartoons of Blair, week after week, and I think that's what drove me blind.'

ISSUE 116, NOVEMBER 1998 BY TROG

Major Family Values

unprepared stream of consciousness about his often comic life and times.

Sadly some of the distinguished company were laughing at him, not with him. Nicholas Soames, then a junior defence minister, was beside himself. His generous form was heaving with mirth and his face was red. The louder the minister laughed, the longer the big brother rambled on about his garden gnome manufacturing adventures. I wondered then whether a junior member of Margaret Thatcher's government would have found it so funny if the Iron Lady had had a garrulous older brother.

Terry was usually able to provide colourful detail about his brother, though was often guarded in his revelations

JAMES HUGHES-ONSLOW, *The Oldie's Memorial correspondent, remembers the loyalty, decency and eccentricity of his friend, Terry Major-Ball, elder brother of John Major, who died in March 2007*

IN 1995 Terry Major-Ball received unique recognition for his memoirs, *Major Major: Memories of an Older Brother*. He was given the first Oldie Big Brother of the Year Award at a ceremony at Simpson's-in-the-Strand. The prize has not been awarded since, maybe because no older brother has distinguished himself in quite the same way.

At the Oldie of the Year Awards Terry received his gong from Terry Wogan, and had the terrifying ordeal of speaking immediately after Spike Milligan had brought the house down with his anarchic wit. A lesser man would have sat down quietly and said 'thank you very much but I can't follow that'. But, as so often in his life, such as when the family garden gnomes business collapsed and he was the main breadwinner with two elderly parents and a young brother to look after, Terry was not a man to shirk his obligations. He got to his feet and began a long

I came across Terry when I was a reporter on the *Evening Standard* in the early 1990s. When John Major first became Prime Minister his background was something of a mystery, although it was known that his parents had been music hall comedians, trapeze artists and gnome makers. (Terry once told a radio interviewer in Melbourne: 'How do you expect me and my brother to be grey men when both our parents were professional comedians?') Terry was usually able to provide colourful detail on the new PM, although he was often guarded in his revelations. He told me that one day on his way to Victoria Station to catch the train home, he decided to drop in at Downing Street to see his young brother. He was by this time a familiar figure with the policemen at the gate. The PM was busy, but Norma Major was hosting a drinks party. Terry was given what he thought was orange juice but turned out to be Buck's Fizz. As a result, he fell asleep on the train to Croydon and ended up at Gatwick, the first time he had ever been to an airport. In fact he had never flown in an aircraft, stayed in a hotel or been abroad, except on National Service.

It led to the *Evening Standard* and Virgin Atlantic putting this right, by flying us both to New York for a four-day stay at the Churchill Hotel in Manhattan. Never having been to New York myself, I was also an innocent abroad. But this was an essential part of our relationship; Terry would never have tolerated me patronising him with superior knowledge about places I had been to before, as I learned when I took him to New Zealand and later to Australia.

'We've been born into a surveillance society'

In his six and a half years in Downing Street, John Major never tried to curtail his brother's antics, although they nearly always attracted publicity which may have been unwelcome to the control freaks in the No 10 press office. I suspect this was because the Prime Minister was a kind-hearted man who knew his brother had had a tough life and deserved a bit of fun. But he also knew how stubborn Terry could be and that it was unwise to try telling him what he could or could not do. Certainly John knew how much he owed Terry for keeping the family together in his teenage years when everything could have fallen apart. Although Terry had a reputation for long-windedness, he never gave away any of the secrets which might have made life very precarious for a Prime Minister with a knife-edge majority. He never mentioned Edwina Currie, who could have sunk the Tory back-to-basics campaign for family values single-handed. Nor anything about the landlord in Brixton, who

lent them two rooms in Coldharbour Lane when the family business went bust and they had to move from their bungalow. It later transpired, when the ex-PM wrote his own memoirs, that this was a secret half-brother.

Another person who played a key role in the young life of the future Prime Minister was Jean Kierans, who Terry describes as 'a friend of Mother's'. Although thirteen years older, Mrs Kierans taught young John all he needed to know about life, and she remained on the scene until he met his wife Norma. When John was a disenchanted teenager, applying unsuccessfully for a bus conductor's job at Camberwell Bus Garage and watching the same film over and over again at the Ritzy Cinema, Mrs Kierans told him to do some exams and get a proper job. He spent a lot of time in Mrs Kierans's house and duly ended up working for the Standard Chartered Bank where he met the chairman Anthony Barber, a former Chancellor of the Exchequer, who introduced him to politics.

Who knows what else this generous lady taught him? But, whatever the truth, he seems to have learned how to handle older people, and particularly older women, with astonishing self-assurance, a skill which came in handy when he became

chairman of the housing committee in Brixton Council, and later a member of Margaret Thatcher's Cabinet. Not many of us would have had the aplomb to carry off that consoling embrace of Mrs Yeltsin at her husband's funeral.

What has all this to do with Terry? Well, the loyal older brother kept one essential insight from us throughout the Major years in government. When in 1967 John Major seriously injured his leg in a car crash in Nigeria while working for Standard Chartered, he returned to south London to be with his family. In *Major Major* Terry records that John couldn't stay with them long because he couldn't bend his leg and this prevented him using the outside lavatory as he couldn't shut the door. 'So John went to stay with friends,' wrote Terry, in a cover-up worthy of Downing Street spin doctors. The friend he went to stay with was in fact Jean Kierans, the revelation of whose existence could have helped Terry sell many more copies of his own memoirs if he hadn't been so discreet.

When Terry died of cancer in March, his death remained unreported for over five weeks. No one had thought to put an announcement in the papers. The fact only emerged when Beryl Bainbridge met Sir John at a party in Hatchard's and naturally asked after Terry. Needless to say, he received huge obituaries in all the serious newspapers. How could anyone have thought the passing of such a decent man, and such a eccentric one-off character, should be kept from his many friends and admirers all over the world?

Left: John Major and Terry Major-Ball: 'John knew how much he owed Terry for keeping the family together in his teenage years when everything could have fallen apart'

Gotta lotta bottle

Can a milkman's life really be full of spies, sexual intrigue and skulduggery?
Well yes, actually, it can, reveals recently retired milkie, **PHIL WARK**
Illustrated by AXEL SCHEFFLER

I know what you are thinking. Is it true what they say about milkmen? All those house-wives? Well, it's not a myth, though I think that it's rare. But when a lady in her forties regularly pays you stark naked, you have to wonder. Is she a naturist? Has she got early Alzheimer's, or is she looking for a bit of fun? With a young, nubile partner at home, I wasn't really interested.

Then there was a pleasant Dutch lady whose sexual frustration was manifest, although her approach was somewhat surreal. 'My husband is away. I drove him to the airport today.

He's in Japan. And look what I found on the floor after he had gone.'

She places a two-inch screw on the table next to my cup of tea.

'It's a nice screw, isn't it?' she says.
'It's... very nice.' I sip my tea.
'Would you like this nice screw?'
'Actually, I've got lots of screws at home.'

I began my career on London's milk rounds in 1982. Friends told me it was a dying business. They were right, but it was a slow death, and I've only just given up the ghost. In those days if you drove north from central London there was a milk depot in every metropolitan village. Supermarket giants like Sainsbury's sold milk, but at the same price as your milkman. Virtually every household had their milk delivered.

Today all but one of those depots have closed down and there are none in central London – the temptation for the main players to cash in on prime property locations having been too great to resist. The big companies have also abandoned retail deliveries, leaving them to franchisees, few of whom have survived.

And so, after a week at Milkman University, being schooled and examined in milkman paperwork and customer relations, I turned up at West Hampstead depot to begin my hands-on training. After a week with a roundsman, I was given a round in Hampstead.

'Mr Foot. Call daily,' read the roundsbook. 'Would you like some tea?' asked the Leader of the Opposition.

'Yes, please.' I was left of Militant at the time and he was an old-time socialist, and we had fine talk and numerous arguments. It was close to election time and I inevitably asked him about Labour's chances of defeating the Iron Lady. He predicted a Labour win with a majority of fifty to sixty seats.

The coda to this story is that I was once approached by a well-known Hampstead vagrant after a cup of tea with Mr Foot.

'Been to see Michael?' he asked.

'Yes,' I answered. 'He thinks Labour can win.'

'He ain't got a bleedin' clue,' said the prescient vagrant.

The judgment was harsh but Foot did lose heavily in the election of 1983. The tramp was rather better dressed than Michael.

Subsequently I worked on a round in NW1 where I served a legendary actor who, I believe, is still just about alive, so I can't really offer a name. One day, on receiving his pint of gold top, he made an unusual request. It seemed that he wanted to see my 'willy'. Just see it, no touching. I answered that there wasn't a lot to see but he was insistent, telling me that Bob, his regular milkman, always showed him

his 'willy'. I obliged. He gave me a £10 tip. All part of the service, though I hadn't been briefed about such occasions at Milkman University.

The Serious Crimes Squad raided the depot at West Hampstead: six milkmen were arrested, lockers and cars searched. There had been a post-train robbery at Euston. Apart from cash and cards, many thousands of milk tokens had been purloined. These traceable tokens began to be presented by roundsmen at West Hampstead. Milkmen working in affluent areas like Golders Green, where tokens were rarely offered in payment, suddenly began presenting eighty or ninety a week, each worth about £2.50.

Then there was the Sunday overtime: well paid, about thirty calls, mainly shops, and one perk, the London Zoo Trojan Horse job. Although I never indulged in this scam, others did. The drops on Sunday were done in a truck, the back of which was covered. It was the last call and the vehicle was almost empty. At the zoo, you pressed a bell at the tradesman's entrance and spoke into an intercom. The staff in the restaurant let you in. You drove in and dropped about one hundred pints of milk off. Nice people, cup of tea, 'Cheerio, see you next week.' Outside you could reverse the truck about twenty yards, which left you next to an alley which led into the zoo. A quick look around; open up the back. 'Quickly kids!' Out they would stream – fifteen to twenty kids, four or five mothers, grannies, aunties, neighbours.

M15 was a strange drop. Naturally there was heavy security. 'Please state the nature of your business.' 'It's the milkman.' Long pause. 'Your entrance is confirmed.' Once through the remotely controlled doors, you drove down a ramp and parked in a slot with underground illumination. Security emerged with what looked a little like a lawn strimmer and poked about underneath the vehicle looking for bombs. It took about five minutes to be cleared. These security men never looked in the back of the vehicle. I could have had bin Laden and thirty Taliban with grenades and Kalashnikovs in the back.

Nothing lasts forever. The supermarkets introduced the cheap four-pint poly-bottle, sales dropped as the working and lower-middle classes started to buy milk with the weekly shop; rounds were broken up, depots closed down. History marches on.

RANT

I HATE QUAINT market towns, cut off from the rest of humanity when Beeching tore up the train tracks. The West Country and the Welsh Marches are full of them. You know the kind of place – the peeling Georgian terraces, the merchants' villas divided into flats for Bulgarian asparagus-pickers on benefits, the shops selling unpalatable jam and novelty scented candles, the smallholders' stalls in the Corn Exchange, where root-faced lesbians or argumentative queers in mail-order wax jackets sell gone-off organic sausages and eggs flecked with authentic chicken ordure.

There's nothing to do in such a town.

I end up poking around in the Spastics' Charity Shop trying on dead people's blazers or examining the videos of the second series of *Oh No! It's Selwyn Froggitt*, starring Bill Maynard. In the local museum, now called the Heritage Centre, I gaze uncomprehendingly at agricultural implements.

Maybe there'll be a few watercolour views of Taormina, nine times out of ten done by a nineteenth-century paedophile vicar.

Quaint market towns are a gastronomic black hole. Apart from the chippy, which will usually be named The Cod Father, The Merrie Fryer or Batterlicious, the only halfway-decent places are Balti Towers and Call Me Halal, neither of which is open at lunchtime. At The Holly Bush everything comes out of the microwave. The lamb I had was frozen at the centre and covered with ice crystals. The waitress kept saying 'Not a problem!' and when she dropped the butter on the floor she picked it up covered with dog hairs and popped it back on my plate.

There is always a grander establishment in the Town Square with a Les Routiers plaque, where you can be guaranteed a frosty reception. At the bar will be the local auctioneer, an alcoholic proud of his canary-yellow waistcoat. Next to him are burly people with loud piercing laughs who have personal cider tankards kept on a hook and an ancient squadron leader sounding off about golf and chemotherapy.

The pavements are filled with under-age putty-faced girls with snout-studs who push pushchairs containing plump, ugly toddlers called Kellan or Kallum, Kyle or Keanu.

None of this lot will be missed.

ROGER LEWIS

Filming Bill Deedes

MICHAEL COCKERELL *was the man who persuaded Lord Deedes – and his friend Denis Thatcher – to step in front of the camera for the 1994 BBC film 'Dear Bill'*

Bill Deedes was not a man who liked to say 'no'. I felt reasonably confident when we met for lunch some years ago at Paradiso e Inferno, a restaurant he favoured in the Strand, that he would agree to my making a television portrait of him.

But he was not at all keen on the idea. 'The past is gone, you can't have it again: tomorrow is more important than yesterday,' he told me. But he had seen and quite enjoyed some of the other TV profiles I had made. A couple of bottles of Verdicchio and eighteen grilled king prawns later, Bill agreed; but on condition that the film reflected his present life and concerns and did not dwell unduly on the past.

Bill Deedes was then eighty and well established in his latest incarnation. The former war hero, Cabinet minister and *Daily Telegraph* editor had become the paper's oldest roving reporter – with a penchant for world trouble spots – and its best-loved columnist.

'I believe there is a future life,' he told me, 'but I do not let that discourage me from getting the best out of this one.' What kept him going as a journalist, he said, 'is not being sure what lies around the next corner.'

Deedes was already a legendary figure and the inspiration for two comic literary characters: Henry Boot in Evelyn Waugh's *Scoop* and the eponymous recipient of the 'Dear Bill' letters that *Private Eye* attributed to Sir Denis Thatcher. The magazine (then edited by *The Oldie*'s own Richard Ingrams in his previous incarnation) had also provided Deedes's character with a catchphrase based on his singular speaking style: 'Shome mishtake, shurely? – Ed.'

'Yes, I am a bit of a slurrer,' Bill told me. 'If a policeman ever stops me in my car, he takes the breathalyser out almost instantly, because he thinks I must be drunk. And occasionally I get abusive letters saying why can't you pronounce words properly? But there is nothing I can do about it. I'm encouraged by the thought that Winston did it.'

It seemed important to find out how close to the mark were the 'Dear Bill' letters – which depicted Bill Deedes and Denis Thatcher as dyed-in-the-gin reactionaries. Although the pair were golfing partners and the closest of friends, they had never been filmed together on a golf course.

Bill agreed – but how to persuade Sir Denis? His policy was to turn down all media requests – and according to *Private Eye* saw all journalists as 'reptiles'. Bill told me: 'Denis has very pronounced views about the BBC which he sees as the strongest-held Marxist citadel of the lot.'

I was pondering the best way to Sir Denis when I bumped into him at John Paul Getty's cricket ground, where I was playing. He was not, I suppose, expecting to be approached by a reptile in flannels. But when I told him about the film and asked if he would appear, he responded: 'I'd do anything for Bill.'

When we filmed them playing golf, the pair discussed the etiquette of replacing divots on different courses round the world. 'In Japan,' said Sir

PHOTOGRAPHS COURTESY OF: MICHAEL COCKERELL

Denis, 'they have these little caddy girls with spades who replant the divots – they are very highly trained.'

Both men played well. Sir Denis told me later how pleased he was that the *Daily Telegraph* TV critic wrote he had a better swing than Bill, who would each morning hit a hundred golf balls in his practice net at home.

I asked Sir Denis how accurate the 'Dear Bill' letters were. 'Oh, not at all. In the beginning they were quite amusing; after a year or two they got a bit boring – in my opinion. But they didn't do Bill any harm and they didn't do me any harm.'

Deedes claimed that the 'Dear Bill' letters had transformed his own social standing and had actually done his friend some good. 'It established an image of Denis as a genial buffer playing golf and drinking gin – an image which he had every right to dislike. But it made it impossible for the press to pin the label of *éminence grise* upon him when Margaret was at Number 10.'

Among the many elements to the lifelong Deedes–Thatcher friendship was their shared experience of the Second World War. Both had ended up as majors with distinguished records. In 1939 Deedes had swapped Fleet Street for the front line – and was soon leading a company of riflemen. 'You had to look after young soldiers who found it very difficult to keep awake through battle exhaustion. I was twenty-seven, nightclub-hardened, and broadly could go a couple of days and nights without sleep. But anyone around eighteen or nineteen, just out of school, it was very difficult to keep them awake.'

I found Bill, like many of his generation, extremely reluctant to talk about his battle experience. He sought to shrug off the MC he won, as his Company tried to take a bridge near Arnhem in 1944, as 'a survivor's medal'. But when I read him the official citation, he told me – with characteristic understatement – what had happened: 'It was a hump-backed bridge, so the tanks couldn't lower their guns to give us any covering

fire. That's asking for trouble. About halfway across the bridge we reported rather heavy casualties, and I was told, "You'd better come back". Well, getting back was worse than going out, because we had to collect the wounded and carry them back. So it was a rough day.' In fact, the citation says that Deedes had displayed 'a complete disregard of his personal safety'.

Half a century on, that characteristic was on display when we filmed with the eighty-year-old Deedes in an African war zone. His age in no way seemed to have dulled his appetite for travelling to some of the nastiest and most difficult war zones and famine areas. He prided himself on being able to get into places other journalists could not reach.

He was convinced there was a good story to be found in Angola – where a particularly brutal, but virtually unreported, civil war was raging. The

Foreign Office was advising against travel to Angola and, in any case, the Luanda government was refusing journalists entry. But Bill had a way in. He was a dedicated fundraiser for relief charities – and wearing that hat was able to secure us visas.

Flying into the besieged city of Lubango was a stimulating experience. Our hired plane circled the military airport from high in the sky, then, to avoid enemy guns, made a sudden dive straight down to the runway. On the ground we found a wretched picture of corruption, brutality and malnutrition.

We watched a government helicopter arrive at the airport, filled with wounded civilian women and children: the raw flesh hung off their open wounds. 'The sight of those wounded being carried off the helicopter reminded you of what a cruel war this is,' said Deedes.

I asked him why he had returned to foreign reporting in his seventies and begun work for international charities. 'When you are as close as I am to giving an account of one's life to St Peter at the heavenly gates, I don't much fancy being able to claim nothing more than fifty years of newspaper journalism.'

Bill never flagged while filming in Angola, despite the boiling sun and the dawn starts to our day. He told me what kept him going: 'If I can get into a dangerous country and get out alive to tell the tale – that remains truly exciting. It's better than sex,' he laughed. 'And if you can guess right, or guess partly right, what's going to happen tomorrow – where the story's going to be – there's enormous satisfaction.' So it keeps you young? I asked. 'Oh yes, absolutely. I like a warm climate too.'

when I get out I'm gonna go straight, ma

The best thing about living alone is you can watch the telly without switching it on

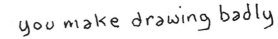

you make drawing badly look easy

Ged Melling
1927–2003

Ged Melling was one of *The Oldie*'s most brilliant cartoonists. Born in Stirling, Ged (real name Gerard) left school at fifteen to become an apprentice house painter. He later studied at St Martin's School of Art and developed his own distinctive style of drawing.

Though he contributed to many papers and magazines in the course of a long career, in the last years before his death in 2007 his work appeared almost exclusively in *The Oldie*. He was a prolific cartoonist and his drawings arrived by fax almost daily.

In common with many humorists, Ged suffered from manic depression and several of his best jokes were based on his experience in self-help groups and Alcoholics Anonymous. The battle of the sexes also provided him with continual inspiration.

RICHARD INGRAMS

Have you seen my razor?

Are you having an affair?

What you must realise is . . . that farmer's wife is a very sick person

March wasn't the best month to come off my medication

Whiteboard jungle

*When aggressive boys get violent, **KATE SAWYER** tries her best to manage the situation – but underneath, she's terrified*

People are fascinated by the idea of a small woman facing up to the huge thugs of popular imagination. And it does happen. I have been frightened by pupils. Once it was a boy half my size but with an aggression in him worthy of a ratting terrier. He had crept up behind a boy and tried to strangle him with his tie. I persuaded him to drop his victim and leave the room. Outside in the corridor, despite my best attempts at reasoned discussion, something happened in his eyes and I realised I had lost any connection with him and I was in trouble. He picked up a desk and held it over his head. Instinct took over. I just said his name, very calmly. He still hurled the desk, but at the last minute he shifted his aim and threw it to one side.

The question should be, why should a child have such rage in him? But believe me, when the desk is whistling past your ear you don't really care.

I met this boy's mother a few times. She wasn't very satisfactory. When her boy was suspended for the day she took him shopping. When he lived through a day without trouble his reward was cigarettes. (The social workers' faces when this was announced were wonderful. I comforted them by pointing out that he could not be getting many cigarettes if that was the criterion.) As the years went by and he became taller, dirtier and more entrenched in drugs, he became more frightening. Until he stopped coming to school at all. Then we had to pretend to care, but it was a huge relief every time he wasn't in class.

This boy was one of the few that did not last the course. It is almost impossible to exclude children from state schools. No matter how bad, even dangerous, their behaviour, they seem to stay. The worse they behave, the more

In teaching it comes down to a simple truth: if they believe you mind about them they will lay down their arms at your request

staff they have running around after them making excuses for them. Part of the reason is that the school is fined thousands of pounds for an expulsion. The only way to recoup the money is to take on some child who's been thrown out of another school (they come with a bounty on their heads) and the thinking is that it is usually easier to deal with your own trouble-maker, whom you have to some degree nurtured, than to start afresh with someone else's. So when they do disappear, either to another school or to one of the very few Pupil Referral Units available, you can be sure they are Serious Trouble.

Another boy, with better reasons for rage (dead father, bullying stepfather) and a conviction or two for assault behind him, also put the fear of God into me. A child burst into my classroom pursued by Bad Boy.

I stood between the two, trying to shield one and reason with the other. It worked. Later Bad Boy apologised, saying he was sorry if I'd been frightened but I should know he would never hit me. 'I respect you, Miss.' I had fought for this boy, defended him from staff with less naïve faith in human nature, and spent hours sweet-talking him into working.

I knew he respected me, but it was the first time I had seen his rage and I was shocked. I didn't really believe he'd hit me, but I did fear he would attack the other boy and I would be caught in the middle.

My most recent encounter was the most terrifying. Again, I stood between two boys. One was pushed against the wall, purpling with the pressure on his throat. I tried, but had no hope of pulling them apart. I talked, but Angry Young Man could not hear. In the end I took hold of his face and pulled it around until we were eyeball to eyeball. 'Drop him,' I said without (to my pride) a quaver. Finally he did. But in doing so, he raised his fist to me, swore fluently and viciously, and shoved me aside before running from the school.

Trembling and perplexed, I tried to work out where it had all gone wrong. And the answer was simple. It lay in the fact that we were all strangers to each other. Because again and again in teaching it comes down to a simple truth: if they believe you mind about them they will lay down their arms at your request. If they believe that, they will listen.

And that has nothing to do with power, or size, or whatever punishment might lie ahead. It has everything to do with humanity. Which doesn't take away anything from the fact that sometimes naughty boys are just naughty – but occasionally, they are terrifying.

Left: John Betjeman and Edward Mirzoeff during filming in Felbrigg Church

Right from top: Betjeman with lighting man John Collins (behind) and sound recordist Simon Wilson, who could, Betjeman said, 'record the sound of flowers growing'; Betjeman reading in the pews of St Mary, Bylaugh; in 'Swaffham' and boater by the ancient ruin of St Benet's Abbey; and with cameraman John McGlashan, whom he nicknamed 'The Bishop'.

Sir John's PASSION

EDWARD MIRZOEFF *on his 1974 film 'A Passion for Churches', which celebrates John Betjeman's love of the Church of England and its places of worship*

PHOTOGRAPH COURTESY OF EASTERN DAILY PRESS

Everyone adored John Betjeman but, as I came to discover, he wasn't the 'teddy-bear' of popular imagination. *Metro-land*, our 1973 film about the joys of suburbia, had gone down well, and the BBC wanted another. What was it to be about? I had an idea close to Betjeman's heart – the Church of England. I thought up a title: *Failed in Divinity*. John had been sent down from Oxford for failing a minor examination in the subject he loved best of all:

Failed in Divinity! Oh count the hours
Spent on my knees in Cowley, Pusey House,
St Barnabas', St Mary Mag's, St Paul's,
Revering chasubles and copes and albs!

The older Betjeman, described by Anthony Powell as having 'a whim of iron', was not amused, and I couldn't win him round. But he had no doubt about the subject: the C of E was a good thing, and the essence of Englishness.

We wanted to make it within and about a single diocese. John suggested Southwark, whose Bishop was his close friend Mervyn Stockwood: they went on holiday together, calling themselves The Church of England Rambling Association. I didn't like the idea of Southwark, a large inner-city diocese with more than its share of social problems, but John was keen that I should meet the Bishop. A dinner was arranged at his palace in Tooting Bec. It was a disastrous evening. The Bishop was high-handed, arrogant and astonishingly rude. I didn't care for his household of young Arab serving-boys, nor was he prepared to offer much help. Betjeman wrote to say that 'the old Bishop woke up yesterday morning in a penitent mood and thought he'd gone a bit far.' Indeed he had.

Where then? Our film editor said that East Anglia had the densest collection of medieval churches in Christendom, unequalled in visual richness. And Norfolk was the home of one of John's dearest friends, Lady Wilhelmina 'Billa' Harrod, to whom he had briefly been engaged.

We set out to research the diocese of Norwich. In the car, driven by my PA, Jane – by whom, as usual, he claimed to be smitten – John read us ghost stories by M R James, often set in remote Norfolk rectories. Towards the climax of one story, a police car stopped Jane for speeding. The Poet Laureate sank lower and lower down the front seat, hoping not to be recognised.

When filming began, John seemed slower than before, and needed more looking after. Billa Harrod lent him a Puffa jacket to keep out the cold, which I forbade him to wear in shot because it made him look fat. Instead we bought a long blue plastic mac from a gents' outfitters in Swaffham. He called it his 'Swaffham' and it trailed after him like a stiff gown, and was sometimes worn with a straw boater.

Elizabeth Jane Howard, then married to Betjeman's friend Kingsley Amis, turned up to write a piece for the *Radio Times*. Her manner was on the grand side and she seemed to notice no one but John, which didn't endear her to the rest of us. She took him off to the local antique shops, and persuaded him to buy a small oil of a windmill. With his usual generosity, Betjeman handed it to me the moment she left.

An unexpected visitor was Betjeman's wife Penelope, who stayed for several days. Her presence unsettled John, perhaps stirring feelings of guilt and anxiety. The night she left, we dined together. There followed an extraordinary outpouring of grief and regret about the sadness of his relationship with her and the alienation of his son Paul – 'the Powlie', as he called him. For once the laughter was stilled, the public act abandoned.

I had to find a way to begin the film. Betjeman told me that as a young boy out sailing with his father he had noticed Belaugh church tower, so beginning a life-long passion for churches, and I asked him to row a dinghy down the Bure while telling the story. During one take he hit the river bank and toppled slowly into the bow, with his feet in the air. He was soaked, and we rushed him to the nearest house – inevitably a rectory. The door was opened by an ancient clergyman, with egg-stains down his front, and John was wrapped in a dressing-gown while his clothes dried.

After filming a wedding in Lyng, we decided to give the happy couple a coffee-maker as a present, together with a wedding ode from the Poet Laureate. John kept putting it off, but eventually scribbled down what must be his shortest poem:

> *Nigel and Celia, may you be*
> *Fonder of coffee than of tea.*

Neither, it turned out, cared much for coffee.

Betjeman's funny and moving commentary, much of it in verse, was composed with the film already cut. He would sit in front of the editing machine in the cutting-room in Soho, running film sequences backwards and forwards to allow their rhythms to sink in, waiting for inspiration from the 'Management' above. He retired regularly to 'the composition cell' – a broom cupboard – to help concentration. Page after page was painstakingly filled with indecipherable handwriting, thrown on the floor and re-written. Occasionally he would consult intimate chums like Margie Geddes, nervously checking their responses and beaming with relief when they approved.

Sometimes the film editor, Ted Roberts, overcame a block by supplying pastiche verse in the poet's own style. For the church fête at South Raynham he suggested:

> *We must dip into our pockets*
> *For our hearts are full of dread*
> *There's all the more to pay for now*
> *The roof's been stripped of lead.*

Betjeman was delighted – 'Oh, that's frightfully good' – but altered the final lines to:

> *At the thought of all the damage*
> *Since the roof was stripped of lead.*

He became increasingly fearful, combining the usual paranoia about reviews with worries about how his churchy friends, and the Anglican community generally, would respond. 'It is my religion which is being filmed,' he wrote, 'and I will be held responsible for views expressed.' How, for example, should he treat the potentially controversial scenes at the Romish shrine at Walsingham, with its candles, images and processions? After much agonising, he found a solution in a series of rhetorical questions: 'I wonder if you'd call it superstitious... Or do you think that forces are around, strong, frightening, loving and just out of reach, but waiting, waiting, somewhere to be asked?'

John could not find the right words for a brief passage linking medieval brasses with modern marriage. Elizabeth Jane Howard observed that 'he has a proper aversion to being hectored, bullied and made to do things, and somewhere, very deeply hidden, one suspects a streak of that ruthlessness essential for the self-protection of any working artist' – and so it proved. I kept telling Betjeman that time was running out when suddenly he snapped, shouting in red-faced rage and frustration. It was terrifying and embarrassing, and took days to get over. After which, needless to say, the little phrase was easily found.

A Passion for Churches was shown in December 1974. 'I need not have worried about the film at all,' John wrote. 'You have made it marvellous and deep and rich and sad and funny and local... It will not get good notices. The Church of England never does. But it is the Church of England and it ambles along like the fat old commentator who signs himself, Yours ever, John Betjeman.'

Modern life

What is...
a life coach?

LIFE IS HARD. Life is a struggle. Life is a hard struggle punctuated by bouts of fear and uncertainty. Life is such a hard and uncertain fearful struggle that most of the time we're happy to keep our heads down, our aspirations low and our backsides parked on the sofa.

Sometimes, we wonder what life might be like if we quit our jobs, followed our dreams, reached for the stars. But what with all the fear, struggle, uncertainty and whatnot sloshing around reminding us how difficult life is, we mostly decide that we're better off staying within our comfort zone, staying safe, staying on the sofa.

But maybe life needn't be like this. Maybe we really can do extraordinary things... Once this seed of dissatisfaction is planted, it eats away at you. But what to do about it? Call a life coach, that's what.

Having a life coach is a bit like being an athlete and having a sports coach, except instead of working with you to achieve better levels of fitness and performance in races and competitions, life coaches are coaching you towards a better performance in the race of life (sorry, once you begin spending time with life coaches, you start saying things like that).

It works like this: you tell them what you want to achieve in life (to have the courage to start your own company, or to write that novel, or whatever) and they help you achieve it. They do this by helping you address not only the practical issues involved in life changes (you want to start your own company? Then stop faffing around and go and talk to the bank manager), but also the emotional and psychological steps involved (have you procrastinated for years about starting your own company because you believe you won't be any good dealing with the finances? What can be done to change these beliefs?)

First off, you sign a contract agreeing to give one hundred per cent effort, and together with your life coach you draw up a plan of action, with weekly goals to be met by you. Regular sessions are scheduled, which usually take place over the telephone, in order to monitor progress. You are responsible for doing all the running, with your coach providing the support and constructive advice and an endless stream of motivational claptrap such as 'There's no such thing as failure, only opportunities for personal growth'.

Life coaching homes in on a simple truth about modern living for the comfortably off: life is in fact neither hard, nor difficult, nor a struggle – it is merely that most people subscribe to a 'better the devil you know' attitude, fear change and lack faith in their own abilities. Life coaching subscribes to the view that, when challenged, people generally rise to the challenge and exceed expectations. (Life coaches are fond of citing the example of the role of the little ships at Dunkirk here.) It mixes this belief with a dash of elementary psychology (the power of positive thinking), a dose of common sense (time management), a smattering of self-help speak ('it is by spending yourself that you become rich'), and tops the lot off with what is surely coaching's most powerful weapon – namely that once you've paid someone else a king's ransom to believe in you, it would be a humiliating waste of time and money not to pull your finger out and go for it.

The examples of successful life coaching are too numerous to mention. Careers have been changed, lives turned around, ruts resoundingly got out of. You can even be your own life coach these days. Fiona Harrold, one of the UK's most successful life coaches (although you'd have to be suspicious of an under-achieving life coach, wouldn't you?), has published a book called *How To Be Your Own Life Coach*. It positively brims over with enthusiasm and self-esteem-enhancing case studies.

And although my cynical mind hates to admit it, life coaching is actually pretty hard to knock: OK, you can't help feeling that there's something a bit sad about paying a perfect stranger to tell you you're the greatest and give you a gentle kick up the arse, but if it brings about a demonstrable change in your life, then what's there to complain about?

Anyway, must finish here, as I'm off to step outside my comfort zone, embrace my fears as challenges, and get that dream job I've always wanted.

I've always really wanted to be a life coach.

NICK PARKER

AND FOR A BONUS POINT WHAT'S THE NAME OF HIS WIFE?

OOH, ER...

Olden life

What was...
a List of Visitors?

IN THE MIDDLE of the nineteenth century, local weekly newspapers in holiday resorts and spa towns included lists of visitors who were staying in hotels and boarding establishments within the circulation area of the publication. In fact some weekly newspapers started life simply as a list of visitors, with little more information than coach and rail arrival and departure times and details of religious services. At many resorts, the presence of summer season visitors was one of the major reasons for the establishment of a local paper, and it was quite common for owners of stationery and printing businesses to be the promoters of these early 'start-ups'.

The summer season ran from around the middle of May until early October, and some of the early weeklies restricted publication to that particular period. A natural development was the late and early visitors' lists which, together with news features and advertising, resulted in the establishment of year-round publication. Some of the earliest local papers to be published all-year-round appeared in towns where there was a proliferation of hydropathic establishments, with constant occupancy irrespective of season.

But what was the point or value of these lists of visitors? It seems strange to us today that readers apparently preferred to read long lists of visitors' names, rather than local or national news. But there was much more to it than that – these lists played an important role in the business and social mores of the time. Many holiday-makers purchased a list of visitors as they were eager to see who was staying in the town, and where – part of their holiday entertainment being spotting titled visitors or leading dignitaries from their home towns.

From the visitors' point of view, it was pleasing to their vanity and helpful to them in meeting, or avoiding, persons of their acquaintance whilst promenading in the resort or spa. It was an added bonus if they could inform friends that their place of residence contained a satisfactory clutch of Reverends, a doctor or two, a military title, and ideally some addresses containing the magical words 'Park', 'Hall', 'Manor', etc.

Initially, mainly the gentry and aristocracy visited seaside resorts and spas, as early 'lists of visitors' indicate, but as time went on, more clients came from the rising Victorian middle classes – manufacturers, tradesmen, merchants and professionals. For instance, the visitors staying at the Royal Crescent Hotel, Filey, in August 1872 included Their Royal Highnesses,

It seems strange to us today that readers preferred to read long lists of visitors' names rather than news

the Grand Duke and Duchess of Hesse and Servants, and Her Royal Highness Princess Louise of Battenberg and Servants. Some thirty-eight years later, however, visitors listed as staying at the same hotel included Captain Gascoigne of the Scots Fusiliers, Charles Gold Esq of the Middle Temple and Sam Hollins Esq of Astley Bridge, Bolton (the last named probably engaged in cotton spinning).

The collation of visitors' names was quite a business, with representatives from the publishers visiting the hotels and boarding establishments on a regular basis. Publishers of the lists were anxious to ensure as many names as possible were included, and new lodging houses and others not visited regularly were requested to send a postcard or to telephone for one of their collectors to obtain a list of their guests.

Anxious to correct any mistakes, the *Bridlington Free Press* stated in 1910: 'The utility of a list of visitors can only be proportionate to its correctness; therefore we will feel obliged if parties observing inaccuracies will give notice

List of Visitors.

Crescent Hotel.	
Viscount and Lady Folkestone and suite	Nunappleton, Tadcaster
Lord Lascelles	Harewood House
Captain Brabazone	London
The Hon and Rev the Dean of Windsor	Windsor Castle
Herbert Fordham, Esq Mrs and fam	Odsey, Royston
Major-General Hutchinson	London
Mrs Hutchinson and family	London
Colonel Ford and Party	Hereford Gardens, Park lane, London
G W Alder Esq	Wakefield
William Peach Esq	Hornsey, London
Mrs Peach and fam	do
Charles Gould Esq	Inner Temple
Captain Gascoigne	Scots Fusileer Guards
Wm Greetham Esq	Stainsfield Hall, Lincolnshire
Thomas Greetham Esq	London
Thomas Barber Esq	Huddersfield
Samuel Shepherd Esq	London
— Laforne Esq	Denmark Hill, London
Mrs Laforno and fam	do
Charles Allison Esq	London
Mrs C Allison	do
Mrs George Blunt	do
— Farquhar Esq	London
Mrs Farquhar	do
Sam Hollins Esq	Astley Bridge, Bolton

A real List of Visitors

to the collector, or to the publishing office, in order that they may be remedied in our succeeding number.'

The publication of lists of visitors ceased in the mid Fifties, although they had been in decline for many years. However, by this time, many of the enterprises had become firmly established as weekly newspapers and, over a period of years, any reference in their titles to being a list of visitors was removed.

With the present-day paranoia about identity theft, when even that voyeur's delight, the hotel registration book, has disappeared from most reception desks, it is difficult to imagine there was a time when people were quite happy to let everyone know where they were staying on holiday.

ALAN THOMAS

LATEST ARRIVALS

Hotel Barnsley: *Colonel and Mrs Edward Rabbit, Sir Walter Mainwopple, Mr Oswald Thake, Miss Shovel, Mrs Utter and Miss Desdemona Utter, Herr Hugo Schwarnheit, the Hon. Mrs Fudge and Master Eric Fudge, Mrs Nargle and family, Captain Fowlhouse, Miss Nodd, Rear-Admiral Sir Arthur Anymore, Lady Ough, Mr Forbes-Melon, Miss Netta Forbes-Melon, Mr Ulyate A. Niceman and Miss Sukie A. Niceman, Senator Rowle, Mrs Grist, and Mlle Rose Duchanel.*

Hotel Barnsley
Paris

...and a spoof list from 'Beachcomber'

'I'm sexing up my confessions'

'Don't read too much into it, Mr Perkins, it's just a hole in the roof'

The **Oldie** AT PRAYER

DIG YOUR OWN

'Powerful sermon, Reverend'

St Bartholemew

JESUS DIED FOR YOUR SINS

'Now look what you've done'

Profitable Wonders
by James Le Fanu

The butterfly and the ant

The Large Blue butterfly is in truth not very large at all, its two-inch wing span being only slightly greater than that of the Common Blue. It does, however, occupy a special place in the affections of all lepidopterists by virtue of its unusual life history, which ranks amongst the strangest of any creature. In the last week of June and early July the female deposits her minuscule pearl-like eggs on the petals of wild thyme flowers. When the caterpillar emerges it feeds on the thyme's downy blossom. Then the caterpillar, after its third skin-casting, becomes restless, drops to the ground and begins to walk, 'as though,' comments naturalist E L Grant Watson, 'it wants something but is not quite sure what.'

The caterpillar walks and walks until it meets and is recognised by a red ant of the species *Myrmica sabuleti*, who starts to caress and stroke it with feet and antennae. The caterpillar responds by secreting from a pore on its tenth segment a sweet honey-like dew much to the ant's liking. After a time, 'prompted by some unexplained and mystic sympathy', the caterpillar rears up – a signal it wants to be carried off. The ant seizes it gently in its jaws and heads for its underground home, placing it in one of the chambers where its own progeny – eggs and larvae – are being nurtured. The caterpillar will feed on these while continuing to produce its honeydew secretions as payment for its host's generous food and lodging.

They hibernate together for the winter and, come the spring, the caterpillar pupates, forming the chrysalis from which it will emerge as a butterfly, its wings at first unexpanded, like limp and shrivelled leaves drooping on each side of its body. How unlikely a place – the dark underground of an ant's nest – for a butterfly to find itself.

And then the host, in a final act of inexplicable altruism, escorts this one-time devourer of its children through the dark passages of its home up towards the light, encircling it to ward off any predators as the butterfly fills the veins of its wings with its pale yellowish-green blood. And off the Large Blue flies for the few short weeks of its adult existence, just time enough to seek a mate and produce its eggs, before the life cycle starts over again.

How unlikely a place – the dark underground of an ant's nest – for a butterfly to find itself

The transition from egg to adult depends on so many bizarre and fortuitous events it seems astonishing that the Large Blue exists at all – and indeed just over thirty years ago it became extinct in Britain. But that is not the end of the matter, for when Jeremy Thomas, Professor of Ecology at Oxford University, sought to reintroduce it back into this country, he discovered its survival is predicated not only on the close proximity of colonies of red ants, but on other factors as well: as the ants are heat-dependent, the grass must be kept short by grazing animals so as to warm the soil; but at the same time, the summer cannot be too dry, as rain encourages the ants to forage, thus increasing the likelihood of that chance encounter with the caterpillar.

It has taken Professor Thomas the best part of a decade of intense effort to recreate the right ecological balance for butterfly and ant to renew their surprising relationship – and now once again the Large Blue can be seen fluttering across the meadows of Devon and Somerset. 'The extravagant idiosyncrasies of its life,' suggests Grant Watson, should cause all 'to pause and wonder'.

'Good morning! My name's Julian and I'll be your torturer today!'

GOOD LUCK FROM NEWPORT, IOWA

High Street, Newport, Isle of Wight

My Island in the Rain

The Isle of Wight has not changed much since the days of Queen Victoria, says **BEN MALLALIEU** – *which means that today it's old-fashioned and thoroughly depressing. And yet he continues to holiday there...* **Illustrations by PETER BAILEY**

There isn't a new Wight. Like the old joke about 'where do you find a tortoise with no legs?' the island is pretty much where you last left it, which in most people's case was a long time ago in the days before cheap flights, when family holidays were spent in 'sensible' places, usually the same place every year, until the children became teenagers and complained. 'But you always loved Seaview,' their mother would say, rather sadly.

It still has that old-fashioned, Christopher Robin and sand between the toes air, but it isn't as good as Cornwall,

There is something that calls itself 'Brading: The Experience of a Lifetime', but if that is the ultimate that life has to offer, then it might be best to call it a day

which in turn isn't as good as Brittany; the sea is still that particularly uninviting shade of gun-metal grey; over-cluttered gift shops still sell undesirable objects made of seashells (exactly the same but now made in China) and display large signs saying 'All breakages

must be paid for', perhaps their main source of income; and no one is any closer to solving the problem of what to do when it rains, which it usually does. There is something, possibly a waxworks, that calls itself 'Brading: The Experience of a Lifetime', but if that is the ultimate that life has to offer then it might be best to call it a day.

160

VENTNOR

The Labour Prime Minister 'Sunny Jim' Callaghan, as he was called by *Private Eye*, was probably no admirer of Queen Victoria but he too came to the island for his holidays. One summer in the early 1950s, my family unexpectedly ran into him in Seaview and he invited us for a swim at what I now realise was Whale Chine. He had been my father's mess orderly during the War, and in 1945, just after they had all been elected as Labour MPs, he and my father's old schoolfriend, Hugh Gaitskell, had taken my father to lunch to pick his brains about how they might become Parliamentary Private Secretaries, the lowest rung on the ladder of political power. But their paths had deviated, Callaghan rising as a party apparatchik, my father wandering out on a limb, a rebel and a romantic.

The bonhomie of the Isle of Wight meeting was perhaps more forced than I noticed at the time, a bit like the Bukharin family running into Stalin at Yalta, I would imagine. My mother took one look at the steep steps down the chine and went back to the car pleading vertigo, which was probably a bad move politically. My strongest memory of that afternoon was that Callaghan, like my father, did not believe in changing behind a towel, perhaps to show his contempt for 'Victorian' values.

Worst of all is a very old-fashioned class structure, the kind you hoped had gone for good: the rich in Cowes, Seaview, Bembridge and Bonchurch; the working class – and not in a good sense – in Ryde, Shanklin, Sandown and Blackgang Chine. Restaurants are, with only a few exceptions, expensive, pretentious and bad, or cheap (but overpriced), cheerless and very bad. You don't see many black faces anywhere and you realise what a positive contribution immigrants have made to the rest of the country in the last fifty years.

Queen Victoria came most summers to Osborne House for her holidays and has left a hefty legacy. But who was Victoria and what exactly are Victorian values?

The past is preserved like the fossils in layers of sedimentary clay on the south-coast beaches: Templar relics in the old inland churches, former TB sanatoria clearly recognisable. Queen Victoria came most summers to Osborne House for her holidays and has left a hefty legacy. But who was Victoria, and what exactly are Victorian values?

I grew up in an era when Victorian stock was at its lowest. 'I'm afraid it's only Victorian,' people would say in a rather shamefaced way about a house or a piece of furniture, much as they would say 'I'm afraid it's only Cyprus' when offering a glass of inferior sherry; Victorian paintings after Turner were almost worthless, and the era was condemned as an age of prudery and hypocrisy. Perhaps it was their affluent self-confidence that was so disliked by a generation that had to pick up the tab for two world wars.

the sand' and he wrote eloquently about her budding breasts and the soft, exquisite curves of her 'rosy dimpled bottom'. Few modern vicars would dare write anything of the sort, even in their private diaries. The girl that Kilvert admired was probably about fourteen, which made it more acceptable in those days, less so now. And nowadays nobody above the age of four or five stands naked on Shanklin beach, despite these supposedly more liberal times. The effect is claustrophobic and rather unpleasant.

But Victoria herself had, I would think from reading between the lines, a very healthy sexual appetite. And on June 12th 1874, the Victorian country curate Francis Kilvert went swimming at Shanklin: 'One has to adopt the detestable custom of bathing in drawers,' he complained in his diary. 'If ladies don't like to see men naked why don't they keep away from the sight?' The following year on a beach somewhere between Sandown and Shanklin, he saw a beautiful girl who 'stood entirely naked on

But I still go to the island because, for reasons interesting but not worth explaining at length, we were there one New Year nearly twenty years ago in the company of an opera singer and her lute-playing husband, and someone had said that I might be interested in an unusual garden on the most windswept corner of the island where nothing taller than a cabbage usually thrives; and, because I wrote about gardening at the time, we went and knocked on the door very early one morning, which was a bit cheeky. The house looked nothing special, a pre-War suburban London semi except that it wasn't attached to anything and it was a long way from London, but the garden was something else. It had been made by a retired engineer and his wife and they spent an hour showing us round, oblivious to the pouring rain. When we went inside he said, 'You'll need something to warm you up after that', and instead of the expected cup of coffee he handed me a full tumbler of rum; it was only ten o'clock in the morning and I wished I'd known them all my life. But we often saw them and their garden afterwards, and later, when they had both died, their daughter, who works as a care nurse and is one of the few entirely good people I have ever met, took over the garden. My wife and I and our children, now grown-up, still stay there, often in tents, and get lost in the dark; and the garden keeps getting better every time we see it.

WORLD'S WORST DUMPS :15

Carcassonne

Fairytale city? Dream on, says **LANCE BUTLER**

In the days when there were travel agents they sometimes had on their office walls a large colour poster of a fairytale city in France that made your heart stop and your mind go 'Can there still be anywhere like that?' Nowadays one would suspect computerised enhancement.

The city was Carcassonne, perfect on the horizon with its medieval towerscape, unruined turrets and banners stunning the sky of Languedoc against the low hills. 'I must go *there!*' you cried – and now, in the age of Ryanair, you can fly there twice a day, straight to the Middle Ages.

The airport and surroundings are low-industrial scruffy, and the autoroute is not entirely silent in the distance, but you *almost* don't mind because you still have that silhouette of the city in your mind. There is, unexpectedly, a whole town at the foot of the hill on which the Cité (as you learn to call it) stands; not a bad southern French town but no more than that.

As you climb the hill you enjoy, first, an immense car-park full of coaches out of which come many, many people: they have charged the drawbridge and are looting the bric-a-brac shops. At first this doesn't matter because you are here, at last, in a medieval town! It's so entire, so finished. It's also very large, and you can *wander*. Then the evidence of modern slatework makes you smell an enormous rat. It comes back to you: this is a fake, a Disney-en-Languedoc nineteenth-century idea of what the Middle Ages were, a highly approximate reconstruction of what never actually looked quite like this Loire-château-style monster.

Well at least it is *based* on an original. This is what it must have been like, at some point, to some extent. But those Second Empire restorers were very approximate gentlemen indeed, and your confidence begins to wane. Eugène Viollet-Leduc constructed something that he knew would evoke a general past rather than restore anything that had ever really been there. A bit like Tennyson reworking the Arthurian legends.

So perhaps you can just enjoy *being* here? Again, not a hope. Pouring from the souvenir shops, young persons emerge waving plastic swords and pretending to fight in a medieval sort of way. This involves an electronic device in the blades that makes them sound like steel clashing on steel every time they make contact. The noise is painful and maddening – a whooshing, snapping affair. The entire Cité is full of these youngsters and their noise, of shops involved in the sort of commerce that is both cheap (i.e. shoddy) and expensive, involving Peruvian ponchos and effigies of the Eiffel Tower, also of cafés (many closed in that strange French manner), exhibitions and vague 'entertainments' designed to dull your senses.

In the main *place* there is a hotel which offers refuge, and you plunge in clutching your much-battered credit card. Looking out from the bar, you realise that it reminds you of a smaller version of the Covent Garden Piazza – old London all right, but not really old at all; only theoretically romantic; also filthy and full of tourists.

In despair you take a room for the night – surely the crowds will go. The room isn't too bad, the sun begins to go down, a drink helps a bit. Then the events begin. French local authorities are always dreaming up wheezes to put (or keep) their towns on the map – jazz and ballet festivals, sheepdog trials, a musical thing they call *le folklore*, celebrations of garlic, aeroplanes, invasions, beef, melons, oysters. For Carcassonne tonight it's a rock concert. From early evening the bands start tuning up and testing their immensely powerful amplifiers just outside the good-enough-to-fool-the-casual-observer walls. You have put up with much during a long day and now, during a long night, you are going to get Led Zeppelin (for it is they, in person, also resurrected from an earlier time) at maximum decibels.

Back at the airport more planeloads of excited Britons are jetting in for an authentic, perhaps even spiritual, experience. As if. And don't even *mention* the Cathars.

James Michie

James Michie, formerly The Oldie's literary editor and originator of the 'I Once Met' column, was the magazine's only in-house poet from 1999 until his death in 2007

True or False?

I bald, she grey, we met – was it again? –
Drinking atrocious corporate champagne.
She had good eyes. After some vapid chatter
She, suddenly: 'Look, it doesn't really matter,
But did we once, in the Sixties, sleep together?'
You could have knocked me down with the old feather.
'You must remember that old men forget,
Especially veterans of the Chelsea set.'
'My memory's hopeless, too.' Rocked by amnesia,
We held hands, which made the rest much easier.

For a Hypochondriac

Blood pressure: fine. Coagulation:
Neither too thin nor yet too thick.
Pacemaker: works. Some consolation
To know you'll die in perfect nick!

TO MY BEARSKIN

I like dead pets the best – and, Bruin,
You're my ideal, a gorgeous ruin
Whose fulvous pelt and claws and head
Exoticise my Willesden bed
Where, winter-happy, underneath
Your harmless snarl and futile teeth
I sleep without one twinge of guilt
At making you my ursine quilt.
I scorn political correction:
You're mine by natural selection.

A Light Dose

Around my skeletal, black-boughed fig
Snowflakes waltz, caper and jig.
A robin balances on a twig,

While I, ancient, infected bard,
Relish the pane-framed, powdered yard,
January's late Christmas card.

It brings back the old boyhood thrill
Of being trivially ill
In my bed under the window-sill.

A happy if not holy ghost,
I take delight in playing host
To a mild germ, with gruel and toast.

APRIL

The spring was sprung,
The grass was riz
When I was young,
When was was is.

But now the spring
Don't spring because,
Though birdies sing,
The is is was.

Is There Nobody Gay in Glamorgan?

'Is there nobody gay in Glamorgan?'
Was the minuscule wail on the wall,
And my heart and the sensitive organ
I dangled were moved by this scrawl.
Is there not one good man in the county,
I thought, from here to Worm's Head,
Who out of mere bisexual bounty
Could take the poor bugger to bed?

Or mightn't some dating computer
Or dial-a-pal telephone find
A compatible person to suit a
Lost cause in the back of behind?
Then I saw (as I gave it a final
Shake in the manner of males),
Even lower case on the urinal:
'There's nobody gay in all Wales!'

WHEN...

When grass grows grey
And mouths don't mean
The words they say
And the future has been,

When jokes don't work
And nor can you,
When you're bored by the Turk
and sick of the Jew,

When you've lost the beat
Of the drums of advance,
Rediscover your feet,
Invent a dance.

Looking for Cherry Tree Lane

JOSEPH HONE *remembers Pamela Travers, the steely author of Mary Poppins who always got what she wanted – including one of his twin baby brothers*

Pamela Travers *c.*1968

Anthony. Pamela was very big on gurus. This was tough on Anthony, who was abandoned once more to my mother's impoverished parents in Ireland.

Pamela was also very big on doubles, believing in the essential duality of life. But her own essential quest was simpler: she was always looking for a Mr Banks, a solid but sensitive and engaging man like her creation, the banker of Cherry Tree Lane – surely an idealised version of her own unsatisfactory father. Travers Goff was a small-town bank manager in rural Australia before he was demoted to bank clerk; he had abandoned Pamela when she was eight, dying after a long association with the bottle.

If Mr Banks was a fanciful version of her father, then Mary Poppins was a whimsical, bossy reflection

'Y ou should never use the words "With love" in a dedication unless you mean it,' the witchy, keen-eyed woman with a flounce of curly white hair and a jangle of silver bangles up each wrist told me after I'd inscribed the words in a novel of mine I'd given her. Miss P L ('Mary Poppins') Travers was right. I didn't love her. But that was her life-long unrealistic hope – for a secure, unconditional, untroubled love. Instead, for lack of this, she created Mary Poppins and a million-dollar fortune. But she wasn't really happy with her success. Pamela was a contrary, divided, hypochondriacal woman, and Mary Poppins was her cure-all, magic nanny – a wonderful tonic for millions of children, but one who never quite cured her creator.

> **She invented a dead father for her new off-the-shelf son, and motherhood for herself. She would be the magic nanny**

Pamela was a friend of my grandfather and she adopted my younger brother Camillus in 1940. He was one of twins abandoned by our parents; she picked him up in Dublin from my grandfather's house. My grandfather, having been landed with me and my sister previously, was anxious to get shot of the twins as soon as possible, so when Pamela arrived in the nursery and saw the two tiny babies, he said to her, like a grocer, 'Take two, they're small.' She didn't – she went away and had both babies' horoscopes prepared by an astrologer in California, who recommended she take Camillus and not

of Pamela herself. Pamela had an unhappy, disrupted childhood. And so she set out in her life, and in her Mary Poppins fantasies, to set her two worlds to rights: to create a magic childhood in the books and, with the help of her gurus, to find a happy life in reality. It was a tall order. She succeeded wonderfully in the first quest but not the second. She found the real world pretty awful. And so she further immersed herself in fairytales, myths, dodgy health cures and Jungian blather – encouraged by a wild assortment of charlatans, most notably the caviar-guzzling, Armagnac-tippling

Russian mystic Gurdjieff in his exotic Paris flat, who told her she should have a daily enema and took her money for his advice.

In the late Fifties she asked me to stay in her Chelsea house to set Camillus to rights. He had become a difficult youth – not surprising, since she had never told him who his real parents were, saying she was his mother and his father had died of a fever in the colonies. This lie had been uncovered in dramatic circumstances shortly before my arrival, when Anthony, intent on finding his twin brother, finally discovered Pamela's address and turned up on her doorstep. Camillus opened the door. 'I'm your twin brother,' Anthony told him. Sensation!

Truth never had a firm root in Pamela's nature. First and foremost she was a storyteller, a fantasist to the tip of Mary Poppins's parrot-headed umbrella. Like Carroll with Alice and Barrie with Peter Pan, Pamela found herself in possession of a universal figure, a magic nanny who has roused the wonder and delight of generations of children. But Pamela had none of the nannying and mothering skills of her creation. Rather the opposite. Despite her airy-fairy fantasies, Pamela was a steely, self-centred, very controlling woman. She got what she wanted – an oven-fresh, ready-packed baby boy. Being without a secure family background of her own, husbandless and loverless, she wanted to create a real family for herself. Just as she had imagined the Banks family, so she would invent a conveniently dead father for her new off-the-shelf son, and motherhood for herself. And if not actual motherhood, then she would be the magic nanny: she could be Mary Poppins in reality. The victim in all this was Camillus, who wasn't a character in a fairytale.

Pamela asked me to stay with her, in the hope that in meeting his more secure elder brother, Camillus might steady himself. I don't know that I helped him much, for I saw very little of him in the three weeks I stayed with them. I was working all day in a bookshop, and Camillus was usually out gambling all night. Of an evening, in the hope that Camillus might join us, Pamela and I sat in her first-floor drawing-room chatting over drinks that she mixed from a cupboard on the landing: fifty-fifty, sweet and dry vermouth.

Camillus made quite a success of his gambling. In the small hours one morning I heard a to-do in the hall. Looking down the stairwell I saw Camillus gesticulating, then saying to Pamela, 'You think I don't apply myself, don't earn any money!' and then throwing a snowfall of old white five-pound notes in the air.

Camillus was far better off in his adoption by Pamela than he would have been with his real parents or grandparents. With her patience, love, and money, she gave him many practical and priceless things that he would never otherwise have had. I remember looking at this small, fragile woman and thinking, 'You're a tough one all right'. But she was a real artist, and she had the application. She lived to be ninety-six and left over two million pounds. Mary Poppins and Pamela Travers: airy-fairy and down to earth – the same little lady of Cherry Tree Lane.

'We feel the less said about this one the better'

House Husbandry
with Giles Wood

G DU BOIS

In which Mr Wood gets his head examined

Mary has started reading aloud self-diagnosis decision charts from our new *Family Doctor Home Adviser*. The other evening she opened up the book at 'Forgetfulness and Confusion'.

'Question: "Have you noticed two or more of the following symptoms: change in personality, decline in standards of hygiene, difficulty in following complex conversations and instructions, and inability to cope with everyday matters?"' she probed.

'Yes to the last two,' I agreed. 'Follow the arrow.'

'That takes us to Dementia,' said Mary.

Lately it has become fashionable to suffer from bipolar disorder or to be a coeliac, but Mary has sought in vain to find out what may be wrong with me. For want of a formal diagnosis she has called it VID, or Variable Intelligence Disorder. She notes that I can show occasional signs of normal, even high intelligence. For example, I can identify all the aberrant forms of the silver-washed fritillary butterfly (*Argynnis Paphia*). Yet I regularly ask her questions such as 'What Time is *News at Ten* on?' or 'Why are you laughing?' when she is watching *Fawlty Towers* reruns.

In my defence I would say this: I spend so many hours on my own keeping the show on the road while Mary is gallivanting in London, that I simply enjoy the novelty of hearing my own voice, and I make such remarks for want of anything else to say.

She worries also that I have suddenly started to enjoy Michael Winner's *Death Wish* films which, when they first

came out, I considered risible. Does this point to a reduction in intelligence or could the explanation be more prosaic? These films have a beginning, an end and a very simple plot. One good guy takes on a sequence of punks and baddies who get their comeuppance in exponentially increasing fire power. Modern films, by contrast, often start with the conclusion before fragmenting into confusing flashbacks. Moreover, it is well known that a heavy meal washed down with strong ale can lead to dull wittedness. This may be the reason why aesthetes enjoy seeing a concert, play or opera on an empty stomach but I generally watch these late-night Winner reruns when fully sated.

This VID is nothing new. At prep school I remember a Cassell's Intelligence Test leading me into a classic heffalump trap: 'Which weighs most, a ton of feathers or a ton of bricks?' Naturally the bricks got my vote and secured my entry into that exclusive cadre, DENSA – the polar opposite of MENSA.

On a train to London recently, most of my brain power was being absorbed by filling in a seed order. I realised we had been motionless for some time but assumed we were stuck in a tunnel. It fell to a cleaner to alert me that we had arrived in Paddington twenty minutes earlier. For Mary, the final straw came when she told me as I came through the cottage door, 'Tony just rang' and I replied, 'Why didn't you tell me?'

The evidence, according to Mary, was pointing either to depression or to early-onset dementia. She wanted our doctor to refer me for a test where blood-flow to the frontal lobes is monitored by electrodes attached to the scalp – the wrong type of blood-flow can be an early indicator of dementia. The art of marriage is compromise, so I agreed to

> ***Mary worries that I have started to enjoy Michael Winner's 'Death Wish' films, which, when they first came out, I considered risible. Does this point to a reduction in intelligence?***

attend the doctor's appointment she had booked. We walked into the surgery together.

Alas for Mary, the doctor said that the problem was not a medical one. I was neither mad, nor would anti-depressants be suitable for what he deemed to be a simple lack of focus. Pointing helpfully in the direction of a life coach, he was laughing a traditional belly-laugh. For me this was rewarding – a patient does not often have the chance to provide therapy for his doctor.

Mary was nonplussed. 'So you can just tell instinctively he doesn't have dementia or depression?' she asked.

'Yes,' beamed the doctor, clapping me on the back in collegiate manner as he showed us out of the surgery.

'I would now like to read out a few text messages'

'Are we nearly there yet, Dad?'

'I've been shopping all day –
my fingers are killing me'

'I'm sorry, but according to my database
you're just one sugar'

'I've wired the email to the toaster'

Unwrecked England

Tickencote, Rutland

Candida Lycett Green

You would never notice Tickencote. Just north of Stamford, where the counties of Lincolnshire, Rutland and Northamptonshire meet, the Great North Road slices through the landscape and merges with Ermine Street, the Roman road which ran from London to Lincoln and on to York.

Below the highway and the low roar of traffic, Tickencote lies hidden on a gentle slope of the Gwash valley, a world away from the hurrying rush. The village street leads down past the sheltered churchyard, stone barns and cottages

to the mill with its handsome miller's house close by. Beyond, the River Gwash widens into an ornamental lake beside a sweeping stretch of parkland and the ghost of Tickencote Hall, an early eighteenth-century mansion which was pulled down in the Fifties. Its dynasties of le Daneys, Dales and Greshams are long gone but a handsome stable block remains, sympathetically converted into a large house by Ogden and Dodd of Leicester. The river loops upstream through soft Rutland country towards Empingham and beyond it to the vast expanse of Rutland Water, the biggest man-made lake in Europe, through

which the Gwash still flows from its source on the western side of the county.

Tikencote's great glory is its church. No photographs could prepare you for the real thing. The horseshoe-shaped chancel arch, which has spread under the great weight it upholds, is the most dazzling showcase of Norman art imaginable. The arch is adorned with six rows of different designs – stylised foliage, zigzags, beak-heads, chevrons, cable moulding – but my favourite arch of all is set among foliage with grotesque faces. There are muzzled bears (a particular favourite with the Normans), a strange cat's head, a fox's head holding that of a monk, several semi-human monsters and the two crowned heads of King Stephen and Queen Maud, rival claimants to the English throne, looking in opposite directions. The chancel itself is sprung with the most spectacular ribbed vaulting covered in zigzag decoration: it's as though you are standing under an enormous starfish with six tentacles drooping down around you. The centre is set with a round boss with three strange heads carved on it. It is extraordinary that such a small church should house such wonder.

There is a stunning Norman font and beside the altar lies the wooden effigy of Sir Roland le Daney, an early owner of Tickencote. The wife of a later incumbent of the lost hall beside the river is remembered on a plaque in the porch and tells how Eliza Wingfield, 'with the true sense of religion and reverence for her Maker which ever distinguished her life, repaired this church in the year 1792.' St Peter's was then in a perilous state. She employed the services of S P Cockerel, the wacky architect of Sezincote in Gloucestershire with its exotic onion domes. Not surprisingly the outside of St Peter's has some eccentric neo-Norman touches.

H V Morton in his book *In Search of England* describes Tickencote as 'a pocket edition of a Norman church – I stood in the shady churchyard and thought this solid little building, planted in the lovely soil soon after the Conquest, is one of the fairest things I have seen... there is nothing that I am aware of like it in all England.'

★ Great Bores of Today ★ No.42

'...so that's two Lottos and a Lucky 5 for Sunday please squire ok? and I'll have a Euro Millions while I'm at it make that two 'cause it's a quadruple rollover this week £130 million or something mental oh and ten powerballs you won't believe this but I missed winning Saturday by only three numbers I had 12 23 and 5 and the numbers that came up were 2 27 and 8 and I've got some old ones that need checking don't expect I've won anything but you never know it could be my lucky day couldn't it I've got just as much chance as the next man...'

© Fant and Al

I once met...

Samuel Beckett

IT WAS 1955, and *Waiting for Godot* was transferring from the Arts Theatre to the Criterion following good reviews by Harold Hobson and Kenneth Tynan. My father, a literary agent, and I met Samuel Beckett for lunch. I can't remember the name of the restaurant, but it had to be near the theatre. He was staying in what we thought was a slightly seedy hotel only because it was also near the theatre. It was clear that he was not interested in his surroundings, or his comfort, or even in being in London for any reason other than seeing the play put on, and didn't intend to go anywhere other than Piccadilly.

He was instantly recognisable when he walked in – slightly hesitantly – thin, even gaunt, with the distinctive greyish crew-cut hair. He ate very sparingly, and drank little.

For some reason he spoke of Paris in the 1930s, when, as well as being close friends with James Joyce, he was also his assistant. Joyce used to dictate to Beckett. 'We were working on what became *Finnegans Wake*, and there was a knock on the door. I didn't hear it, so when Joyce said "Come in" I wrote down "Come in". I never took it out. It made as much sense as anything else. I like to imagine earnest literary students writing theses on the meaning and implications of that "Come in" in the book.'

My father asked him if he was a happy man. Beckett looked surprised at the naivety of the question. 'No, no. Why would anyone be happy?'

PHOEBE WINCH

Wojtek the Bear

When **JOHN McEWEN** was four, he was taken to meet the six-foot mascot of the 22nd Company of the Artillery Supply Comand, 2nd Polish Corps

Researchers at Hull University have discovered that a fifth of us invent our earliest memories. One volunteer even claimed to have seen a living dinosaur. But at the age of four in Berwickshire I really did meet Wojtek (pronounced 'Voytek') the bear. I know because I checked. 'Am I dreaming or did you take me to meet a bear just after the war?' I asked the bear-like Auberon Herbert, himself worthy of an I Once Met, at a party in the Sixties. 'I certainly did, and that's exactly why – because I knew you'd always remember it,' he replied.

In Iraq he caused mayhem by making off with the precious, non-army issue smalls of the Women's Signals Company

Wojtek was loosely chained to a tree. He stood upright while jolly Polish soldiers put him through his party routine. What sticks in the memory was his relish for swallowing lit cigarettes. He no doubt also quaffed a bottle or two of his favourite beer, opened his mouth to inhale exhaled smoke and indulged in a bit of bear play. My recollection is of a fierce, dark presence, whereas he was brown and renowned for gentleness. It grieves me in old age that no one thought to bring a camera.

Wojtek was unique, as witness the exhibition in his honour and, by association, the wartime Polish army, at the Polish Institute in 2010. The exhibition told Wojtek's story in film, photographs, cuttings and books, including two biographies (one for children).

PHOTOGRAPHY COURTESY OF © ANDREW POZNIAK

Wojtek, bought as a starving cub in Persia, became the mascot of the 22nd Company of the Artillery Supply Command, 2nd Polish Corps, and served with them from 1942 until 1947, by which time he weighed 250 pounds and stood over six feet tall. When the Company travelled, Wojtek sat in the cab between Peter, his guardian, and Stanislav the driver. In Palestine he almost died from a scorpion sting. In Iraq he caused mayhem by making off with the precious, non-army issue smalls of the Women's Signals Company, which he had discovered on a washing-line. But his antics could also be militarily productive. In Egypt he sneaked into his favourite hang-out, the washhouse, and flushed out an Arab with some stolen rifles. The terrified man was captured. Wojtek earned himself a legitimate shower.

By the time he reached Italy in 1944 Wojtek had a name, rank and number. In the battle for Monte Cassino, won by the Poles on 18th May, he helped carry ammunition boxes and twenty-five-pound shells from truck to battery. His action inspired the Company insignia: a bear carrying a shell against the background of a steering wheel.

In Glasgow, at the war's end, he marched at the head of the regiment and was then posted to Berwick-shire, where he took swims in the River Tweed and was elected an honorary member of the Scottish-Polish Society. He continued to make himself useful carrying logs and crates, and rolling barrels. When the Polish army was 'demobbed' in 1947 he was sent to Edinburgh Zoo. His old comrades often visited him, horrifying visitors and bringing the keepers running by climbing into his cage. Wojtek died in 1963.

'Caught anything?'

The Worm's Head seen from the ruined radar station

The Past is Myself

Famous for its walks and views, the Gower Peninsula is also full of history, says **SONALI CHAPMAN**

STANDING ON the rocky summit of the Worm's Head, about one hundred and fifty feet above the sea, feels like standing on the edge of the world. Ahead there is nothing but water: the village of Rhossili, which sits on the cliff-top behind, seems a world away. Surrounded on three sides by water, the Worm's Head is a long promontory joined to the mainland by a rocky causeway which is cut off at high tide. Shaped like a giant sea serpent with its head sticking out of the water, the Worm apparently took its name from the Norse word for 'dragon' – *wurm* – and marks the outermost point of the Gower Peninsula.

The Gower is a walking paradise: there is a walk in every direction, and the small village of Rhossili on the Gower's southwestern tip is an excellent base from which to explore the area. The hike from the village to the end of the Worm is a favourite, though the trek across the jagged rocky outcrop to the headland can be tricky. On the Worm itself, you'll pass a natural blow hole and cross Devil's Bridge, a narrow and vertiginous rock bridge which leads to the 'outer head'. It's important to check the tide tables: Dylan Thomas once spent a night on the Worm's Head, having been cut off, and he later recounted the tale in the short story 'Who Do You Wish Was With Us?'

Rhossili Bay, an expansive sandy beach stretching for three miles, was voted Best British Beach in 2010. With its panoramic views and dramatic backdrop, it's easy to see why. The skeletal wreck of the *Helvetia*, a timber ship which ran aground in 1887 during a terrible storm, is dug into the sand and is still visible at low tide. To the north of the village is Rhossili Down, from where there are breathtaking views of the Worm's Head and the beach. On its western side are the concrete remains of a World War Two radar station which was operational between 1942 and 1945 – 'a lovely place to sit out the war,' as one local remarked.

The whole area is steeped in history, a snapshot of our existence from the beginning of time. At the northernmost end of Rhossili Bay is the tiny tidal island of Burry Holms, on which there are the remains of an Iron Age hill fort and ditch, and of a medieval monastery. The land was previously home to Mesolithic hunters: at the beginning of the last century archaeologists discovered flint and bone tools there. On the Eastern slope of Rhossili Down are 'Sweynes Howes', a collection of stones used as communal burial chambers by settlers nearly six thousand years ago. Further down the coast towards Port Eynon is Paviland Cave, where the remains of the mistakenly named 'Red Lady of Paviland' were discovered in 1823: the thirty-thousand-year-old male skeleton had been stained red with ochre.

Wales is famous for its castles, and the Gower is no exception. Rhossili is a short drive from many of them, including the eerie remains of Pennard Castle, a Norman ruin high on the cliff above Three Cliffs Bay, and Weobley Castle, a fortified medieval manor house with stunning views across the Loughor Estuary.

'I have been all men known to history,' began R S Thomas in 'Taliesin 1952'. The Gower Peninsula has been them all too.

STRICTLY BALLROOM

*The palais glide, the conga, anxious boys and waiting girls: ballroom dancing
in 1941 was both exhilarating and nerve-wracking*

Written and illustrated by SHIRLEY HUGHES

Slow, slow, quick-quick slow; slow, slow, quick-quick slow; now the tricky bit, a double reverse turn at the corner and off again smoothly down the room. This was serious stuff demanding heavy concentration. We were not yet aiming at the sequined glamour we had seen in the Rita Hayworth/Gene Kelly movies, the swoops and twirls of satin evening dresses, the layers of stiff petticoats, the impeccable white tie and tails. This was mid-afternoon in the school hall and at this point in my life, aged about fifteen, a rudimentary skill in ballroom dancing had to be acquired somehow before you ever got near a boy or a proper dance hall.

It was an all-girls high school. The big, tall girls (I was one) had to take the men's part, wheeling our smaller, daintier partners along while counting under our breath. One problem with this method was that when, at a later stage, you made it onto the floor at a proper dance you had to resist the urge to propel your male partner firmly backwards. The art of anticipating the man's every move a split second before he makes it, and attempting light conversation while doing so, was one I had yet to acquire. And I was nowhere near realising what fun ballroom dancing could be, once you had got the hang of it.

Our Eton-cropped gym mistress operated the wind-up gramophone and called out the steps. The music provided was played by Victor Silvester and his dance orchestra. It was brisk, strict tempo stuff, arguably about the most un-sexy dance music ever recorded. We longed for the big American Swing bands, Benny Goodman, Glenn Miller and Artie Shaw, but no such luck. This was England during the Second World War, the era of stoicism, austerity and the stiff upper lip (or so they kept telling us) so we could jolly well make do with Victor Silvester. We were not being encouraged to aim at anything too ambitious, such as a tango or a rumba, let alone jitterbugging. Just the basic stuff, quicksteps, foxtrots or perhaps an old-fashioned waltz. We hoped that it might lead to something hotter if we persevered.

What it actually led to, as far as the school was concerned, was a daringly conceived event involving a dance with the boys from the grammar school. We were not supposed to talk to them on our way to and from school, and this invested them with a glamour they might not otherwise have had. When they bicycled past our school gates (they were experts at nonchalantly riding with no hands on the handlebars) one of them sometimes flicked a note written on a bit of screwed-up paper, an invitation to go to the pictures perhaps, at a girl as she walked by. This struck me as rather romantic, but unfortunately these notes were usually aimed not at me but at Joan Robinson. She was in my class, and whatever you had to have as far as boys were concerned, Joan certainly had it. It did not seem to have much to do with ballroom dancing.

The school dance was not a success, perhaps because, like our practice classes, it took place in the afternoon and was heavily policed by the teaching staff. The boys arrived and stood about sheepishly on one side of the hall while we girls clustered together in groups at the other. A few brave lads attempted a dance or two with us, but under the beady-eyed gaze of our teachers it was quite difficult to get any warmth into it. Conversation was minimal when we took to the floor, owing to our counting under our breath, and we trod heavily on one another's toes from time to time. Victor Silvester droned on, but the event ended early.

The really serious stuff happened when at last we got to the Saturday night hops down at the church hall. There was a live band, local boys on piano, drums, saxophone and clarinet. Sometimes there was also an accordionist. Roddy, the pianist, was also the bandleader who held it all together. The glamour of the guitar had yet to hit us, unless you happened to be a fan of Django Reinhardt.

The blackout curtains were well in place as we girls hung up our coats and titivated our hair in the draughty cloakroom. The boys turned up wearing suits or tweed sports jackets and grey flannel trousers, hair slicked back with a heavy application of Brylcreem. For girls, clothes were a tremendous problem. All clothing was rationed and the most touching token of true love then was a gift of precious clothing coupons. I knew I had got it wrong when I turned up at my first dance wearing my long-sleeved Viyella dress with polka dots and a demure Peter Pan collar. Joan Robinson always seemed to manage something more clinging and décolleté.

When the band struck up, the girls, seated together in a row at one side of the room, affected a sophisticated detachment as to whether or not they would be invited onto the dance floor. The boys loitered and joshed about in groups. They knew that a formidable ordeal awaited them, which was having to cross the room and invite a girl to dance. If she said 'yes' they were away, launching out across the floor with varying degrees of expertise. But if she did not fancy him and refused, turning her back to chat with her friends, he had to return to his buddies, embarrassed, and attempt to pluck up the courage to try another girl. An equally daunting exposure faced the girls who were not asked. There was no worse fate than being left stranded as a 'wall flower'. Better to dance with another girl.

Somehow or other, though, the event got going. The glamorous glass-faceted ball which hung from the ceiling slowly turned, reflecting myriad tiny coloured lights onto us as we foxtrotted, quickstepped and samba-ed to the numbers we all knew from listening to the big American dance bands on the radio. We linked arms for the palais glide, and formed a conga line, hanging onto one another's waists and kicking our legs out sideways. There was the 'Excuse Me' dance in which a boy (but never a girl) could cut in on any couple on the floor and dance with the girl he fancied, leaving her partner to try his luck elsewhere. Also, rather unnervingly, there was the Paul Jones in which boys and girls circled each other in opposite directions and, when the music stopped, you danced with the nearest person. This, of course, resulted in a traffic jam in front of Joan and other girls who were rated as top glamour.

Sometimes, towards the end of the evening, a few young servicemen who were stationed at the nearby RAF camp looked in. They were lonely, far from home and usually rather drunk. Though they were not much older than the boys we were dancing with they seemed to us like people from another planet, grown men who had seen action or were soon going to. They were scared stiff although they tried not to show it. They usually stood in the doorway for a while, looking on and listening to the band, then turned and drifted away, back to the pub to see if the landlord had any beer left and perhaps to find older and more willing female company.

> *There was the 'Excuse Me' dance in which a boy (but never a girl) could cut in on any couple on the floor and dance with the girl he fancied*

When the last waltz came – early, if the Liverpool Blitz had already started – the lights were dimmed, the coloured ball turned and Roddy and his band played 'Goodnight Sweetheart' and 'Who's Taking You Home Tonight?' As we struggled into our coats we all knew that Joan would be accompanied home by her four regular escorts, nicknamed 'The Convoy'. One carried her bag, another wheeled her bicycle and the other two walked on either side of her. What kind of complex rivalry this must have involved when they reached her front doorstep was a matter for conjecture. Joan herself never let on. Humiliatingly, girls who had no escorts were often met by anxious parents who had braved the blackout to see that they got home safely. The boys who were not in The Convoy got on their bicycles and melted away into the darkness.

Everyone, young and old, danced during World War Two. All over the country dance halls kept open in spite of the Blitz. They were sometimes bombed to rubble, but people were still prepared to risk it. I can never hear those tunes, 'Moonlight Becomes You', 'Begin the Beguine' and 'In the Mood', without remembering what ballroom dancing meant to us then.

Brief encounters

NIGEL FOUNTAIN *looks at the lives of others*

'My dear brothers,' says Mr Boateng, 'my dear sisters. We have, once again, come to share the House of God with you.' Mr Boateng is standing just down from Greggs the bakers, under the vile concrete canopy attached to the Electric Avenue branch of the Iceland supermarket in Brixton, south London. 'And we will talk,' he continues, 'of Jesus Christ of Nazareth, our saviour.'

The supermarket, like the Boots over the way, is a brutal appendage to the magical, late-Victorian sweep of the Avenue. Until the 1980s its shops had their own splendid 1880s canopies, but now the Africa Shopping Centre, Kace Afro-Hair and Beauty, Danny's Greengrocer and all the other stores make do without.

Mr Boateng has been preaching since 1995. He is fifty-four, amiable, open, baseball-capped, in striped lumberjack shirt and blue trousers. He was born in Asante-Bekwai in what was the Gold Coast, a country on the verge, in 1957, of becoming Ghana. 'Ghana,' he says, 'is a British colony.' Not any more, I reply, that is all over.

'It is a British colony,' he says. 'I can say, Britain and Ghana, we are friends.' His parents were Christians and farmers, he left school at eighteen – he was a good student – and he, too, became a farmer. Then, in 1995, he was accused, wrongly, he explains, of a theft within the family. 'The police came to my house with guns and other things, and I was informed that somebody may kill me.'

So he came to London with $1,500, stayed in Stockwell with friends and took odd jobs. 'Somebody invited me to his Pentecostal church. I became an active Christian when I came to this country.'

I say London can be unfriendly, racist and cold. Sometimes it is cold, he says. 'If we are not born in this country – well, we are not very used to it. But today, this is very good weather.'

It is a grey Wednesday Brixton afternoon, misty rain is seeping into everything. Mr Boateng takes his cap off. 'This is good weather for you?' I say. We laugh.

'Racism, this thing happens to everyone,' he says. 'As a human being, I have to love you.' You don't, I say.

'I have to love you as a Christian,' he says, 'you are a human being. That is why Jesus Christ of Nazareth died for us.'

When Mr Boateng was in Ghana he did not give his life to Jesus. 'I did not know Jesus, I was in the world, when you do whatever you want – you understand what I mean?' A bit, I say.

Back in 1995 he was working as a night-time casual at Sainsbury's. 'It was near South Bank University. I was cleaning two and a half hours a night, and it was around four in the morning and I heard a voice, somebody was mentioning my name and saying that "I was looking for you for so many years, you don't want to give your life to me. This is the time I want you to give your life to me. I want to use you." Then I give my life to Jesus because I know that God is calling me.'

When Mr Boateng is preaching outside Iceland, and not being questioned by me, a stream of Brixtonians come by. Some small children are taken by the oddity of a man making a speech outside a supermarket, but no one pauses. As if in orbit, at intervals, a dishevelled rasta-haired man – about Mr Boateng's age – approaches, talking of the blood of the Virgin, and vanishes back into Electric Avenue. I ask Mr Boateng if he gets discouraged, and he says no, not at all, and I almost believe him.

'When Jesus Christ of Nazareth was preaching, they are saying he is a madman, a drunkard, he is deceiving people.' Mr Boateng adds that 'Jesus says not to panic or be afraid.'

People can be unkind to the likes of him, I say. 'No,' he says, 'I am not thinking about that because I am saying the word of God for people to repent because Jesus of Nazareth came for the sinners, not the righteous, to turn away from their wicked ways.'

Is this, I ask, a moral country? 'The leaders,' says Mr Boateng, 'are very, very good people, I am praying for them all the time, the Prime Minister and the Queen, they have a passion for people, they care.' Blair and Brown? 'Blair and Brown.'

Nobody is stopping, I say, as the distracted, poor and worried surge past. 'I have to preach the word of God,' he says, 'whether you listen or not listen. That doesn't bother me. People listen to me very well. They listen to me.'

I become Mr Boateng's congregation. I should have heckled – that can pull in a crowd – but I did not want to. There was, in truth, a smack of *Finnegans Wake* about his address, as he reiterates that God, and Satan, are about to do something. Things are always about to happen.

I wander off up Electric Avenue, stopping by a shabbily dressed African lady, with a fine face, full of sorrow. She is looking at Mr Boateng out of the corner of her eye. 'It is the word of God,' she says, matter-of-factly. 'It comes with the power to transform.'

Virginia Ironside

Men have their practical uses – but their greatest virtue is that they are not women

I want a man. Don't get me wrong. I don't want a man *per se* and I'm *certainly* not looking for a partner or a lover. No thanks! No, I mean I want to be able to ask, when I'm advertising for people – teachers, say, or lodgers – for a man rather than a woman.

But I think it might now be illegal, and as I don't want to be clapped in irons, I never specify which sex I want.

The reason I want a male lodger is that I've already got a female one, and then there's me – and experience has told me that a house full of women is an icky business. There tends to be bitching in the bathroom, carping in the kitchen. And anyway, I don't like female-only enclaves. I once sat through *The Vagina Monologues* with an all-female audience, and the smug superiority of it all, the 'us and them-ness', made me feel as if I was drowning in a sea of Tampax.

I worked for a long time at *Woman* magazine, and when someone told me that when a lot of women get together for long periods, as they do in convents, they all start to menstruate at the same time, I'd hold my breath in the lifts, just in case any of the lunar hormones, or whatever they were, got to me, and I'd start working in some ghastly physical unison with the fashion Ed, the knitting Ed, the cooking Ed and even, heaven forbid, the daunting Ed herself.

Blokes are useful in the house. They can kill rats and frighten burglars away

Then, on a more practical level, blokes are extremely useful in the house. They can kill rats, unstick windows, put bulbs in inaccessible sockets and, with their heavy footsteps and booming voices, they can frighten burglars away when they get in. (They can also keep burglars away *before* they get in, just by being spotted regularly at the front door as they butchly shove their keys into the locks.)

Talking of rats, I'm sure there was some experiment done with the pesky beasts to show that if you get a box of male rats and shove a female in, all the males instantly start behaving better, applying deodorant, twirling their whiskers and saying 'After you' before entering the sewers. Similarly, take a box of female rats and add a male and all the females stop gossiping and shopping and, instead, behave like normal human beings – if a rat can ever behave like a normal human being.

I like a bit of difference. On the rare occasions I'm to be found in a church, I feel depressed at the sight of a female vicar. Of course she's got every right to preach, but at least with a male vicar he's a bit of a mystery. He's male for a start and therefore baffling. And also, startlingly, he's usually encased in a long gold-stitched dress. Weird. Makes him look as if there's a real possibility he could be in touch with some mysterious 'other'. Females, on the other hand, are too familiar to me to hold any magic. And in their embroidered dresses, instead of appearing as the channellers of spiritual wisdom, they look like women on their way to Glyndebourne.

Anyway, I've got the male lodger, I've got a male music teacher up my sleeve if I need one and now there's the German teacher to cast around for, because I've decided to learn it. It's not that I mind being taught by a woman, but obviously a woman German teacher is going to remind me of one of the teachers I had at school, all female, and I shall start, as a result, to skip prep and write fake notes in my late mother's handwriting to say I'm ill. Give me a man, however, and I shall check my make-up in the mirror, see my tights are unladdered, and open the door with a cheery '*Ich habe alle meine Hausaufgaben gemacht und freuen uns auf unsere Lektion zusammen.*'*

And as a result will be fluent before I can say 'Fritz Müller', being the nearest I can get, in German, to Jack Robinson.

Who was, you may notice, a bloke.

*'I have done all my homework and look forward to our lesson together.' At least, according to Google Translate.

The Queen and I

CHARLES ELLIOTT, *who grew up with a bit of a crush on the Queen, finally got within chatting distance when he was reporting for 'Life' magazine. How did it go?*

The Queen and I go way back, though I suspect she may be ignorant of the fact. I can date the connection to childhood. She is a few years older than I am, but I was an infant Anglophile. I can remember being overcome with admiration (as only a five-year-old American raised on Christopher Robin and such could be) for the pictures I saw of two extremely fetching little girls said to be princesses. Nobody like Elizabeth and Margaret in Michigan.

We both grew up and went our own ways. I became a journalist working for the weekly picture magazine, *Life*. She became a queen. As fate would have it, one of my earliest assignments was to accompany the photographer Alfred Eisenstaedt to Canada for the opening of the St Lawrence Seaway in 1959. Elizabeth and President Eisenhower would jointly do the honours.

It has to be understood that a *Life* reporter was not your ordinary sort of journalist, but someone combining the skills of a railway porter and a stenographer (mostly the former). A reporter's duty was to tag along with the photographer, keep track of the pictures he shot, and deal with problems as they arose. In Eisie's case, the main problem was his height. Without some way to add to his five foot two, he could see neither the Queen nor the President. We had no ladder. I was the solution. Perched on my shoulders, he produced a memorable shot of a pretty dark-haired monarch having a laugh with an avuncular President. I saw very little but Eisie's right shoe.

Given my intense interest in Elizabeth, this would have been extremely disappointing except for the fact that despite my menial status I was officially classed as a member of the

The Queen and President Eisenhower at the St Lawrence Seaway opening – as covered by *Life* magazine in July 1959

press corps. I even had a badge. This qualified me to go aboard the Royal Yacht *Britannia* for the traditional drinks party given during the course of a royal tour. The point of the party was to thank the hacks and perhaps to alleviate the boredom. After all, unless something dreadful happens – say a streaker or a fainting guardsman – a royal tour is not the most exciting source of copy.

The yacht was splendid and the drink abundant, but I never got anywhere near the Queen, although I did offer a word to Prince Philip and he grunted in response.

It might be better to pass quietly over my next contact. The episode was *lèse majesté* at best and possibly illegal. In pursuit of her queenly duties, Elizabeth and Philip found themselves at their first American football game. The University of Maryland was playing North Carolina. One of the editors got the smart idea of reporting what she said during the game. The only people close enough to hear her were the college president and the state governor, who were unlikely to be forthcoming. So we engaged a lip-reader, equipped him with binoculars and got a couple of hours of truly banal questions and answers, many of which we printed in the next issue of the magazine.

In 1963 I was stationed in Hong Kong. Someone in New York with a weak command of geography decided that the photographer Larry Burrows and I should travel five thousand miles to Fiji for a royal tour that would go on to New Zealand and Australia. This time we really did become part of the entourage, covering endless parades, flag-waving, military tattoos, folk dances and demonstrations of sheep-shearing. It was exhausting, and I can only admire the patience with which the royals put up with it. For three weeks Burrows and I doggedly photographed the festivities in the heat of Auckland and the rains of Dunedin, the little England of Christchurch and the Maori paradise of the Bay of Islands, securing in the end (at what must have been a staggering overhead cost) just two pages in the magazine. The Queen got sunburn.

We were again invited on board *Britannia* for a press party and this time I actually met Elizabeth, having planned better on this occasion. With two or three others I stood nervously on the deck talking with her. She was animated and easy. She joked about a young vicar who had shown her around a church that day and had forgotten his lines. He was embarrassed to the point of speechlessness, she said. It was at this point that the fellow next to me, a Fleet Street photographer, dropped his drink on her foot. The conversation, needless to say, ended.

The Queen and I have not had an opportunity to meet again for some years now. She has of course been very busy. But perhaps the opportunity will arise. It would be nice.

MIND THE AGE GAP

LIZZIE ENFIELD, *daughter of Edward, took over his column in 2010. Her subject? Her parents, of course...*

MY PARENTS were concerned about food miles long before it became fashionable to tell the world you were spending the month eating only things that had been grown within a five-mile radius.

They never refer to food miles as such – they simply have an innate sense of wrong-doing if they eat anything out of season. Were I to invite them for a meal at the end of April, for example, and dish up strawberries for pudding, they would raise their eyebrows and say 'Strawberries!' in a tone suffused with all the moral authority of an Ayatollah.

The implication would be clear: that I lacked the strength of character to wait until strawberries came into season. The fact that the strawberries might have been flown from Kenya in a plane churning out huge amounts of gunk into the atmosphere would be secondary to their concern that I would be eating strawberries before 30th May, the date they have decided signals the official start of the strawberry season.

I recently watched an episode of *That Mitchell and Webb Look* in which they performed a sketch based on Scott of the Antarctic. Oates had gone walkabout and those who remained had only a strip of dried puffin for food, which even the wasted Scott could not stomach.

'There's nothing then,' said his colleague. 'Unless ...' He reaches behind him and produces, from a hamper overflowing with food, a Christmas pudding. 'The Christmas pudding,' says Scott. 'Have you gone mad? It's only August!'

My parents would have been the same. Even if they were staring starvation in the face they would not sustain themselves with a chunk of Easter egg if it was still Lent.

In the days when he had a full-time job, my father would boycott the office Christmas dinner on the grounds that there was turkey on the menu and it was only the middle of December. The carpet in his living room is worn out in the spot directly in front of the drinks cabinet, as this is where he paces during the time when he is desperate for a drink but will not pour himself one as it is 'not yet six-thirty'. After Eights might have been invented for my parents: chocolates that expressly prohibit you from eating them at certain times – perfect! Forget sell-by and use-by dates. What they would really appreciate are clearly labelled 'not-to-be-eaten-before' dates.

The season for strawberry debacles is now past: tangerines are allowed, chestnuts are on sale in the local farmers' market, and my phone is ringing.

It is my mother.

'Can you look up something on your computer for me?' She always gets straight to the point – partly because she is a direct person, but also because she likes to keep the cost of phone calls down. She wants me to surf the net on her behalf because both she and my father are computer illiterate.

'I need to get hold of some cranberry liqueur,' she tells me. 'They don't sell it in the village. Can you find out where we can get some?'

'Now?' I ask. It is 9.30 in the morning, a good nine hours before official drinking time begins but, more to the point, I am trying to work.

'Yes,' she says. 'As soon as possible. We can't find any anywhere.'

'What do you need it for?' I ask, envisaging a pre-Christmas drinks party.

'To drink,' she says. This might have been reason enough, but there is a qualifier: 'There's going to be a frost at the weekend. The first in December.'

This, I suspect, signals the official start of the cranberry liqueur-drinking season. Don't ask me why.

ILLUSTRATION BY **MARTIN HONEYSETT**

Third time unlucky

After two failed marriages, a Very Stupid Woman found Rupert through an 'upmarket' introduction agency. He looked like Toad of Toad Hall but he was charming, ardent and well connected, writes **ANNE HOWELLS**

Once there was a stupid woman who paid £4,000 to an upmarket introduction agency in order to be introduced to upmarket men. Seeing herself as some sort of phoenix arising from the ashes of two failed marriages, she was sure that in the company of men who said 'lavatory' instead of 'toilet' and 'what'

instead of 'pardon', she would find that elusive someone who would share her passions for music, art, literature, documentaries about air crashes and Geeta's Lime and Chilli Chutney.

She didn't have the four grand to join up, so she borrowed the money from Lloyds Bank, telling them it was for double-glazing.

After a couple of lunches with pleasant, unremarkable men, she

met Rupert. Tall, and upper-class of bearing, Rupert was intelligent, articulate and charming. Educated at Charterhouse, he had trained as a solicitor. He had been chairman of a famous gentlemen's club in St James's, also of several well-known companies. He wrote speeches for a distant relative who was a member of the House of Lords. He was also a sailor and member of a renowned sailing club in Cornwall. More importantly, as far as the stupid woman was concerned, he could make her laugh.

He courted her to within an inch of her life. Flowers arrived and the phone never stopped ringing. Overlooking his penchant for checked suits and braces with gold stars on that made him look like Toad of Toad Hall, the stupid woman was all of a dither, for Rupert pursued her with ardour. He clutched her to him and when his hot breath fogged up her glasses as well as his own, he whispered in her ear instead. He murmured passionately of nights spent lying on deck gazing at the stars, of travel to places she had only dreamed of. Tired of being alone and fighting her own battles, she decided to accept his suit (but not the braces). Reader, she married him.

Rupert turned out to be a superlative cook but always left the kitchen looking like an abattoir. His new wife once came home to find him stooped secretively over the corpse of the Christmas turkey from which he was gleaning the wherewithal for a turkey curry. He looked wild and dishevelled, with bits of turkey hanging off his spectacles and prune stuffing trampled into the drawing-room carpet.

His cooking was aided and abetted by more than a glass or two of whatever bottle happened to be open – so much so that his discourse over dinner often took a repetitive turn, but the stupid woman didn't mind. They had rented a house with a wonderful view which made up for the odd conversational dead-end.

He took over her financial and tax matters, which was an enormous relief to the stupid woman, who was numerically challenged. 'My darling,' he boomed, 'women of passion and beauty do not concern themselves with Value Added Tax.'

He often went shooting with the Lord and came home with his briefcase stuffed full of small corpses and bloody feathers. Indeed, Rupert and dead birds seemed destined to spend time with each other, like some living tableau by an artist of the Dutch Renaissance.

Though stupid, the woman began to realise that things were not exactly as Rupert had advertised them to be. They went down to Cornwall to look

at a cottage that Rupert had seen in *Country Life*. It turned out to be lovely. 'I can have the money on the table by Monday morning,' Rupert told the estate agent. The stupid woman was delighted and began to give the address to friends and mentally to draw up a rota of who would visit and when – so she was staggered to learn, after finding letters from solicitors stuffed down behind the sofa, that the deal had never been done and the cottage had been sold elsewhere.

She felt rather silly. And cheated. She also finally admitted to herself that the flutter of activity from Rupert's study when she arrived home, which could have been her husband quickly tidying up, was in

fact the stashing of his bottles of booze in one of the drawers of his desk. Or hiding paperwork that he didn't want her to see.

She had bought him a mobile phone as a present, so that they could keep in touch when Rupert was out of the country 'doing his deals'. Rupert seemed surprisingly irritated by the gift. 'Darling, I am not of an age for these gadgets – I find them intrusive and, in fact, an irrelevance.'

One day an ex-business partner of Rupert's rang with shattering news. Rupert was involved in a £2 million case of embezzlement. The 'partner' had done his homework thoroughly and all the pieces of the puzzle were almost in place but not quite – he suspected the presence of a 'third player'. Would Rupert's wife see what she could find out? The phoenix nosedived with a thump.

Seriously alarmed to find herself married to a con-man, the stupid woman hired a private detective to follow him. She met this individual in a coffee shop in Godalming. 'Bernie' had a cadaverous look about him that seemed entirely in keeping with his profession. He also seemed to have a sinus condition.

'It'll all be on his phode,' he said.
'On his what?'
'His bobile phode. I bet he's got wud.'

The stupid woman began to do a little scouting around, and lo! In the leather briefcase, nestling among the feathers and beaks, there was indeed a mobile phone – so much for 'irrelevant' and 'intrusive'. When she played Rupert's messages back, they included several from a lady solicitor with whom her husband was apparently carrying on. And imagine her feelings when, in a terse conversation with the 'other woman', she discovered that her husband had killed her off to suit his scenario – that he had reported her death to his paramour, from breast cancer. She also discovered that despite having told our heroine that he was divorced when they first met, he had in fact

obtained his decree absolute only two weeks before their wedding.

The black comedy turned even blacker. Unsurprisingly, the stupid woman threw him out and he rented elsewhere – but she felt sorry for him in spite of everything and allowed him to visit for weekends. His rented house featured an extremely steep staircase and when Rupert was found dead at the foot of it after another bottle of vodka, the stupid woman was genuinely distraught.

She would love to have finished this story with the words 'Reader, I buried him', but in fact Rupert's ashes were scattered on the River Dart at sunset while the stupid woman and two friends poured champagne on the water to Ella Fitzgerald's recording of 'There may be trouble ahead/ But while there's moonlight and music/ And love and romance/ Let's face the music and dance.'

The stupid woman still sees herself as a phoenix but has given up any thought of maximum lift-off. To those lone women who are over the hill but not over the rainbow, she has this advice: if music, love and romance are what you are after, don't go anywhere near expensive introduction outfits. Go instead to the cinema – it's much cheaper, the men are better looking and where else can you indulge your fantasies while eating a hot dog?

> *Rupert turned out to be a superlative cook but always left the kitchen looking like an abbatoir. His cooking was aided and abetted by more than a glass or two*

A land of dark hills

On a journey through the foothills of the Carpathian mountains in Poland,
COLIN THUBRON *discovered the haunting tale of a nearly forgotten people*

The Carpathian mountains stretch south in a broad arc from the borders of Poland, circling the Great Hungarian Plain, and turn west at last into the heart of Romania. Their massif is often broken and rarely reaches higher than 8,500 feet. But where they shelve south into Slovakia, you can see them rising to their zenith in corrugations of bleak, grey rock.

In the Polish foothills, where the Carpathians begin, I found myself driving through valleys soft with birch and oak and opening onto bright grasslands. Here the roads disappear without notice into Slovakia, and there is scarcely a car or lorry about. The land is silent, as if half-inhabited.

A Polish woman tells me: 'These hills are where the Lemko used to live.'

I had never heard of the Lemko. But mountains, of course, have always been the refuge of the sectarian and

All that is left in the underbush are the tall stone crosses of their dead; they were fine stonemasons

the oppressed. The Lemko are a Slavic people, the woman says, who lived here as farmers for centuries. But in 1947, when Ukrainian nationalists in these mountains were fighting against the Soviets, the Lemko were deported en masse by Poland's Stalinist government, who accused them of partisan sympathies.

I ask: 'Where were they taken?'

'From here they were transported to Siberia, I think, and to distant parts of Poland in the north, thousands of them. Many never returned.'

The land seemed suddenly changed. The low houses with their tangled orchards and steep-pitched roofs looked in long decay. Most were owned by Poles now. And the region was full of graveyards. Some of them survived from the First World War, where soldiers of the Austro-Hungarian empire lay buried beside their Russian enemies. But others were more strange. You clamber through thickets to empty clearings where churches once stood. This absence in itself is rare. The congregations in Catholic Poland are so huge that often a new church

PHOTOGRAPHS © HEMIS / ALAMY AND PIOTR HORNUNG

has been raised beside the old, and Sunday worshippers spill out to kneel in the cemeteries.

But the Lemko were not Roman Catholic. They clung to the Orthodox rite. Only officially had some of them made union with Rome, and this, of course, could not save them. All that is left in the underbush are the tall stone crosses of their dead – they were fine stonemasons – standing high on their plinths in the grass, inscribed with long-off dates. Nearby you may still glimpse the hollows and swellings in the ground where burnt or abandoned villages had been, and marshy ponds.

In Poland now the Lemko are divided between the shores of the Baltic Sea, to which many were deported, and these secret valleys, to which a few returned. Every year some hundreds converge on a meeting-place – a wide field edged by new buildings – and share news and memories.

Among the nations deported wholesale under Stalin – Volga Germans, the peoples of the north Caucasus, the Crim Tartars – the Lemko occupy barely a footnote. In Poland they have become divided, diffused, half-integrated. But their old homeland among the forested hills is still a site of nostalgic longing; here and there a dilapidated wooden church survives, and under the lichened crosses lie artificial flowers.

Main picture: the Carpathian mountains in Poland
Above: stone Lemko crosses

GOOD DAY DAW!

JANUARY 2012

Notes from the sofa
Apoplectic Christmas opulence

Written and illustrated by **RAYMOND BRIGGS**

CHARLES DICKENS is a great writer. We all know that, but he certainly could do with some editing. He wouldn't survive long under the iron editorship of Ingrams and his bevy of teenage acolytes.

Take this paragraph from *A Christmas Carol*: 'There were great, round pot-bellied baskets of chesnuts, shaped like the waistcoats of jolly old gentlemen, lolling at the doors, and tumbling out into the street in their apoplectic opulence. There were ruddy, brown-faced, broad-girthed Spanish Onions, shining in the fatness of their growth like Spanish Friars; and winking from their shelves in wanton slyness at the girls as they went by...'

Blimey! Was he on something? Chesnuts (spelled wrong, but never mind), pot-bellied baskets shaped like waistcoats, lolling at doors, and apoplectic opulence!

Apoplectic opulence sums up this writing quite well. Beginner writers are always being told to cut down on adjectives, yet Dickens uses six adjectives to describe onions, which most of us have seen before. And the onions are like lecherous Friars; well, that does sound remarkably up to date, so he did have foresight.

'...there were Norfolk Biffins, squab and swarthy, setting off the yellow of the oranges and lemons, and, in the great compactness of their juicy persons, urgently entreating and beseeching to be carried home...' They sound like illegal immigrants, except that they are 'to be carried home in paper bags and eaten after dinner.' At least we haven't started eating immigrants... yet. Even if they are juicy persons.

'...while the Grocer and his people were so frank and fresh that the polished hearts with which they fastened their aprons behind might have been their own, worn outside for general inspection, and for Christmas daws to peck at if they chose.'

Aprons fastened with polished hearts? Couldn't they just tie a knot? Their own hearts for general inspection? Why? Jackdaws pecking at the back parts of grocers? This is borderline barmy. Almost time for the men in long white coats.

'The very gold and silver fish, set forth among these choice fruits in a bowl, though members of a dull and stagnant-blooded race, appeared to know that there was something going on; and, to a fish, went gasping round and round their little world in slow and passionless excitement.'

Passionless excitement? (Bit of a contradiction? Ed.) Stagnant-blooded? (They'd be dead, wouldn't they? Ed.) Went gasping? (Fish? they don't breathe air, do they? Ed.)

'... the candied fruits so caked and spotted with molten sugar as to make the coldest lookers-on feel faint and subsequently bilious.' (Quite. Say no more. Ed.)

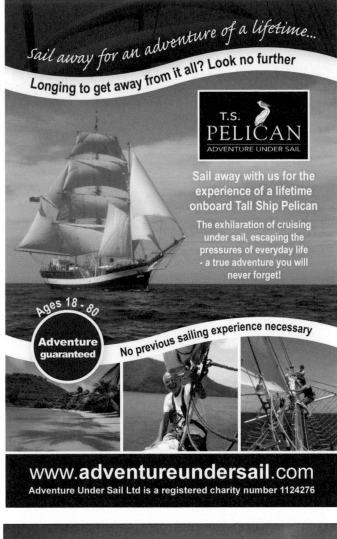

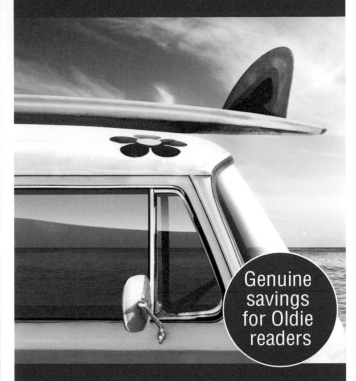

Does your will provide for **everyone** you care about?

Making a will is the best way to provide for your family and friends in years to come, but it's also an opportunity to protect the future of your brothers and sisters in developing countries.

However you've supported CAFOD in the past, a gift in your will means your faith and values will live on. You can supply clean drinking water, send children to school, provide healthcare to the sick and dying; and give training and tools to people struggling to feed their families. When future disasters strike, you could provide emergency aid and long-term support to families as they rebuild their homes and lives.

Your legacy, large or small, could change lives forever.

For a free copy of our will-making guide or to discuss the difference your gift could make call Heather on **020 7095 5367**, email **legacy@cafod.org.uk** or write to Heather Vallely, CAFOD, Romero House, 55 Westminster Bridge Road, London, SE1 7JB. For more information visit: **www.cafod.org.uk/legacy**

Please remember CAFOD in your will and help us build a better world for all God's children.

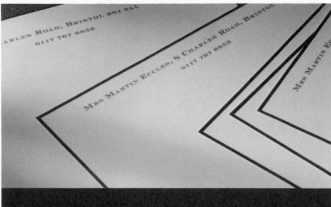

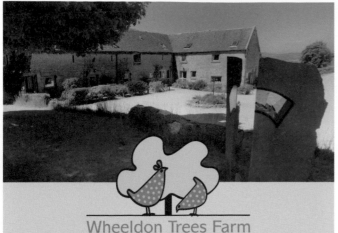

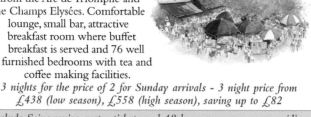

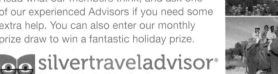

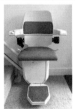

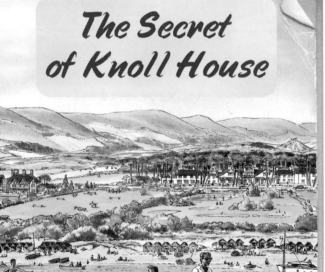